Oxford PAT Guide 2020

Dr Matthew French

Contents

Chapter 1

Introduction

The new printed version of this book brings together a wealth of help for those preparing for sitting the Oxford University PAT. It will be useful both to teachers and students alike.

1.1 Useful Maths Equations

There is an easy way to remember the pattern for values of $\sin\theta$, $\cos\theta$ and $\tan\theta$ which you should know. Notice how the number under the square root starts at zero (for sin) and goes up by one each time. The pattern for cos is reversed. The values for tan are found by remembering $\tan\theta = \frac{\sin\theta}{\cos\theta}$.

θ	0	30	45	60	90
$\sin\theta$	$\frac{\sqrt{0}}{2}=0$	$\frac{\sqrt{1}}{2}=\frac{1}{2}$	$\frac{\sqrt{2}}{2}=\frac{1}{\sqrt{2}}$	$\frac{\sqrt{3}}{2}$	$\frac{\sqrt{4}}{2}=1$
$\cos\theta$	$\frac{\sqrt{4}}{2}=1$	$\frac{\sqrt{3}}{2}$	$\frac{\sqrt{2}}{2}=\frac{1}{\sqrt{2}}$	$\frac{\sqrt{1}}{2}=\frac{1}{2}$	$\frac{\sqrt{0}}{2}=0$
$\tan\theta$	$\frac{0}{1}=0$	$\frac{1\times 2}{2\sqrt{3}}=\frac{1}{\sqrt{3}}$	$\frac{\sqrt{2}}{\sqrt{2}}$	$\frac{2\sqrt{3}}{2\times 1}=\sqrt{3}$	∞

Trig identities:

$$\sin^2\theta + \cos^2\theta = 1 \tag{1.1}$$

$$\tan\theta = \frac{\sin\theta}{\cos\theta} \tag{1.2}$$

$$\sin 2\theta = 2\sin\theta\cos\theta \tag{1.3}$$

$$\cos 2\theta = \cos^2\theta - \sin^2\theta \tag{1.4}$$

$$= 2\cos^2\theta - 1 \tag{1.5}$$

$$= 1 - 2\sin^2\theta \tag{1.6}$$

Maclaurin Series

$$\sin x = x - \frac{x^3}{3!} + \frac{x^5}{5!} \tag{1.7}$$

$$\cos x = 1 - \frac{x^2}{2!} + \frac{x^4}{4!} \tag{1.8}$$

Quadratic Formula solutions of $ax^2 + bx + c = 0$

$$x = \frac{-b \pm \sqrt{b^2 - 4ac}}{2a} \tag{1.9}$$

The binomial expansion:

$$(1+x)^n = 1 + nx + \frac{n(n-1)}{2!}x^2 + \dots + \frac{n(n-1)\dots(n-r+1)}{r!}x^r + \dots + x^n \tag{1.10}$$

Integration by parts

$$\int u\,dv = uv - \int v\,du \tag{1.11}$$

Logs

$$x = b^y \tag{1.12}$$

$$y = \log_b x \tag{1.13}$$

$$\log x + \log y = \log xy \tag{1.14}$$

$$\log x - \log y = \log \frac{x}{y} \tag{1.15}$$

$$\log_b a = \frac{\log_c a}{\log_c b} \tag{1.16}$$

Angles in a triangle:

$$\frac{a}{\sin A} = \frac{b}{\sin B} = \frac{c}{\sin C} \tag{1.17}$$

$$a^2 = b^2 + c^2 - 2bc \cos A \tag{1.18}$$

Area of a Triangle:

$$A = \frac{1}{2}ab \sin C \tag{1.19}$$

Equation of a circle with centre (a,b) and radius r

$$(x-a)^2 + (y-b)^2 = r^2 \tag{1.20}$$

Area of sector a circle

$$A = \frac{1}{2}r^2\theta \tag{1.21}$$

Arithmetic Series

$$S_n = \frac{1}{2}n(a+l) = \frac{1}{2}n\left[2a + (n-1)d\right] \tag{1.22}$$

Geometric Series

$$S_n = \frac{a(1 - r^n)}{1 - r} \tag{1.23}$$

$$S_\infty = \frac{a}{1 - r} \tag{1.24}$$

1.2 Useful Physics Equations

$$E = mc\theta \tag{1.25}$$

Where E is energy (J), m is mass (kg), c is specific heat capacity ($4200 Jkg^{-1}K^{-1}$) and θ is change in temperature (K).

$$E = Pt \tag{1.26}$$

Where E is energy (J), P is power (W) and t is time (s).

$$P = Fv \tag{1.27}$$

Where P is power (W), F is force (N) and v is velocity (m/s).

$$v = f\lambda \tag{1.28}$$

Where v is wave speed (m/s), f is frequency (Hz) and λ is wavelength (m).

$$F = ma \tag{1.29}$$

Where F is force (N), m is mass (kg) and a is acceleration (m/s^2).

$$a = \frac{v - u}{t} \tag{1.30}$$

Where a is acceleration (m/s^2), v is final velocity (m/s), u is initial velocity (m/s) and t is time (s).

$$W = mg \tag{1.31}$$

Where W is weight (N), m is mass (kg) and g is $9.81 m/s^2$.

$$F = kx \tag{1.32}$$

Where F is force (N), k is the spring constant (N/m) and x is extension (m).

$$E = \frac{1}{2}Fx = \frac{1}{2}kx^2 \tag{1.33}$$

Where E in the energy stored in a spring (J), F is the force (N) and x is the extension (m).

$$W = Fd \qquad (1.34)$$

Where W is the work done (J), F is the force (N) and d is the distance moved in the direction of the force (m).

$$E = mgh \qquad (1.35)$$

Where E is the gravitational potential energy (J), m is the mass (kg), g is 9.81m/s^2

$$E = \frac{1}{2}mv^2 \qquad (1.36)$$

Where E is the kinetic energy (J), m is the mass (kg) and v is the velocity (m/s).

$$p = mv \qquad (1.37)$$

Where p is momentum (kgm/s), m is the mass (kg) and v is the velocity (m/s).

$$Q = It \qquad (1.38)$$

Where Q is the electric charge (C), I is the current (A) and t is the time (s).

$$W = QV \qquad (1.39)$$

Where W is the work done (J), Q is the electric charge (C) and V is the potential difference (V).

$$V = IR \qquad (1.40)$$

Where V is the potential difference (V), I is the current (A) and R is the resistance (Ω).

$$P = IV = I^2R = \frac{V^2}{R} \qquad (1.41)$$

Where P is the power (W), I is the current (A), R is the resistance (Ω) and V is the potential difference (V).

$$v = \frac{d}{t} \qquad (1.42)$$

Where v is the velocity (m/s), d is the distance (m) and t is the time (s).

$$f = \frac{1}{T} \qquad (1.43)$$

Where f is the frequency (Hz) and T is the time period (s).

$$M = Fd \tag{1.44}$$

Where M is the moment (Nm), F is the force (N) and d is the perpendicular distance (m).

$$P = \frac{F}{A} \tag{1.45}$$

Where P is the pressure (Pa), F is the force (N) and A is the area (m^2).

$$\frac{V_p}{V_s} = \frac{N_p}{N_s} \tag{1.46}$$

Where V_p is the voltage across the primary coil of a transformer, V_s is the voltage across the secondary coil, N_p is the number of turns on the primary coil and N_s is the number of turns on the secondary coil.

$$s = ut + \frac{1}{2}at^2 \tag{1.47}$$
$$s = \frac{u+v}{2} \times t \tag{1.48}$$
$$v = u + at \tag{1.49}$$
$$v^2 = u^2 + 2as \tag{1.50}$$

Where s is the distance (m), u is the initial velocity (m/s), v is the final velocity (m/s), a is the acceleration (m/s^2) and t is the time (s).

$$R = \frac{\rho L}{A} \tag{1.51}$$

R is resistance (Ω), ρ is the resistivity (Ωm), L is the length (m) and A is the area (m^2).

$$\rho = \frac{m}{V} \tag{1.52}$$

Where ρ is the density (kgm^{-3}), m is the mass (kg) and V is the volume (m^3).

$$n\lambda = d\sin\theta \tag{1.53}$$

Where n is the order, λ is the wavelength (m), d is the slit width (m) and θ is the angle of the maxima in degrees.

$$\lambda = \frac{dx}{L} \tag{1.54}$$

Where λ is the wavelength (m), d is the slit width (m), x is the fringe spacing (m), and L is the distance from the slits to the screen (m).

$$E = mc^2 \tag{1.55}$$

Where E is the energy (J), m is the mass (kg) and c is the speed of light ($3 \times 10^8 m/s$).

$$E = hf \tag{1.56}$$

Where E is the energy (J), h is Planc's constant ($6.63 \times 10^{-34} Js$) and f is the frequency (Hz).

$$\lambda = \frac{h}{p} \tag{1.57}$$

Where λ is the wavelength (m), h is Planc's constant ($6.63 \times 10^{-34} Js$) and p is the momentum (kgm/s).

$$PV = nRT \tag{1.58}$$

Where P is the pressure (Pa), V is the volume (m^3), n is the number of moles, R is the gas constant (8.31 Jmol^{-1}K^{-1}) and T is the temperature (K).

$$a = \frac{v^2}{r} \tag{1.59}$$

Where a is the acceleration in a circle (m/s^2), v is the velocity (m/s) and r is radius (m).

$$v = \omega r \tag{1.60}$$

Where v is the velocity (m/s), ω is the angular velocity (rad/s) and r is radius (m).

$$F = \frac{mv^2}{r} \tag{1.61}$$

Where F is the force (N), m is the mass (kg), v is the velocity (m/s) and r is radius (m).

$$F = \frac{GMm}{r^2} \tag{1.62}$$

Where F is the gravitational force (N), G is the gravitational constant ($6.67 \times 10^{-11} Nm^2kg^{-2}$), M is the mass (kg), m is the other mass(kg) and r is the distance between the masses (m).

Chapter 2

Oxford Physics Aptitude Test 2006 Answers

2.1 Part A - Maths

2.1.1 Question 1

2.1.1.1 part i

There are a number of ways to tackle this problem. You can just multiply these numbers on paper, but there is a quicker way. Re-express as two brackets:

$$
\begin{align}
2007^2 - 2006^2 &= (2000 + 7)^2 - (2000 + 6)^2 \tag{2.1} \\
&= 2000^2 + 2 \times 7 \times 2000 + 49 \tag{2.2} \\
&\quad -2000^2 - 2 \times 6 \times 2000 - 36 \tag{2.3} \\
&= 14 \times 2000 - 12 \times 2000 + 49 - 36 \tag{2.4} \\
&= 2 \times 2000 + 13 \tag{2.5} \\
&= 4013 \tag{2.6}
\end{align}
$$

A even quicker way is to think about it spatially. Think of a first square with edges 2007 long and the second square with edges 2006 long laying over the top of the first square. You want the difference in area of these two squares i.e. the area of the think strip around the edges with width 1. You simply need to add the numbers together (2007+2006=4013).

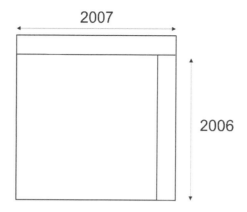

2.1.1.2   part ii

This is only required to 1 significant figure, so doesn't need to be expanded fully:

$$(1.001)^6 - (1.001)^5 = (1.001)^5(1.001 - 1) \tag{2.7}$$

$$= \frac{(1.001)^5}{1000} \tag{2.8}$$

$$\approx \frac{1}{1000} \tag{2.9}$$

$$\approx 0.001 \tag{2.10}$$

Since $1.x^5$ will always be $1.y$ and then it's divided by a thousand, the first figure will always be a 1, provided that x is sufficiently small. Alternatively you can use a binomial expansion.

2.1.2   Question 2

Simply use the gradient formula:

$$m = \frac{y_2 - y_1}{x_2 - x_1} \tag{2.11}$$

$$= \frac{-2 - 8}{5 - 4} \tag{2.12}$$

$$= \frac{-10}{1} \tag{2.13}$$

$$= -10 \tag{2.14}$$

2.1.3   Question 3

Remember that:

$$\log x^y = y \log x \tag{2.15}$$

$$\log_x x = 1 \tag{2.16}$$

2.1.3.1 part i

$$\log_e e^{3x} = 6 \tag{2.17}$$

$$3x \log_e e = 6 \tag{2.18}$$

$$3x + 6 \tag{2.19}$$

$$x = 2 \tag{2.20}$$

2.1.3.2 part ii

$$\log_3 x^2 = 2 \tag{2.21}$$

$$\pm 2 \log_3 x = 2 \tag{2.22}$$

$$\log_3 x = \pm 1 \tag{2.23}$$

$$x = \pm 3 \tag{2.24}$$

2.1.4 Question 4

Split up the equation given in the question:

$$x = \tan^{-1} \frac{12}{5} \tag{2.25}$$

$$y = 13 \sin(x) \tag{2.26}$$

Now using the first equation above, rearrange and consider a triangle:

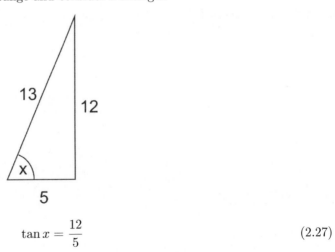

$$\tan x = \frac{12}{5} \tag{2.27}$$

Now you need $13 \sin x$ which is easily given from the triangle as $13 \times 12/13 = 12$ since $\sin x =$ opposite/hypotenuse.

2.1.5 Question 5

2.1.5.1 part i

This is simply:

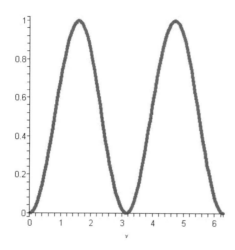

2.1.5.2 part ii

The graph on the left shows $1/x^2$ (which you should know) and the graph on the right shows $1/(x^2-1)$. Look carefully and you will see there must be a singularity where $x^2 = 1$ as the bottom of the fraction is then 0. So it's a regular graph on the outsides. Between -1 and 1 use a binomial expansion:

$$(1+x)^n = 1 + nx + ... \tag{2.28}$$
$$(x^2 - 1)^{-1} = -(1-x^2)^{-1} \tag{2.29}$$
$$= -(1-x^2)^{-1} \tag{2.30}$$
$$= -\left[1 + (-1)(-x^2)\right] \tag{2.31}$$
$$= -1 - x^2 \tag{2.32}$$

so this if the form of the graph in this region.

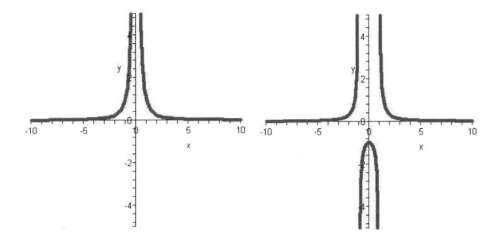

2.1.6 Question 6

Work in cm^2. Write down equations for the facts stated in the question.

$$r_a = r_b + 1 \tag{2.33}$$

$$\pi r_a^2 = \pi r_b^2 + 2\pi \tag{2.34}$$

Divide by π and substitute for r_a in the second equation, using the first equation:

$$(r_b + 1)^2 = r_b^2 + 2 \tag{2.35}$$

$$r_b^2 + 2r_b + 1 = r_b^2 + 2 \tag{2.36}$$

$$2r_b = 1 \tag{2.37}$$

$$r_b = \frac{1}{2} \tag{2.38}$$

using the first equation gives

$$r_a = \frac{3}{2} \tag{2.39}$$

2.1.7 Question 7

2.1.7.1 part i

You must multiply the probabilities of each separate die giving a six. Think of a tree diagram if you find it helpful.

$$\frac{1}{6} \times \frac{1}{6} \times \frac{1}{6} = \frac{1}{216} \tag{2.40}$$

2.1.7.2 part ii

There are six paths on a tree diagram for this - each identical to the path in the previous question:

$$6 \times \frac{1}{216} = \frac{1}{36} \tag{2.41}$$

2.1.7.3 part iii

You need the probability of getting:

$$\text{not a } 6 \times \text{not a } 6 \times \text{a } 6 \tag{2.42}$$

$$\frac{5}{6} \times \frac{5}{6} \times \frac{1}{6} = \frac{25}{216} \tag{2.43}$$

2.1.8 Question 8

The volume increases by 1cm^3 per second and $V = \frac{4}{3}\pi r^3$. Therefore:

$$\frac{dV}{dt} = 1 \tag{2.44}$$

and you need to find

$$\frac{dr}{dt} \tag{2.45}$$

Now using the chain rule:

$$\frac{dr}{dt} = \frac{dr}{dV}\frac{dV}{dt} \tag{2.46}$$

and

$$\frac{dV}{dr} = 4\pi r^2 \tag{2.47}$$

$$\frac{dr}{dV} = \frac{1}{4\pi r^2} \tag{2.48}$$

so:

$$\frac{dr}{dt} = \frac{1}{4\pi r^2} \tag{2.49}$$

Now the surface area of the balloon is given by $4\pi r^2$ so when this is 100 the rate of growth of the radius is:

$$\frac{dr}{dt} = \frac{1}{100} \tag{2.50}$$

$$= 0.01\text{cm per second} \tag{2.51}$$

2.1.9 Question 9

The question asks for an area - so you should be thinking about integrating something. Note that an integral gives the area between the graph and the x-axis. The function $|x^n|$ will be even therefore the integral (area) between -2 and 2 will be twice the integral (area) between 0 and 2. For positive x you can remove the modulus sign as x^n will always be greater than zero.

$$y \quad = \quad |x^n| \tag{2.52}$$

$$\int_{-2}^{2} y dx \quad = \quad 2 \times \int_{0}^{2} y dx \tag{2.53}$$

$$= \quad 2 \times \int_{0}^{2} x^n dx \tag{2.54}$$

$$= \quad 2 \times \left[\frac{x^{n+1}}{n+1} + c \right]_{x=0}^{x=2} \tag{2.55}$$

$$= \quad 2 \times \left[\frac{2^{n+1}}{n+1} - 0 \right] \tag{2.56}$$

$$= \quad \frac{2^{n+2}}{n+1} \tag{2.57}$$

You also need to add the area between the x-axis and the line y=-2. This is a rectangle of height 2 and width (2-(-2)=4) giving an area of 8. The total area is:

$$A = \frac{2^{n+2}}{n+1} + 8 \tag{2.58}$$

2.1.10 Question 10

2.1.10.1 part i

This is a geometric progression with first term $a = 1$ and common ratio $\exp^y$. SO:

$$\Sigma_\infty \quad = \quad \frac{1}{1-r} \tag{2.59}$$

$$= \quad \frac{1}{1-e^y} \tag{2.60}$$

2.1.10.2 part ii

Firstly note that:

$$\log_2 1 = \log_2 2^0 = 0 \log_2 2 = 0 \qquad (2.61)$$

$$\log_2 2 = \log_2 2^1 = 1 \log_2 2 = 1 \qquad (2.62)$$

$$\log_2 2 = \log_2 2^2 = 2 \log_2 2 = 2 \qquad (2.63)$$

$$\log_2 2^n = n \log_2 2 = n \qquad (2.64)$$

$$\qquad (2.65)$$

So you need the sum of the integers between 0 and n.

$$\frac{n(n+1)}{2} \qquad (2.66)$$

2.1.11 Question 11

The stationary points are found by differentiating the equation and setting the differential equal to zero. The points can be classified by considering the second differential: if this is positive then its a minimum and if its negative then its a maximum. (Where necessary, points of inflection can be found by considering the second derivative a little bit each side of the point in question. If this has the same sign on both sides (i.e. both negative or both positive) then you have a point of inflection.)

$$y = 5 + 24x - 9x^2 - 2x^3 \qquad (2.67)$$

$$\frac{dy}{dx} = 24 - 18x - 6x^2 = 0 \qquad (2.68)$$

$$0 = 6x^2 + 18x - 24 \qquad (2.69)$$

$$0 = x^2 + 3x - 4 \qquad (2.70)$$

Use the standard quadratic equation:

$$x = \frac{-b \pm \sqrt{b^2 - 4ac}}{2a} \qquad (2.71)$$

$$= \frac{-3 \pm \sqrt{3^2 - 4 \times 1 \times (-4)}}{2} \qquad (2.72)$$

$$= \frac{-3 \pm \sqrt{9 + 16}}{2} \qquad (2.73)$$

$$= \frac{-3 \pm 5}{2} \qquad (2.74)$$

$$= -4 \ and \ 1 \qquad (2.75)$$

Now for the second derivative, you must use the original first derivative to ensure the signs are correct and set the result equal to zero:

$$\frac{d^2y}{dx^2} = \frac{d}{dx}\left(24 - 18x - 6x^2\right) \tag{2.76}$$

$$= -18 - 12x = 0 \tag{2.77}$$

For $x = -4$:

$$-18 + 48 = 30 \tag{2.78}$$

This is positive and so corresponds to a minimum. (You can also check for inflection points by checking with $x = -3: -6$ and $x = -5: 42$. Now for $x = 1$:

$$-18 - 12 = -30 \tag{2.79}$$

so this corresponds to a maximum. Again points of inflection can be checked for in a similar way.

2.1.12 Question 12

The area of the small circle is:

$$A_s = \pi r^2 \tag{2.80}$$

and the area of the large circle is:

$$A_s = \pi(2r)^2 = 4\pi r^2 \tag{2.81}$$

Now you need the area of the square. Consider this diagram:

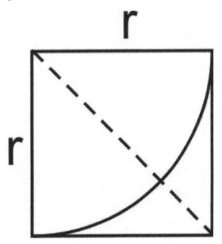

The radius of the circle and the sides of the square are r. So the diagonal is given by pythagoras:

$$\sqrt{r^2 + r^2} \tag{2.82}$$

$$\sqrt{2}r \tag{2.83}$$

In a similar way the diagonal of the corresponding square for the large circle is

$$\sqrt{(2r)^2 + (2r)^2} \tag{2.84}$$

$$\sqrt{8r^2} \tag{2.85}$$

$$\sqrt{8}r \tag{2.86}$$

$$2\sqrt{2}r \tag{2.87}$$

Now the diagonal of the full square is given by the sum of the two diagonals you've just calculated and the radii of the two circles:

$$D = \sqrt{2}r + 2\sqrt{2}r + 2r + r \tag{2.88}$$

$$= (3 + 3\sqrt{2})r \tag{2.89}$$

Imagining a triangle consisting of the diagonal of the large square and two other sides the area of the square is:

$$A = 2 \times \frac{1}{2} \times \text{base} \times \text{height} \tag{2.90}$$

$$= \text{base} \times \text{height} \tag{2.91}$$

$$= (3 + 3\sqrt{2})r \times \frac{(3 + 3\sqrt{2})r}{2} \tag{2.92}$$

$$= 9 + 18\sqrt{2} + 18 \times \frac{r^2}{2} \tag{2.93}$$

$$= \frac{27 + 18\sqrt{2}}{2}r^2 \tag{2.94}$$

So the ratio of the areas is:

$$= \frac{\text{Area Circles}}{\text{Area Square}} \tag{2.95}$$

$$= \frac{2 \times 5\pi r^2}{(27 + 18\sqrt{2})r^2} \tag{2.96}$$

$$= \frac{10\pi}{27 + 18\sqrt{2}} \tag{2.97}$$

$$= \frac{\pi}{2.7 + 1.8\sqrt{2}} \tag{2.98}$$

2.2   Part B - Physics

2.2.1   Question 1

u is a speed and t is a time. A speed multiplied by a time gives a distance. You can also notice that x is a distance and each component added or subtracted on the right hand side of the equation must also have the same units as x. The answer is C - a displacement.

2.2.2 Question 2

Remember the equations:

$$\text{Pressure} = \frac{\text{Force}}{\text{Area}} \qquad (2.99)$$

and

$$\text{Density} = \frac{\text{Mass}}{\text{Volume}} \qquad (2.100)$$

The force will be given by:

$$
\begin{aligned}
F &= \text{mass} \times \text{gravity} & (2.101) \\
&= \text{density} \times \text{volume} \times \text{gravity} & (2.102) \\
&= 8570 \times 0.03 \times 0.04 \times 0.05 \times 10 & (2.103) \\
&= 5.142 & (2.104)
\end{aligned}
$$

The maximum pressure will be when the area is smallest - so you need the area of the smallest face:

$$
\begin{aligned}
\text{Pressure} &= \frac{5.142}{0.03 \times 0.04} & (2.105) \\
&= 4285 Pa & (2.106) \\
&= 4.3 kPa & (2.107)
\end{aligned}
$$

Therefore the answer is A.

2.2.3 Question 3

Compare this to comets which have similar elliptical/elongated orbits. A comet travels fastest when closest to the sun therefore A is false.

2.2.4 Question 4

The answer is C - the level stays the same. When in the boat, an object displaces its weight in water. When in the water the object displaces its volume in water. If the object in question is more dense than water, the water level is higher when the object is in the boat. If the object is question is a teaspoon of water, it will make no difference to the water level. There may, however, be an effect due to the boat sitting lower in the water as a result of the extra mass inside. In this case there would be more water displaced (and assuming the boat is made of a material less dense than water) the level will rise slightly, so that answer may be B.

2.2.5   Question 5

If you don't recognise the equation immediately, work it out. Equate potential and kinetic energy and then take out momentum (mv) as a factor:

$$eV = \frac{mv^2}{2} \tag{2.108}$$

$$2eV = mv^2 \tag{2.109}$$

$$2meV = m^2v^2 \tag{2.110}$$

$$2meV = p^2 \tag{2.111}$$

$$\sqrt{2meV} = p \tag{2.112}$$

$$\lambda = \frac{h}{p} \tag{2.113}$$

$$= \frac{h}{\sqrt{2meV}} \tag{2.114}$$

Therefore the answer is B.

2.2.6   Question 6

Apply SUVAT to both cars. For the first car:

$$u = 0 \tag{2.115}$$

$$v = 20 \tag{2.116}$$

$$t = t \tag{2.117}$$

$$s = d \tag{2.118}$$

$$s = \frac{u+v}{2}t \tag{2.119}$$

$$d = 10t \tag{2.120}$$

For the second car:

$$u = 0 \tag{2.121}$$

$$v = 20 \tag{2.122}$$

$$t = 2t \tag{2.123}$$

$$s = ? \tag{2.124}$$

$$s = \frac{u+v}{2}t \tag{2.125}$$

$$s = 10 \times 2t \tag{2.126}$$

$$= 20t \tag{2.127}$$

$$= 2d \tag{2.128}$$

Therefore the answer is D - note that $d = 10t$ was substituted into the penultimate line to give the final answer.

2.2.7   Question 7

Write out the sequences:

$$D = 1, 4, 9, 16, 25 \tag{2.129}$$

$$Y = 1, 8, 27, 64, 125 \tag{2.130}$$

and now ask yourself what the pattern is that relates Y and D. You should easily see that if you multiply D by its square root you get Y. Therefore the answer is C.

2.2.8   Question 8

The scales don't actually measure mass - they measure a force and use a pre-set magnitude of gravity to convert the force into a mass using the equation:

$$\text{Force} = \text{Mass} \times \text{Gravity} \tag{2.131}$$

So on Mars, but using the gravity on Venus:

$$F = 93 \times 8.8 \tag{2.132}$$

$$= 818.4\text{N} \tag{2.133}$$

Now you have the force exerted by the alien on his scales on Mars, use the correct gravity for Mars to calculate his mass:

$$m = \frac{818.4}{3.8} \tag{2.134}$$

$$= 215\text{kg} \tag{2.135}$$

Therefore the answer is C.

2.2.9 Question 9

Firstly note that the mass does not change (no atoms of metal leave or arrive). Therefore if its mass is constant, but it shrinks, its density must be higher (since density = mass/volume). Therefore the answer is B.

2.2.10 Question 10

Use SUVAT to write down what you know:

$$u = 11 \tag{2.136}$$

$$v = ? \tag{2.137}$$

$$t = 7 \tag{2.138}$$

$$s = ? \tag{2.139}$$

$$a = 10 \tag{2.140}$$

$$s = ut + \frac{1}{2}at^2 \tag{2.141}$$

$$= 11 \times 7 + \frac{1}{2} \times 10 \times 7^2 \tag{2.142}$$

$$= 322\text{m} \tag{2.143}$$

Therefore the answer is C.

2.2.11 Question 11

2.2.11.1 part a

If there are two bulbs, half as much current will flow due to the doubled resistance of two bulbs compared to one. Additionally the voltage drop will be half as much across a bulb. Consider the brightness as the power of the bulb:

$$P = I^2 R = \frac{V^2}{R} \tag{2.144}$$

So power will be less, and the bulb will be less bright than normal.

2.2.11.2   part b

Since there are two cells, the voltage drop across bulb b will be the same as the original bulb. The resistance of bulb b is the same, so the power equation says the power will be the same. Therefore the brightness is the same.

2.2.11.3   part c

It is easier to consider bulb d first. Once you've worked out d, you will see that this circuit is the same as the one containing bulb b, so it has the same answer: the brightness will be the same.

2.2.11.4   part d

Current from the left cell flows up through bulb d. Current from the right cell flows down through bulb d. These currents are equal (the the circuit is the same) and so there is no overall net current through this part of the circuit. Therefore this bulb is off.

2.2.11.5   part e

Each tier of the parallel circuit receives the same voltage. But as there are two bulbs on this tier, the current flowing will be less. The power will be lower and so the bulb dimmer.

2.2.11.6   part f

Each tier of the parallel circuit receives the same voltage. The resistance of bulb f is the same as the original bulb. Therefore the current will be the same and so will the power. The bulb will be the same brightness.

2.2.11.7   part g

The vertical section of the circuit in the centre can be ignored as no net current flows in this part of the circuit (see part d for an explanation of this). In this circuit there are two cells so the voltage across bulb g is twice as big, but the resistance is the same. So the power will be higher, and the bulb brighter.

2.2.11.8   part h

Ignoring the central vertical piece, this is effectively a parallel circuit. So the voltage across this branch will be double, but there are two bulbs to share is. This means the overall voltage is normal, and the resistance is normal. Therefore the power is the same and the brightness is also the same.

2.2.12 Question 12

Firstly write down equations from the details given in the text:

$$r + g = t \tag{2.145}$$

$$2g + b = 2t \tag{2.146}$$

$$r + b = 2g \tag{2.147}$$

$$m_r + m_g + m_b = m_t \tag{2.148}$$

$$t = 0.35 \tag{2.149}$$

$$m_t = 20 \tag{2.150}$$

where r is the length of the red cube, t is the length of the tank etc and m_r is the weight of the red cube and m_t is the weight of the tank etc. So:

$$r + g = 0.35 \tag{2.151}$$

$$2g + b = 0.7 \tag{2.152}$$

$$r + b = 2g \tag{2.153}$$

$$\tag{2.154}$$

Now eliminate b and g, and solve for r:

$$g = 0.35 - r \quad eqn1 \tag{2.155}$$

$$2g + b = 0.7 \quad eqn2 \tag{2.156}$$

$$b = 2g - r \quad eqn3 \tag{2.157}$$

$$\tag{2.158}$$

Substitute eqn 1 and eqn 3 into eqn 2:

$$2g + 2g - r = 0.7 \tag{2.159}$$

$$4g - r = 0.7 \tag{2.160}$$

$$4(0.35 - r) - r = 0.7 \tag{2.161}$$

$$1.4 - 5r = 0.7 \tag{2.162}$$

$$0.7 = 5r \tag{2.163}$$

$$r = 0.7/5 \tag{2.164}$$

$$= 0.14 \tag{2.165}$$

Now substitute this into eqn 1 to find g:

$$r + g = 0.35 \tag{2.166}$$
$$0.14 + g = 0.35 \tag{2.167}$$
$$g = 0.21 \tag{2.168}$$

Finally, substitute r and g into eqn 3 to find b:

$$b = 2g - r \tag{2.169}$$
$$= 2 \times 0.21 - 0.14 \tag{2.170}$$
$$= 0.28 \tag{2.171}$$

If the cubes are floating with half their volume exposed it means that the glowing fluid displaced by (the other) half the volume has the same mass as the whole cube. Since the mass is the same, but the volume of the cube is double, the density of the cubes is half that of the glowing fluid. So:

$$\text{Density} = \frac{\text{Mass}}{\text{Volume}} \tag{2.172}$$
$$\text{density of glowing liquid} = \frac{20}{0.14^3 + 0.28^3 + 0.21^3} \times 2 \tag{2.173}$$
$$= 1178 \text{kgm}^{-3} \tag{2.174}$$

2.2.13 Question 13

2.2.13.1 part a

Started to slow down

2.2.13.2 part b

The acceleration is highest where the gradient is steepest - around $t = 50$sec. This could either be due to a decrease in mass of the rocket as fuel is burnt, or the decrease in air resistance as the air gets thinner.

2.2.13.3 part c

Continues to move forwards but decelerates at a constant rate.

2.2.13.4 part d

Extend the straight line part of the graph until the straight line meets the time (horizontal) axis. Then find the total area between the line (the curved and straight part) and the horizontal axis.

2.2.14 Question 14

2.2.14.1 part a

Electrical energy can be given by power times time. This can be equated to kinetic energy as you are told to consider the motor as a device which converts electrical energy directly into kinetic energy:

$$\frac{1}{2}mv^2 \;=\; Pt \tag{2.175}$$

$$v \;=\; \sqrt{\frac{2Pt}{m}} \tag{2.176}$$

2.2.14.2 part b

Acceleration is the differential of velocity with time:

$$a \;=\; \frac{dv}{dt} \tag{2.177}$$

$$=\; \sqrt{\frac{2P}{m}}\frac{1}{2}t^{-\frac{1}{2}} \tag{2.178}$$

$$=\; \sqrt{\frac{P}{2tm}} \tag{2.179}$$

To find the distance integrate the velocity with respect to time:

$$d \;=\; \int v\,dt \tag{2.180}$$

$$=\; \sqrt{\frac{2P}{m}}\frac{2}{3}t^{\frac{3}{2}} \tag{2.181}$$

$$=\; \sqrt{\frac{8Pt^3}{9m}} \tag{2.182}$$

2.2.14.3 part c

From part a we have that

$$v = \sqrt{\frac{2Pt}{m}} \tag{2.183}$$

so for large times, the velocity will be infinite. This does not seem reasonable - but is due to the neglecting of air resistance and friction.

2.2.14.4 part d

From part b we have that

$$a = \sqrt{\frac{P}{2tm}} \tag{2.184}$$

For small t, the bottom of the fraction will be small, so the fraction as a whole will be large. This suggests that the acceleration will be large, which is probably true as the car is only just beginning to move. For large t, the bottom of the fraction will be large, so the fraction as a whole will be small. This suggests that the acceleration will be small. This is probably also true, as the car won't continue accelerating indefinitely.

2.2.14.5 part e

Equate the energy supplied by the motor to gravitational potential energy:

$$Pt = mgh \tag{2.185}$$

$$h = \frac{Pt}{mg} \tag{2.186}$$

$$v = \frac{h}{t} = \frac{P}{mg} \tag{2.187}$$

2.2.14.6 part f

The kinetic energy is given by:

$$KE = \frac{1}{2}mv^2 \tag{2.188}$$

$$= \frac{1}{2}m\frac{P^2}{m^2g^2} \tag{2.189}$$

$$= \frac{P^2}{2mg^2} \tag{2.190}$$

substituing in for P from $h = Pt/mg$ above:

$$KE = \frac{m^2g^2h^2}{t^22mg^2} \tag{2.191}$$

$$= \frac{mh^2}{2t^2} \tag{2.192}$$

Now divide kinetic energy by potential energy to calculate ratio:

$$\frac{KE}{PE} = \frac{mh^2}{2t^2mgh} \tag{2.193}$$

$$= \frac{h}{2gt^2} \tag{2.194}$$

To ignore kinetic energy you need $h/2gt^2$ to be small: this happens for long times or very small heights.

Chapter 3

Oxford Physics Aptitude Test 2007 Answers

3.1 Part A - Maths

3.1.1 Question 1

The easiest way to work this out is the difference of two squares

$$
\begin{align}
a^2 - b^2 &= (a-b)(a+b) \tag{3.1}\\
6667^2 - 3333^2 &= (6667 - 3333)(6667 + 3333) \tag{3.2}\\
&= 3334 \times 10000 \tag{3.3}\\
&= 3.334 \times 10^7 \tag{3.4}
\end{align}
$$

3.1.2 Question 2

The gradient of the tangent is given by the derivative:

$$
\begin{align}
y &= x^4 \tag{3.5}\\
\frac{dy}{dx} &= 4x^3 \tag{3.6}\\
at \quad &(-2, 16) \tag{3.7}\\
&= 4 \times (-2)^3 \tag{3.8}\\
&= -32 \tag{3.9}
\end{align}
$$

For the equation of the tangent we now have:

$$
\begin{align}
y &= mx + c \tag{3.10}\\
y &= -32x + c \tag{3.11}
\end{align}
$$

You also know it goes through the point $(-2, 16)$ so:

$$16 \quad = \quad -32 \times -2 + c \tag{3.12}$$

$$16 \quad = \quad 64 + c \tag{3.13}$$

$$c \quad = \quad -48 \tag{3.14}$$

Therefore:

$$y = -32x - 48 \tag{3.15}$$

3.1.3   Question 3

Remember that:

$$\log a^b = b \log a \tag{3.16}$$

So:

$$\frac{2 \log 135}{3 \log 25} \quad = \quad \frac{2 \log 5^3}{3 \log 5^2} \tag{3.17}$$

$$= \quad \frac{3 \times 2 \log 5}{2 \times 3 \log 5} \tag{3.18}$$

$$= \quad 1 \tag{3.19}$$

3.1.4   Question 4

Draw yourself a tree diagram (if not on paper, then at least think of one in your mind). Remember than you multiply along the branches, then add the branches together.

3.1.4.1 part i

Identify all combinations which add to six:

1st	2nd	Probability
1	5	$\frac{1}{6} \times \frac{1}{6} = \frac{1}{36}$
2	4	$\frac{1}{36}$
3	3	$\frac{1}{36}$
4	2	$\frac{1}{36}$
5	1	$\frac{1}{36}$

Adding gives a total probability of 5/36.

3.1.4.2 part ii

Similarly, identify all combinations which add to 11:

1st	2nd	Probability
5	6	$\frac{1}{6} \times \frac{1}{6} = \frac{1}{36}$
6	5	$\frac{1}{36}$

so the total probability is 2/36 = 1/18.

3.1.5 Question 5

This question just involves simply multiplying out the bracket and being very careful. Any terms with a power of x greater than 4 don't need to be written down.

$$(2+x)^5 = (2+x)^2(2+x)^2(2+x) \tag{3.20}$$

$$(2+x)^2 = 4+4x+x^2 \tag{3.21}$$

$$(2+x)^5 = (4+4x+x^2)(4+4x+x^2)(2+x) \tag{3.22}$$

$$= (16+16x+4x^2+16x+16x^2+4x^3+4x^2+4x^3)(2+x) \tag{3.23}$$

$$= (16+32x+24x^2+8x^3)(2+x) \tag{3.24}$$

$$= 32+64x+48x^2+16x^3+16x+32x^2+24x^3 \tag{3.25}$$

$$= 32+80x+80x^2+40x^3 \tag{3.26}$$

3.1.6 Question 6

Label the radii of the circles (big, b, and small, s) and the angles of the new triangles.

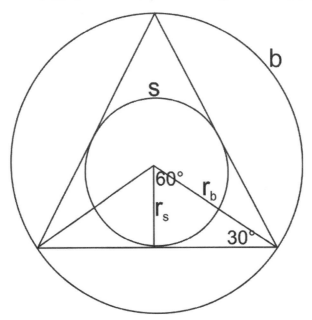

3.1.6.1 part i

Using the small right angled triangle calculate r_s in term of r_b:

$$\sin 30 = \frac{r_s}{r_b} \tag{3.27}$$

$$\frac{1}{2} = \frac{r_s}{r_b} \tag{3.28}$$

$$r_s = \frac{r_b}{2} \tag{3.29}$$

Therefore the area of the small circle is:

$$A_s = \pi r_s^2 \tag{3.30}$$

$$= \pi \frac{r_b^2}{4} \tag{3.31}$$

The ratio is:

$$\frac{A_b}{A_s} = \frac{\pi r_b^2}{\pi r_b^2/4} \tag{3.32}$$

$$= \frac{4\pi r_b^2}{\pi r_b^2} \tag{3.33}$$

$$= 4 \tag{3.34}$$

3.1.6.2 part ii

The area of the big shaded region (A_{bs})is a third of the difference between the areas of the large circle and the triangle:

$$A_{bs} = \frac{A_b - A_t}{3} \tag{3.35}$$

Now:

$$A_t = \frac{1}{2} \text{base} \times \text{height} \tag{3.36}$$

The height is simply

$$r_b + r_s = \frac{3r_b}{2} \tag{3.37}$$

The base is given by considering the small right angle triangle again and using pythagoras:

$$r_b^2 = x^2 + \frac{r_b^2}{4} \tag{3.38}$$

$$x^2 = \frac{3r_b^2}{4} \tag{3.39}$$

$$x = \frac{\sqrt{3}}{2} r_b \tag{3.40}$$

So the base of the large triangle is twice x. Therefore:

$$A_t = \frac{1}{2} \times \sqrt{3} r_b \times \frac{3r_b}{2} \tag{3.41}$$

$$= \frac{3\sqrt{3}}{4} r_b^2 \tag{3.42}$$

The area of the large shaded region is:

$$A_{bs} = \frac{1}{3}\left[\pi r_b^2 - \frac{3\sqrt{3}}{4}r_b^2\right] \tag{3.43}$$

$$= \left[\frac{\pi}{3} - \frac{\sqrt{3}}{4}\right]r_b^2 \tag{3.44}$$

Now the area of the small shaded region (A_{ss}) is given by a third of the area of the triangle minus the area of the circle:

$$A_{ss} = \frac{A_t - A_s}{3} \tag{3.45}$$

$$= \frac{1}{3}\left[\frac{3\sqrt{3}}{4}r_b^2 - \pi r_s^2\right] \tag{3.46}$$

$$= \frac{1}{3}\left[\frac{3\sqrt{3}}{4}r_b^2 - \frac{\pi r_b^2}{4}\right] \tag{3.47}$$

$$= \frac{1}{12}\left[3\sqrt{3} - \pi\right]r_b^2 \tag{3.48}$$

and the ratio is given by:

$$\frac{A_{bs}}{A_{ss}} = \frac{\left[\frac{\pi}{3} - \frac{\sqrt{3}}{4}\right]r_b^2}{\frac{1}{12}\left[3\sqrt{3} - \pi\right]r_b^2} \tag{3.49}$$

$$= \frac{12\left[\frac{\pi}{3} - \frac{\sqrt{3}}{4}\right]}{3\sqrt{3} - \pi} \tag{3.50}$$

$$= \frac{4\pi - 3\sqrt{3}}{3\sqrt{3} - \pi} \tag{3.51}$$

3.1.7 Question 7

You should know immediately how to draw the first two graphs. Remember that is x is replaced by $(x - 2)$ it means the graph is shifted two towards positive x. The final graph can be drawn by 'adding' the other two sketches together. Notice the value when $x = 0$, $y = 4$:

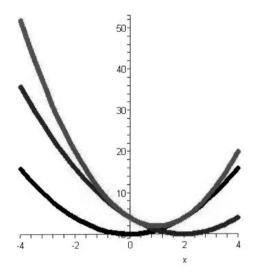

The black line is x^2, the blue is $(x-2)^2$ and the red is $x^2 + (x-2)^2$. Notice that the final graph just had the shape of x^2 as this is still the dominant term - you can multiply out the brackets to check.

3.1.8   Question 8

Draw a sketch of the two graphs:

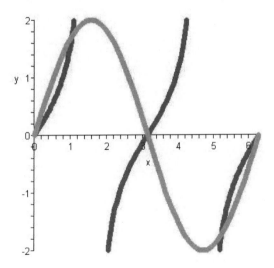

So it is easy to see there are solutions at $\theta = 0$, π, 2π and there are two other solutions.

$$\tan\theta = 2\sin\theta \tag{3.52}$$

$$\frac{\sin\theta}{\cos\theta} = 2\sin\theta \tag{3.53}$$

$$\sin\theta = 2\cos\theta\sin\theta \tag{3.54}$$

$$1 = 2\cos\theta \tag{3.55}$$

$$\frac{1}{2} = \cos\theta \tag{3.56}$$

$$\theta = \frac{\pi}{3} \tag{3.57}$$

By symmetry and looking at the sketch the final solution is at

$$\theta = 2\pi - \frac{\pi}{3} \tag{3.58}$$

$$= \frac{5\pi}{3} \tag{3.59}$$

3.1.9 Question 9

Firstly, draw a sketch and plot the points you know. Work out the orientation of the square.

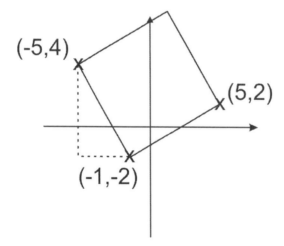

Note that the opposite sides of the square are parallel and therefore have the same gradient. They are also the same length (otherwise it wouldn't be a square!). Using the two points on the left in the sketch the difference in x is $(-5) - (-1) = 4$ and the difference in y is $4 - (-2) = 6$. Now apply this to the $(5, 2)$ point: for x you have $5 - 4 = 1$ and for y you have $2 + 6 = 8$. (You know whether to add or subtract as you have the sketch to indicate roughly what the expected value should be). Therefore the point is $(1, 8)$. Check this agrees with roughly where your sketch says the point should be.

To find the area use the same differences you just worked out - they are two sides of the dashed triangle from the sketch. Using pythagoras:

$$a^2 = b^2 + c^2 \tag{3.60}$$

$$= 4^2 + 6^2 \tag{3.61}$$

$$= 52 \tag{3.62}$$

This of course is the area of the square and there is no need to square root.

3.1.10 Question 10

$$\int_1^9 \left(x^{\frac{1}{2}} + x^{-\frac{1}{2}} \right) dx = \left[\frac{2}{3} x^{\frac{3}{2}} + 2x^{\frac{1}{2}} + c \right]_1^9 \tag{3.63}$$

$$= \left[\frac{2}{3} \times 9 \times 3 + 2 \times 3 + c \right] - \left[\frac{2}{3} + 2 + c \right] \tag{3.64}$$

$$= 18 + 6 - \frac{2}{3} - 2 \tag{3.65}$$

$$= 21\frac{1}{3} \tag{3.66}$$

3.1.11 Question 11

For the geometric progression you have:

$$a, \ ar, \ ar^2 \tag{3.67}$$

and for the arithmetic progression you have:

$$a, \ a + d, \ a + 2d \tag{3.68}$$

Start by writing down what you know from the question:

$$a = a \tag{3.69}$$

$$ar = a + d \tag{3.70}$$

$$ar^2 = 2(a + 2d) = 2a + 4d \tag{3.71}$$

Find two expressions for d - the question hints at then eliminating d. Rearranging the above equations:

$$d = ar - a \tag{3.72}$$

$$d = \frac{ar^2 - 2a}{4} \tag{3.73}$$

Eliminating d:

$$ar - a = \frac{ar^2 - 2a}{4} \tag{3.74}$$

$$4ar - 4a = ar^2 - 2a \tag{3.75}$$

$$0 = ar^2 - 4ar + 2a \tag{3.76}$$

$$0 = r^2 - 4r + 2 \tag{3.77}$$

Now solve for r using the quadratic formula:

$$r = \frac{-b \pm \sqrt{b^2 - 4ac}}{2a} \tag{3.78}$$

$$= \frac{4 \pm \sqrt{16 - 4 \times 1 \times 2}}{2} \tag{3.79}$$

$$= \frac{4 \pm \sqrt{8}}{2} \tag{3.80}$$

$$= \frac{4}{2} \pm \frac{\sqrt{8}}{\sqrt{4}} \tag{3.81}$$

$$= 2 \pm \sqrt{2} \tag{3.82}$$

If you have time you can quickly check your answer by substituting it back in:

$$ar - a = \frac{ar^2 - 2a}{4} \tag{3.83}$$

$$a(2 + \sqrt{2}) - a = \frac{a(4 + 4\sqrt{2} + 2) - 2a}{4} \tag{3.84}$$

$$a + \sqrt{2}a = \frac{4a + 4\sqrt{2}a}{4} \tag{3.85}$$

3.1.12 Question 12

Firstly draw a sketch:

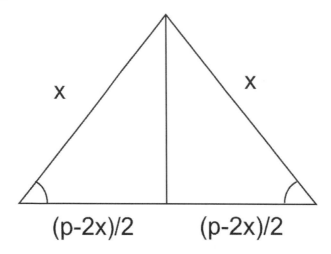

$(p-2x)/2 \qquad (p-2x)/2$

The same x value can produce different isosceles triangles - the top angle can be anything from very small to very large. But if p is fixed, this defines the angle for a given x. The question asks for the value of x which maximises the area. This should lead you think about finding the area and then differentiating it with respect to x. The height is given by considering the right angled triangle from the sketch and pythagoras:

$$h = \sqrt{x^2 - \left(\frac{p-2x}{2}\right)^2} \tag{3.86}$$

so the area of the isosceles triangle is given by:

$$A = \frac{1}{2} \times b \times h \tag{3.87}$$

$$= \frac{1}{2} \times (p-2x) \times \left[x^2 - \left(\frac{p-2x}{2}\right)^2\right]^{\frac{1}{2}} \tag{3.88}$$

$$= \frac{1}{2}(p-2x)\left[x^2 - \frac{p^2}{4} + \frac{4px}{4} - \frac{4x^2}{4}\right]^{\frac{1}{2}} \tag{3.89}$$

$$= \frac{1}{4}(p-2x)(4px - p^2)^{\frac{1}{2}} \tag{3.90}$$

$$\tag{3.91}$$

Use the product rule to differentiate this since x appears in both brackets and set the derivative equal to zero as we are looking for a maximum (or a turning point). In words this is: first bracket multiplied by derivative of the second, plus, differential of the first bracket multiplied by the second.

$$\frac{dA}{dx} = \frac{1}{4}(p-2x)\frac{1}{2}4p(4px - p^2)^{-\frac{1}{2}} + \frac{1}{4}(-2)(4px - p^2)^{\frac{1}{2}} \tag{3.92}$$

$$0 = \frac{1}{2}\frac{p(p-2x)}{(4px - p^2)^{\frac{1}{2}}} - \frac{1}{2}(4px - p^2)^{\frac{1}{2}} \tag{3.93}$$

$$0 = \frac{1}{2}p(p-2x) - \frac{1}{2}(4px - p^2) \tag{3.94}$$

$$p(p-2x) = (4px - p^2) \tag{3.95}$$

$$p(p-2x) = p(4x - p) \tag{3.96}$$

$$p-2x = 4x - p \tag{3.97}$$

$$6x = 2p \tag{3.98}$$

$$x = \frac{p}{3} \tag{3.99}$$

This makes sense as it is then a equilateral triangle - shapes that are more circular have the most area for a given perimeter.

3.2 Part B - Physics

3.2.1 Question 1

Use the equation

$$R = \frac{\rho L}{A} \tag{3.100}$$

since $A \propto L^2$ this gives:

$$R \propto \frac{L}{L^2} = \frac{1}{L} \tag{3.101}$$

Therefore the answer is C.

3.2.2 Question 2

The answer is D. Gravitational force drops with $1/r^2$ - the space station is much closer than the moon which is kept in orbit by the Earth's gravity, so there is still an appreciable amount of gravity where the space station is. Moving objects are still affected by gravity. Since the astronaut is accelerating at the same rate as the station she feels weightless.

3.2.3 Question 3

The current is the rate of flow of charge - 1Amp is 1Coulomb per second. So the current is:

$$
\begin{align}
I &= \frac{V}{R} \tag{3.102} \\
&= \frac{9}{100} \tag{3.103} \\
&= 0.09A \tag{3.104} \\
\text{Number of Electrons per sec} &= \frac{\text{Current}(Cs^{-1})}{\text{Charge on an electron}(C)} \tag{3.105} \\
&= \frac{0.09}{1.6 \times 10^{-19}} \tag{3.106} \\
&= 5.6 \times 10^{17} \tag{3.107}
\end{align}
$$

Therefore the answer is A.

3.2.4 Question 4

If you consider rolling balls down an inclined plane: the acceleration down the plane is given by $g \sin \theta$. Initially with θ large and a steep slope the acceleration is large, as the slope levels out θ becomes smaller and the acceleration down the plane drops. The other component of acceleration perpendicular to the plane doesn't contribute to the motion - think if a stationary object on a flat surface. If the acceleration decreases the only answer available is C.

3.2.5 Question 5

Springs in series behave the same a capacitors in series (or resistors in parallel). So:

$$\frac{1}{k_{new}} = \frac{1}{k} + \frac{1}{k} \tag{3.108}$$

$$= \frac{2}{k} \tag{3.109}$$

$$k_{new} = \frac{k}{2} \tag{3.110}$$

Therefore the answer is A.

3.2.6 Question 6

The equation for power loss is a circuit is:

$$P = I^2 R = \frac{V^2}{R} \tag{3.111}$$

So you need to find R. For resistors in parallel it is:

$$\frac{1}{R} = \frac{1}{R_1} + \frac{1}{R_2} \tag{3.112}$$

Therefore:

$$P = \frac{V^2}{R} = V^2 \times \left(\frac{1}{R_1} + \frac{1}{R_2} \right) \tag{3.113}$$

Therefore the answer is A.

3.2.7 Question 7

The half life is the time taken for the activity (or decays per second) to drop to half its original value. This take 2 hours. But if the body excretes half of the drug every 2 hours then it takes only 1 hour for the amount of radioactive drug to half. Therefore the answer is B.

3.2.8 Question 8

Use the equation:

$$P = \frac{F}{A} \tag{3.114}$$

Remember to get the quantities in their SI units and that the force needed to lift the weight is equal to it's mass multiplied by the acceleration due to gravity.

$$P = \frac{0.125 \times 10}{\pi (1 \times 10^{-3})^2} \tag{3.115}$$

$$= 400,000 \text{Pa} \tag{3.116}$$

$$= 400 \text{kPa} \tag{3.117}$$

The answer is C.

3.2.9 Question 9

The total force on the tow bar if the car is traveling along at constant speed would be zero (think of Newton's first law). However if there is a frictional force on the trailer an equal and opposite force must be supplied by the tow bar. Further, if the car and trailer accelerate, a force must be applied on the trailer (and therefore the tow bar) by the car.

$$F = ma + \text{friction} \tag{3.118}$$

$$= 1000 \times 4 + 2500 \tag{3.119}$$

$$= 6500N \tag{3.120}$$

Therefore the answer is A.

3.2.10 Question 10

3.2.10.1 part a

Use the equation:

$$s = \frac{d}{t} \tag{3.121}$$

$$t = \frac{d}{s} \tag{3.122}$$

$$= \frac{300}{170} \tag{3.123}$$

$$= 1.765 hours \tag{3.124}$$

To convert this into hours and minutes $0.765/100 \times 60$ which give 1 hr 46 min and an estimated arrival time of 1046am.

3.2.10.2 part b

Simply resolve the distance traveled into components north ($153\cos 10$) and east ($153\sin 10$). Since you are considering a time of 1 hour and measuring distance in km and speed in km/h there is no difference in the numbers for distance and speed $s = d/t = d/1$. Now since the plane started north and can travel at 170km/h relative to the wind, the wind has a component south which is $170 - 153\cos 10$ and component east of $153\sin 10$. Making a right angled triangle out of these and using pythagoras gives the resultant as:

$$= \sqrt{(170 - 153\cos 10)^2 + (153\sin 10)^2} \qquad (3.125)$$

$$= 32.9 km/h \qquad (3.126)$$

3.2.11 Question 11

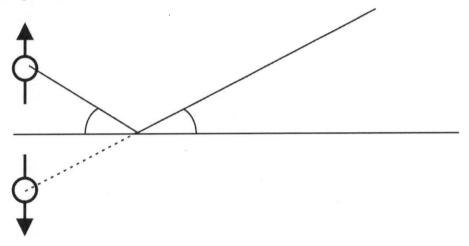

3.2.12 Question 12

Write down equations representing the statements in the question. Use normal letters for colours (M, L, V) and subscripts to represent either $_l$ for length and $_s$ for speed. So:

$$5M_d = 7V_d -\text{eqn 1} \qquad (3.127)$$

$$3L_d + M_d = 8V_d -\text{eqn 2} \qquad (3.128)$$

$$5L_d + 5M_d + 2V_d = 1\,1 - \text{eqn 3} \qquad (3.129)$$

$$L_s = \frac{V_d}{10}1 - \text{eqn 4} \qquad (3.130)$$

$$V_s = 2L_s \qquad (3.131)$$

$$M_s = 2L_s \qquad (3.132)$$

You need to find M_s. Looking upwards from the bottom of the above list of equations, this means you need to find L_s and therefore V_d. Rearrange the first three equations to find V_d:

$$\text{Use eqn 1} \tag{3.133}$$

$$M_d = \frac{7}{5}V_d \tag{3.134}$$

$$\text{Use eqn 2} \tag{3.135}$$

$$3L_d + \frac{7}{5}V_d = 8V_d \tag{3.136}$$

$$3L_d = 6\frac{3}{5}V_d \tag{3.137}$$

$$3L_d = \frac{33}{5}V_d \tag{3.138}$$

$$L_d = \frac{33}{15}V_d \tag{3.139}$$

$$\text{Use eqn 3} \tag{3.140}$$

$$5 \times \frac{33}{15}V_d + 5 \times \frac{7}{5}V_d + 2V_d = 1 \tag{3.141}$$

$$11V_d + 7V_d + 2V_d = 1 \tag{3.142}$$

$$20V_d = 1 \tag{3.143}$$

$$V_d = \frac{1}{20} \tag{3.144}$$

Now using eqn 4:

$$L_s = \frac{1}{20 \times 10} \tag{3.145}$$

$$= \frac{1}{200} \tag{3.146}$$

$$M_s = 2 \times L_s \tag{3.147}$$

$$= 0.01 \text{ms}^{-1} \tag{3.148}$$

Time taken for a mauve caterpillar to crawl around the equator of Pluto is:

$$t = \frac{\text{distance}}{\text{speed}} \tag{3.149}$$

$$= \frac{2\pi r}{0.01} \tag{3.150}$$

$$= \frac{2\pi \times 1180 \times 10^3}{0.01} \tag{3.151}$$

$$= 7.41 \times 10^8 \text{seconds} \tag{3.152}$$

$$/60/60/24/365.35 \tag{3.153}$$

$$= 23.5 \text{years} \tag{3.154}$$

3.2.13 Question 13

If a current of 0.4 A flows in the non-linear resistor then:

$$I = 0.05V^3 \tag{3.155}$$

$$0.4 = 0.05V^3 \tag{3.156}$$

$$8 = V^3 \tag{3.157}$$

$$2 = V \tag{3.158}$$

If the supply is 9V and 2V is across the non-linear resistor, the fixed resistor must have 7V across it since voltages is series add up. The current in a series circuit is the same everywhere. So:

$$V = IR \tag{3.159}$$

$$7 = 0.4R \tag{3.160}$$

$$17.5\Omega = R \tag{3.161}$$

3.2.14 Question 14

3.2.14.1 part a

$$L_{CM} = L \tag{3.162}$$

$$I = ML^2 \tag{3.163}$$

$$P = 2\pi\sqrt{\frac{ML^2}{gML}} \tag{3.164}$$

$$= 2\pi\sqrt{\frac{L}{g}} \tag{3.165}$$

3.2.14.2 part b

$$L_{CM} = L/2 \tag{3.166}$$

$$I = \frac{1}{3}ML^2 \tag{3.167}$$

$$P = 2\pi\sqrt{\frac{ML^2 2}{3gML}} \tag{3.168}$$

$$= 2\pi\sqrt{\frac{2L}{3g}} \tag{3.169}$$

3.2.14.3 part c

Draw a sketch. Remember that the mass of an object can be thought of as acting from its centre of mass (L_{CM}).

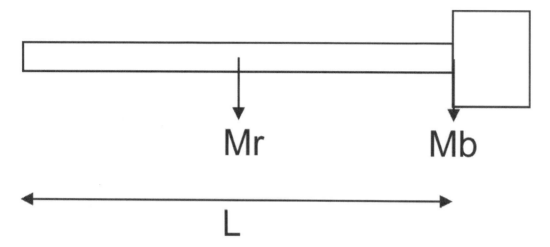

Take moments about the top of the pendulum.

$$L_{CM}(M_r + M_b) = M_b L + \frac{1}{2} M_r L \tag{3.170}$$

$$L_{CM} = \frac{M_b L + \frac{1}{2} M_r L}{M_r + M_b} \tag{3.171}$$

So the period is given by:

$$P = 2\pi \sqrt{\frac{M_b L^2 + \frac{1}{3} M_r L^2}{g(M_r + M_b)\left(\frac{M_b L + \frac{1}{2} M_r L}{M_r + M_b}\right)}} \tag{3.172}$$

$$= 2\pi \sqrt{\frac{M_b L + \frac{1}{3} M_r L}{g M_b + \frac{1}{2} g M_r}} \tag{3.173}$$

$$= 2\pi \sqrt{\frac{L(M_b + \frac{1}{3} M_r)}{g(M_b + \frac{1}{2} M_r)}} \tag{3.174}$$

So as $M_b \to 0$

$$P = 2\pi \sqrt{\frac{L \frac{1}{3} M_r}{g \frac{1}{2} M_r}} \tag{3.175}$$

$$= 2\pi \sqrt{\frac{2L}{3g}} \tag{3.176}$$

and the pendulum behaves like a rod.

44

So as $M_r \to 0$

$$P = 2\pi\sqrt{\frac{LM_b}{gM_b}} \tag{3.177}$$

$$= 2\pi\sqrt{\frac{L}{g}} \tag{3.178}$$

and the pendulum behaves like an ideal pendulum.

3.2.14.4   part d

Start by writing down what you know: The new length will be $(1 + \alpha\delta T)L$. To be accurate to 1 second in 24 hours the change in period needs to be less than

$$\frac{1}{\text{number of periods in one day}} \tag{3.179}$$

But:

$$\text{number of periods in one day} = \frac{\text{number seconds in one day}}{T} \tag{3.180}$$

$$= \frac{A}{T} \tag{3.181}$$

where T is the period. Therefore the biggest change in period permitted is

$$\frac{T}{A} \tag{3.182}$$

This equals the difference between the periods of the pendulum with the longer and shorted length i.e.:

$$\frac{T}{A} = 2\pi\sqrt{\frac{L(1 + \alpha\delta T)}{g}} - 2\pi\sqrt{\frac{L}{g}} \tag{3.183}$$

$$\frac{T}{A} = 2\pi\sqrt{\frac{L}{g}}\sqrt{1 + \alpha\delta T} - 2\pi\sqrt{\frac{L}{g}} \tag{3.184}$$

$$\frac{T}{A} = T\sqrt{1 + \alpha\delta T} - T \tag{3.185}$$

$$\frac{1}{A} = \sqrt{1 + \alpha\delta T} - 1 \tag{3.186}$$

$$\left(\frac{1}{A} + 1\right)^2 = 1 + \alpha\delta T \tag{3.187}$$

$$\frac{\left(\frac{1}{A} + 1\right)^2 - 1}{\alpha} = \delta T \tag{3.188}$$

$$1.22K = \delta T \tag{3.189}$$

(Be careful not to mix up T, the period, and δT the temperature.) A is the number of seconds in a day $60 \times 60 \times 24 = 86400$.

3.2.14.5   part e

Simply substitute in the different value of α giving $\delta T = 19.3K$.

Chapter 4

Oxford Physics Aptitude Test 2008 Answers

4.1 Part A - Maths

4.1.1 Question 1

You can arrange the numbers in pairs:

$$(1 + 100) + (2 + 99) + ... + (50 + 51) \tag{4.1}$$

Each pair adds to 101 and there are 50 pairs so

$$101 \times 50 = 5050 \tag{4.2}$$

In the general case the sum of the integers from 1 to N is given by

$$\frac{N}{2}(N + 1) \tag{4.3}$$

4.1.2 Question 2

$$(0.25)^{-\frac{1}{2}} = \left(\frac{1}{4}\right)^{-\frac{1}{2}} \tag{4.4}$$

$$= 4^{\frac{1}{2}} \tag{4.5}$$

$$= 2 \tag{4.6}$$

and

$$(0.09)^{\frac{3}{2}} = \left(0.09^{\frac{1}{2}}\right)^3 \tag{4.7}$$

$$= 0.3^3 \tag{4.8}$$

$$= 0.027 \tag{4.9}$$

Since $0.3 \times 0.3 = 0.09$ and $0.09 \times 0.03 = 0.27$.

4.1.3 Question 3

Use the expansion they provide to expand the two brackets and then multiply your two expansions together.

$$(1+x)^{m+1} = 1 + (m+1)x + \frac{(m+1)(m+1-1)x^2}{2} \tag{4.10}$$

$$= 1 + (m+1)x + \frac{m(m+1)x^2}{2} \tag{4.11}$$

and

$$(1-2x)^m = 1 + m(-2x) + \frac{m(m-1)(-2x)^2}{2} \tag{4.12}$$

$$= 1 - 2mx + \frac{4m(m-1)x^2}{2} \tag{4.13}$$

Now multiply these together, but only want terms in x^0, x^1 and x^2.

$$= \left[1 + (m+1)x + \frac{m(m+1)x^2}{2}\right]\left[1 - 2mx + \frac{4m(m-1)x^2}{2}\right] \tag{4.14}$$

$$= 1 - 2mx + 2m(m-1)x^2 + (m+1)x - 2m(m+1)x^2 \tag{4.15}$$

$$+ \frac{m(m+1)x^2}{2} \tag{4.16}$$

$$= 1 + (m+1-2m)x \tag{4.17}$$

$$+ \left[2m(m-1) - 2m(m+1) + \frac{m(m+1)}{2}\right]x^2 \tag{4.18}$$

$$= 1 + (1-m)x + \left[2m^2 - 2m - 2m^2 - 2m + \frac{m^2}{2} + \frac{m}{2}\right]x^2 \tag{4.19}$$

$$= 1 + (1-m)x + \left(\frac{m^2}{2} - \frac{7}{2}m\right)x^2 \tag{4.20}$$

4.1.4 Question 4

Rearrange and solve for x:

$$\frac{x^2 + 2}{1 - x^2} < 3 \tag{4.21}$$

$$x^2 + 2 < 3 - 3x^2 \tag{4.22}$$

$$4x^2 < 1 \tag{4.23}$$

$$x^2 < \frac{1}{4} \tag{4.24}$$

$$x < \pm\frac{1}{2} \tag{4.25}$$

But also notice there is a singularity when $x = \pm 1$ since $1 - 1^2 = 0$. By substitution it can easily be found that where $x^2 > 1$ the graph is negative - meaning it must be less than 3. So the set of value for x is:

$$x < -1 \tag{4.26}$$

$$-\frac{1}{2} < x < \frac{1}{2} \tag{4.27}$$

$$x > 1 \tag{4.28}$$

4.1.5 Question 5

Remember the usual log laws:

$$a = b^c \tag{4.29}$$

$$c = \log_b a \tag{4.30}$$

$$\log_b a = \frac{\log_d a}{\log_d b} \tag{4.31}$$

$$\log ab = \log a + \log b \tag{4.32}$$

4.1.5.1 part i

$$\log_2 9 = \frac{\log_9 9}{\log_9 2} \tag{4.33}$$

$$= \frac{1}{x} \tag{4.34}$$

since $\log_b b = 1$.

4.1.5.2 part ii

$$\log_8 3 \quad = \quad \frac{\log_9 3}{\log_9 8} \tag{4.35}$$

$$= \quad \frac{\log_9 9^{\frac{1}{2}}}{\log_9 2^3} \tag{4.36}$$

$$= \quad \frac{\frac{1}{2}}{\log_9 2 + \log_9 2 + \log_9 2} \tag{4.37}$$

$$= \quad \frac{\frac{1}{2}}{3x} \tag{4.38}$$

$$= \quad \frac{1}{6x} \tag{4.39}$$

Since $\log_b bx = x$ - try substituting $a = b^x$ into the two log law equations at the beginning of this answer.

4.1.6 Question 6

An arithmetic progression has the same difference between each term therefore

$$x^2 - 1 \quad = \quad x - x^2 \tag{4.40}$$

$$2x^2 \quad = \quad x + 1 \tag{4.41}$$

$$2x^2 - x - 1 \quad = \quad 0 \tag{4.42}$$

Solve using quadratic formula:

$$x \quad = \quad \frac{+1 \pm \sqrt{1 - 4 \times 2 \times -1}}{4} \tag{4.43}$$

$$= \quad \frac{1 \pm \sqrt{9}}{4} \tag{4.44}$$

$$= \quad \frac{1 \pm 3}{4} \tag{4.45}$$

$$= \quad 1 \text{ or } -\frac{1}{2} \tag{4.46}$$

4.1.7 Question 7

If two lines have the same gradient, they must have equal derivatives. Therefore differentiate and equate the answers.

$$\frac{dy}{dx} \quad = \quad 1 + \frac{2x}{2} + \frac{3x^2}{3} + \frac{4x^3}{4} + \dots \tag{4.47}$$

$$= \quad 1 + x + x^2 + x^3 + \dots \tag{4.48}$$

and for the other equation

$$\frac{dy}{dx} = a \tag{4.49}$$

The first derivative we did is a geometric progression with $a = 1$ and $r = x$ so using the formula for the sum to infinity of a geometric progression and equating this to the second derivative we did:

$$\frac{1}{1-x} = a \tag{4.50}$$

If $x = 0$ then $a = 1$, if $x = 1/4$ then

$$\frac{1}{1 - \frac{1}{4}} = a \tag{4.51}$$

$$\frac{1}{3/4} = a \tag{4.52}$$

$$\frac{4}{3} = a \tag{4.53}$$

4.1.8 Question 8

The general equation for a circle is given by

$$(x - h)^2 + (y - k)^2 = r^2 \tag{4.54}$$

Where the center of the circle is at (h, k) and it has radius r. Therefore you need to find the radius and the centre of the circle. Draw a sketch of the circle.

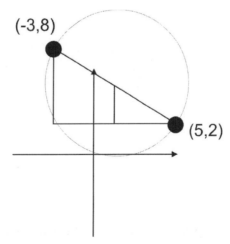

If the two given points are on opposite end of the diameter of the circle then they can form two of the vertices of a right angle triangle. Pythagoras can be used to find the hypotenuse of the triangle which is the circle diameter.

$$a^2 = b^2 + c^2 \tag{4.55}$$

$$a^2 = (5 - -3)^2 + (2 - 8)^2 \tag{4.56}$$

$$a^2 = 64 + 36 \tag{4.57}$$

$$a = \sqrt{100} \tag{4.58}$$

$$a = 10 \tag{4.59}$$

So the radius is 5. A smaller triangle with the circle radius as the hypotenuse is a similar triangle to a triangle with the diameter as the hypotenuse, if you half the hypotenuse (from diameter to radius) you half the other dimensions too. So the triangle has $x = 4$ and $y = 3$. Subtracting these dimensions from the point $(5, 2)$ gives$(5 - 4, 2 + 3) = (1, 5)$. Finally the equation of the circle is

$$(x - 1)^2 + (y - 5)^2 = 5^2 \tag{4.60}$$

4.1.9 Question 9

Draw out a probability table:

Die	Probability	Probability
1	0	0
2	x	$\frac{1}{9}$
3	x	$\frac{1}{9}$
4	x	$\frac{1}{9}$
5	3x	$\frac{1}{3}$
6	3x	$\frac{1}{3}$

4.1.9.1 part i

This can simply be read from the table: $\frac{1}{9}$.

4.1.9.2 part ii

The options for getting 10 or more are 5+5, 4+6, 6+4, 5+6, 6+5 and 6+6. The probabilities can be found in the table above. Note for successive throws probabilities are multiplied.

6 and 4 $\frac{1}{3} \times \frac{1}{9} = \frac{1}{27}$

5 and 5 $\frac{1}{3} \times \frac{1}{3} = \frac{1}{9} = \frac{3}{27}$

4 and 6 $\frac{1}{9} \times \frac{1}{3} = \frac{1}{27}$

5 and 6 $\frac{1}{3} \times \frac{1}{3} = \frac{1}{9} = \frac{3}{27}$

6 and 5 $\frac{1}{3} \times \frac{1}{3} = \frac{1}{9} = \frac{3}{27}$

6 and 6 $\frac{1}{3} \times \frac{1}{3} = \frac{1}{9} = \frac{3}{27}$

The total probability is found by adding the probabilities for each way of getting 10 or more:

$$\frac{1+3+1+3+3+3}{27} = \frac{14}{27} \tag{4.61}$$

4.1.10   Question 10

Taking the base of the triangle and using pythagoras:

$$A^2 = a^2 + a^2 \tag{4.62}$$

$$A^2 = 2a^2 \tag{4.63}$$

$$\tag{4.64}$$

Now taking a diagonal vertical plane through the cube:

$$B^2 = a^2 + A^2 \tag{4.65}$$

$$B^2 = a^2 + 2a^2 \tag{4.66}$$

$$B^2 = 3a^2 \tag{4.67}$$

$$B = \sqrt{3}a \tag{4.68}$$

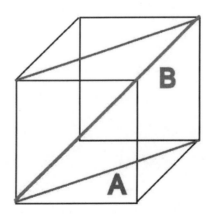

4.1.11   Question 11

4.1.11.1   part i

This is an odd function over limits symmetric about $x = 0$ so the answer is zero. Alternatively, if you don't notice this you need to integrate it:

$$\int_{-1}^{1} x + x^3 + x^5 + x^7 dx = \left[\frac{x^2}{2} + \frac{x^4}{4} + \frac{x^6}{6} + \frac{x^8}{8} + c \right]_{-1}^{1} \tag{4.69}$$

$$= \left[\frac{1}{2} + \frac{1}{4} + \frac{1}{6} + \frac{1}{8} + c \right] \tag{4.70}$$

$$- \left[\frac{1}{2} + \frac{1}{4} + \frac{1}{6} + \frac{1}{8} + c \right] \tag{4.71}$$

$$= 0 \tag{4.72}$$

4.1.11.2   part ii

$$\int_{0}^{1} \frac{x^9 + x^{99}}{11} dx = \frac{1}{11} \left[\frac{x^{10}}{10} + \frac{x^{100}}{100} + c \right]_{0}^{1} \tag{4.73}$$

$$= \frac{1}{11} \left[\frac{1}{10} + \frac{1}{100} + c \right] - \frac{c}{11} \tag{4.74}$$

$$= \frac{1}{11} \left[\frac{10}{100} + \frac{1}{100} \right] \tag{4.75}$$

$$= \frac{1}{11} \times \frac{11}{100} \tag{4.76}$$

$$= \frac{1}{100} \tag{4.77}$$

4.1.12   Question 12

Firstly, set $AD = AB = BC = CA = CE = x$. The area of the triangle is given by:

$$\frac{1}{2} ab \sin C = \frac{1}{2} x^2 \sin 60 \tag{4.78}$$

$$= \frac{1}{2} x^2 \frac{\sqrt{3}}{2} \tag{4.79}$$

$$= \frac{\sqrt{3} x^2}{4} \tag{4.80}$$

since it's an equilateral triangle where all the internal angles are $60°$. To find the area of the circle you needs its radius. Therefore you need the distance $OC = y$.

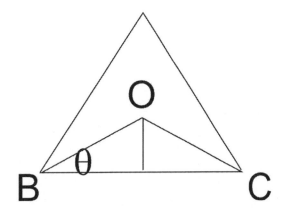

$$\cos \theta = \frac{\text{adj}}{\text{hyp}} \tag{4.81}$$

$$\cos 30 = \frac{x/2}{y} \tag{4.82}$$

$$\frac{\sqrt{3}}{2} = \frac{x}{2y} \tag{4.83}$$

$$\sqrt{3} \times 2y = 2x \tag{4.84}$$

$$y = \frac{x}{\sqrt{3}} \tag{4.85}$$

The area of the shaded 'circle' is given by the two thirds of the total area of the circle with radius $(x + y)$ minus the area of the circle with radius y.

$$= \frac{2}{3} \left[\pi(x + y)^2 - \pi y^2 \right] \tag{4.86}$$

$$= \frac{2\pi}{3} \left[x^2 + 2xy + y^2 - y^2 \right] \tag{4.87}$$

$$= \frac{2\pi}{3} \left[x^2 + 2xy \right] \tag{4.88}$$

$$= \frac{2\pi}{3} \left[x^2 + \frac{2x^2}{\sqrt{3}} \right] \tag{4.89}$$

$$= \frac{2\pi}{3} \left[\frac{\sqrt{3}x^2 + 2x^2}{\sqrt{3}} \right] \tag{4.90}$$

The ratio is given by:

$$\frac{\text{Area Triangle}}{\text{Area Circle}} = \frac{\sqrt{3}x^2}{4} \frac{3}{2\pi} \left[\frac{\sqrt{3}}{\sqrt{3}x^2 + 2x^2} \right] \tag{4.91}$$

$$= \frac{3\sqrt{3}x^2}{8\pi} \frac{\sqrt{3}}{x^2(\sqrt{3} + 2)} \tag{4.92}$$

$$= \frac{9}{8\pi(\sqrt{3} + 2)} \tag{4.93}$$

4.2 Part B - Physics

4.2.1 Question 13

Remember the equation:

$$\text{Moment} = \text{Force} \times \text{distance} \tag{4.94}$$

Remember that the force is the mass times acceleration due to gravity, but we can ignore this extra factor of 10 as it appears on both sides when we equate the moments:

$$20 \times 1.5 \quad = \quad 30 \times x \tag{4.95}$$

$$x \quad = \quad 1\text{m} \tag{4.96}$$

Therefore the answer is D. It's 1m from girl to pivot and 1.5 from boy to pivot. So the girl is 1+1.5=2.5m from the boy.

4.2.2 Question 14

If it's a commercial reactor it must create energy. Since $E = mc^2$ this energy must come from a reduction is mass of the reactants as they break up. (Note fusion is fusing or sticking together and fission is breaking apart). Therefore the answer is B.

4.2.3 Question 15

The total mass is the sum of the mass of dark matter and normal matter:

$$\begin{aligned}
\text{Total Mass} \quad &= \quad \text{Dark Mass} + \text{Normal Mass} & (4.97) \\
&= \quad 20 \times \text{Normal Mass} + \text{Normal Mass} & (4.98) \\
&= \quad 21 \times \text{Normal Mass} & (4.99) \\
\text{Normal Mass} \quad &= \quad 400 \times 10^9 \times 250 \times 10^4 \times 2 \times 10^{30} & (4.100) \\
&= \quad 4 \times 10^{11} \times 2.5 \times 10^{11} \times 2 \times 10^{30} & (4.101) \\
&= \quad 4 \times 2.5 \times 2 \times 10^{52} = 20 \times 10^{52}\text{kg} & (4.102) \\
\text{Total Mass} \quad &= \quad 21 \times 20 \times 10^{52} & (4.103) \\
&= \quad 420 \times 10^{52} & (4.104) \\
&= \quad 4.2 \times 10^{54}\text{kg} & (4.105)
\end{aligned}$$

Therefore the answer is D.

4.2.4   Question 16

A solar eclipse occurs when the moon comes between the Earth and the Sun - this is when there is a new moon (i.e. the moon looks black as the unlit side faces Earth). By contrast a lunar eclipse occurs when the Earth comes between the moon and the Sun and only occurs when there is a full moon. Therefore the answer is A.

4.2.5   Question 17

Use the equation

$$PV = nRT \tag{4.106}$$

If the volume (V), the number of particles (n) and the constant R are fixed, then if the temperature (T) rises, the pressure (P) must also rise. Since:

$$\text{Density} = \frac{\text{Mass}}{\text{Volume}} \tag{4.107}$$

if the mass of particles and volume is constant, the density must be constant. Therefore the answer is C.

4.2.6   Question 18

Very little effort or energy is needed for horizontal motion in the absence of friction (think about dry ice or liquid nitrogen sliding around the desk/floor). Therefore the minimum energy is given simply by the gravitational potential energy

$$mgh = 60 \times 10 \times 4 = 2400 J \tag{4.108}$$

Therefore the answer is B.

4.2.7   Question 19

You need to equate energies. Energy in battery is given using:

$$P = VI \tag{4.109}$$

$$\text{Energy} = \text{Power} \times \text{time} \tag{4.110}$$

So

$$\text{Energy} = VIt \tag{4.111}$$

$$= 3600VI \tag{4.112}$$

since there are 3600 seconds in an hour. The energy output from the solar cell is given by:

$$Energy = \text{Efficiency} \times \text{Incident Power} \times \text{Area} \times \text{time} \tag{4.113}$$

$$= 0.1 \times 1000 \times 0.25^2 \times T \times 3600 \tag{4.114}$$

where T is measured in hours. Equating these energies and making T the subject:

$$3600VI = 100 \times 0.0625 \times T \times 3600 \tag{4.115}$$

$$\frac{3600VI}{6.25 \times 3600} = T \tag{4.116}$$

$$\frac{3.6 \times 0.7}{6.25} = T \tag{4.117}$$

$$\frac{2.52}{6.25} = T \tag{4.118}$$

$$0.4 \approx T \tag{4.119}$$

Therefore the answer is C. Note that

$$0.25^2 = \frac{1}{4} \times \frac{1}{4} \tag{4.120}$$

$$= \frac{1}{16} \tag{4.121}$$

$$= 0.5 \times \frac{1}{8} \tag{4.122}$$

$$= 0.5 \times 0.125 \tag{4.123}$$

$$= 0.0625 \tag{4.124}$$

4.2.8 Question 20

A light dependent resistor (LDR) has a high resistance in the dark and a low resistance in the light. Consider the equation

$$P = \frac{V^2}{R} \tag{4.125}$$

Assume V is constant (since the question says it's an ideal source) therefore when R is high, P is low and when R is low P is high. This means that P is highest when R is lowest (and a large current flows, with power loss I^2R). This is when it is lightest - therefore the answer is C: Noon.

4.2.9 Question 21

The kinetic energy of the bullet ($\frac{1}{2}m_bv^2$) will be dissipated into the water causing a temperature rise given by $E = m_wc\Delta T$. Note that the masses are different, b=bullet and w=water:

$$m_wc\Delta T = \frac{1}{2}m_bv^2 \tag{4.126}$$

$$\Delta T = \frac{m_bv^2}{2m_wc} \tag{4.127}$$

$$= \frac{0.01 \times 400^2}{2 \times 2^3 \times 1000 \times 4200} \tag{4.128}$$

$$= \frac{1 \times 10^{-2} \times 1.6 \times 10^5}{1.6 \times 10^1 \times 10^3 \times 4.2 \times 10^3} \tag{4.129}$$

$$= \frac{1}{4.2} \times 10^{-4} \tag{4.130}$$

$$\approx 0.2 \times 10^{-4} \tag{4.131}$$

$$\approx 2 \times 10^{-5} \tag{4.132}$$

Therefore the answer is A.

4.2.10 Question 22

The mass should be in kg therefore if its given in grams it is 1000 times too much. Therefore E will be 1000 times too much or in mJ. Therefore the answer is A.

4.2.11 Question 23

Substitute $q^2 = C^2V^2$:

$$W = \frac{q^2}{2C} \tag{4.133}$$

$$= \frac{C^2V^2}{2C} = \frac{CV^2}{2} \tag{4.134}$$

Now substitute $C = pA/d$:

$$W = \frac{1}{2}\left[\frac{pA}{d}\right]V^2 \tag{4.135}$$

$$= \frac{pAV^2}{2d} \tag{4.136}$$

Start by considering the density:

$$D = \frac{\text{mass}}{\text{volume}} \tag{4.137}$$

$$D = \frac{m}{dA} \tag{4.138}$$

Now substitute $V_{max} = Bd$ into the equation for the energy stored, noting that the maximum energy is stored when the voltage is a maximum:

$$E = \frac{pAV^2}{2d} \tag{4.139}$$

$$= \frac{pAB^2d^2}{2d} \tag{4.140}$$

$$= \frac{pAdB^2}{2} \tag{4.141}$$

$$= \frac{pmB^2}{2D} \tag{4.142}$$

since $dA = m/D$.

$$E = \frac{2 \times 10^{-11} \times 1 \times (2 \times 10^7)^2}{2 \times 1000} \tag{4.143}$$

$$= \frac{2 \times 10^{-11} \times 4 \times 10^{14}}{2 \times 10^3} \tag{4.144}$$

$$= 4\text{J} \tag{4.145}$$

$1\text{kW} = 1000$ J/s. The time scale of gust of wind will be of the order of 10s - so $10 \times 1000 J = 10,000 J$. Thus a storage capacity of 4J won't help significantly in smoothing an output that varies due to gusts of wind.

4.2.12   Question 24

Draw a sketch:

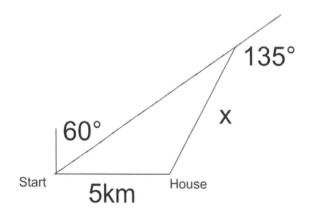

and now label the other points you know:

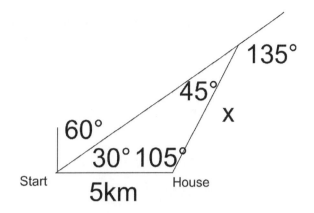

Use:

$$\frac{a}{\sin A} = \frac{b}{\sin B} \tag{4.146}$$

$$\frac{5000}{\sin 45} = \frac{x}{\sin 30} \tag{4.147}$$

$$5000\sqrt{2} = 2x \tag{4.148}$$

$$x = \frac{5000\sqrt{2}}{2} \tag{4.149}$$

$$= 2500 \times 1.4 \tag{4.150}$$

$$= 3500m \tag{4.151}$$

Remember that $\sin 30 = 1/2$ and $\sin 45 = 1/\sqrt{2}$.

4.2.13   Question 25

Write three equations from the three points (a-c) given in the question:

$$c + r = 2s \tag{4.152}$$

$$2c + s = 1 \tag{4.153}$$

$$c^2 + s^2 = r^2 \tag{4.154}$$

Now rearrange to eliminate s and r from the third equation:

$$s = 1 - 2c \tag{4.155}$$

$$r = 2s - c \tag{4.156}$$

$$= 2(1 - 2c) - c \tag{4.157}$$

$$= 2 - 5c \tag{4.158}$$

$$c^2 + (1 - 2c)^2 = (2 - 5c)^2 \qquad (4.159)$$

$$c^2 + 1 - 4c + 4c^2 = 4 - 20c + 25c^2 \qquad (4.160)$$

$$0 = 20c^2 - 16c + 3 \qquad (4.161)$$

Use the quadratic equation to solve for c:

$$c = \frac{16 \pm \sqrt{16^2 - 4 \times 20 \times 3}}{40} \qquad (4.162)$$

$$= \frac{16 \pm \sqrt{256 - 240}}{40} \qquad (4.163)$$

$$= \frac{16 \pm \sqrt{16}}{40} \qquad (4.164)$$

$$= \frac{16 \pm 4}{40} \qquad (4.165)$$

$$= \frac{1}{2} \text{ or } \frac{3}{10} \qquad (4.166)$$

c can't be 1/2 otherwise $2c + s = 1$ would imply that $s = 0$ which can't be correct as it implies a zero length for a scarlet bird so $c = 3/10$. Substituting, this gives:

$$s = 1 - 2c \qquad (4.167)$$

$$s = 1 - 2 \times \frac{3}{10} = \frac{4}{10} \qquad (4.168)$$

$$r = 2s - c \qquad (4.169)$$

$$= 2 \times \frac{4}{10} - \frac{3}{10} \qquad (4.170)$$

$$= \frac{5}{10} \qquad (4.171)$$

4.2.14 Question 26

The most rapid change implies the steepest gradient - this is at 7am. Use the usual equation for a gradient:

$$m = \frac{y_2 - y_1}{x_2 - x_1} \qquad (4.172)$$

$$= \frac{275 - 25}{120} \qquad (4.173)$$

$$= \frac{250}{120} \qquad (4.174)$$

$$= 2.1 \text{cm min}^{-1} \qquad (4.175)$$

Note how the numbers read from the graph are converted into cm and minutes.

4.2.15   Question 27

Draw a sketch:

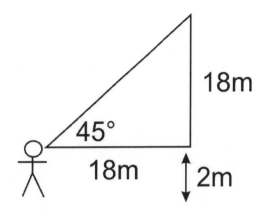

If the angle is 45° and he stands 18m away, you know the height is 18m above his eyes or 20m above the ground.

4.2.15.1   part a

Consider vertical motion:

$$s = 20 \tag{4.176}$$

$$u = 0 \tag{4.177}$$

$$a = 10 \tag{4.178}$$

$$t = ? \tag{4.179}$$

$$s = ut + \frac{1}{2}at^2 \tag{4.180}$$

$$20 = \frac{1}{2} \times 10 \times t^2 \tag{4.181}$$

$$t^2 = \frac{20}{5} \tag{4.182}$$

$$t = \sqrt{4} \tag{4.183}$$

$$t = 2s \tag{4.184}$$

4.2.15.2   part b

$$v^2 = u^2 + 2as \tag{4.185}$$

$$v^2 = 2 \times 10 \times 20 \tag{4.186}$$

$$v^2 = 400 \tag{4.187}$$

$$v = 20ms^{-1} \tag{4.188}$$

4.2.15.3 part c

Force is given by the change in momentum divided by the time taken:

$$F = \frac{mv - mu}{t} \tag{4.189}$$

and the time taken is given by:

$$s = 0.001 \tag{4.190}$$
$$u = 20 \tag{4.191}$$
$$v = 0 \tag{4.192}$$
$$t = ? \tag{4.193}$$
$$s = \left(\frac{u + v}{2}\right) t \tag{4.194}$$
$$0.001 = \left(\frac{20}{2}\right) t \tag{4.195}$$
$$t = 1 \times 10^{-4} \tag{4.196}$$

so:

$$F = \frac{0.02 \times 20}{1 \times 10^{-4}} \tag{4.197}$$
$$= \frac{2 \times 10^{-2} \times 2 \times 10^{1}}{1 \times 10^{-4}} \tag{4.198}$$
$$= 4 \times 10^{3} \text{N} \tag{4.199}$$

4.2.15.4 part d

The work done by the force is given by:

$$\text{WD} = F \times d \tag{4.200}$$
$$= 4000 \times 1 \times 10^{-3} \tag{4.201}$$
$$= 4J \tag{4.202}$$

The gravitational potential energy of the egg is given by:

$$\text{GPE} = mgh \tag{4.203}$$
$$= 0.02 \times 10 \times 20 \tag{4.204}$$
$$= 4J \tag{4.205}$$

The loss is gravitational potential energy is the same as the work done by the force in stopping the egg.

4.2.15.5 part e

Assume the egg still falls 20m otherwise you have to work out new velocities and the maths gets complex - it's only worth 3 marks.

$$s = 0.05 \tag{4.206}$$

$$u = 20 \tag{4.207}$$

$$v = 0 \tag{4.208}$$

$$t = ? \tag{4.209}$$

$$s = \left(\frac{u+v}{2}\right)t \tag{4.210}$$

$$0.05 = 10 \times t \tag{4.211}$$

$$t = 0.005\text{s} \tag{4.212}$$

$$F = \frac{mv - mu}{t} \tag{4.213}$$

$$= \frac{0.02 \times 20}{0.005} \tag{4.214}$$

$$= \frac{2 \times 10^{-2} \times 2 \times 10^1}{5 \times 10^{-3}} \tag{4.215}$$

$$= 0.8 \times 10^2 \tag{4.216}$$

$$= 80\text{N} \tag{4.217}$$

4.2.15.6 part f

The minimum energy he would have to expend is the gravitational potential energy needed to lift his body and the egg:

$$mgh = 100 \times 10 \times 20 = 20,000\text{J} \tag{4.218}$$

$$\text{Total Energy} = 20,004J. \tag{4.219}$$

I have assumed the centre of mass of the bird watcher is at his feet as this simplifies the maths for the next question.

4.2.15.7 part g

Use the usual equation the energy needed to boil the egg

$$
\begin{align}
E &= mc\Delta T \tag{4.220}\\
&= 0.02 \times 4000 \times 80 \tag{4.221}\\
&= 2 \times 10^{-2} \times 4 \times 10^{-3} \times 8 \times 10^{1} \tag{4.222}\\
&= 16 \times 10^{2} \tag{4.223}\\
&= 6400\text{J} \tag{4.224}
\end{align}
$$

The minimum efficiency will be given by

$$
\begin{align}
\text{efficiency} &= \frac{6400}{20000} \tag{4.225}\\
&= \frac{64}{200} = 32\% \tag{4.226}
\end{align}
$$

Chapter 5

Oxford Physics Aptitude Test 2009 Answers

5.1 Part A - Maths

5.1.1 Question 1

Using the trig identities you should know:

$$\tan t = \frac{\sin t}{\cos t} \tag{5.1}$$

$$\sin^2 t + \cos^2 t = 1 \tag{5.2}$$

make substitutions from the equations given in the question.

$$y = \tan t = \frac{\sin t}{\cos t} \tag{5.3}$$

$$= \frac{x}{\cos t} \tag{5.4}$$

and

$$\sin^2 t + \cos^2 t = 1 \tag{5.5}$$

$$x^2 + \cos^2 t = 1 \tag{5.6}$$

$$\cos t = \sqrt{1 - x^2} \tag{5.7}$$

Substituting the second resulting equation into the first:

$$y = \frac{x}{\cos t} \tag{5.8}$$

$$= \frac{x}{\sqrt{1 - x^2}} \tag{5.9}$$

5.1.2   Question 2

Break down the given equation into parts that you can graph easily, then build it up. Finding the stationary point(s) at the beginning will also help. Differentiate and set the derivative equal to zero.

$$y = x + 4x^{-2} \tag{5.10}$$

$$\frac{dy}{dx} = 1 - 8x^{-3} = 0 \tag{5.11}$$

$$1 - \frac{8}{x^3} = 0 \tag{5.12}$$

$$1 = \frac{8}{x^3} \tag{5.13}$$

$$x^3 = 8 \tag{5.14}$$

$$x = 2 \tag{5.15}$$

Substituting back in gives $y = 3$.

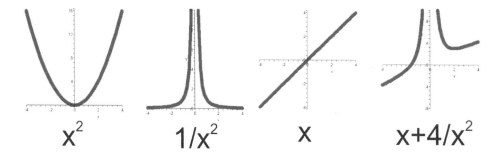

5.1.3   Question 3

For a straight line you need to know two points through which it passes. One is given in the question (0,4), the other you need to work out. A line going radial out from the origin (0,0), must intercept the tangent line and be perpendicular to the it (the tangent line). Therefore their gradients will multiply to -1. Considering the gradients of the radial and tangent lines:

$$\frac{y_2 - y_1}{x_2 - x_1} \times \frac{y_3 - y_2}{x_3 - x_2} = -1 \tag{5.16}$$

$$\frac{y - 0}{x - 0} \times \frac{4 - y}{0 - x} = -1 \tag{5.17}$$

$$\frac{y}{x} \times \frac{4 - y}{-x} = -1 \tag{5.18}$$

$$\frac{y(4 - y)}{x^2} = 1 \tag{5.19}$$

$$4y - y^2 = x^2 \tag{5.20}$$

$$4y = x^2 + y^2 \tag{5.21}$$

Now you also know that the radius of the circle is 2, so making a right angled triangle with the origin and the tangent point (x,y) as vertices, you know

$$x^2 + y^2 = 4 \tag{5.22}$$

Using these two equations gives:

$$4y = 4 \tag{5.23}$$

$$y = 1 \tag{5.24}$$

Using $x^2 + y^2 = 4$ again gives $x = \sqrt{3}$. So the tangent line passes through the points $(0,4)$ and $(\sqrt{3}, 1)$. Its gradient is given by:

$$m = \frac{y_2 - y_1}{x_2 - x_1} \tag{5.25}$$

$$= \frac{4 - 1}{0 - \sqrt{3}} = -\frac{3}{\sqrt{3}} = -\sqrt{3} \tag{5.26}$$

Now you need to find the intercept on the y axis - this is simply 4 given from the point (0,4). So the equation of the right hand tangent line is

$$y = -\frac{3}{\sqrt{3}}x + 4 = -\sqrt{3}x + 4 \tag{5.27}$$

The other tangent line passes through the same point $(0,4)$, but $(-\sqrt{3}, 1)$. This line will have the same magnitude of gradient, but positive, therefore

$$y = \frac{3}{\sqrt{3}}x + 4 = \sqrt{3}x + 4 \tag{5.28}$$

5.1.4 Question 4

5.1.4.1 part i

Remember that:

$$a = b^c \tag{5.29}$$

$$c = \log_b a \tag{5.30}$$

Therefore:

$$\log_2^3 \sqrt{x} = \frac{1}{2} \tag{5.31}$$

$$\log_2 x^{\frac{1}{3}} = \frac{1}{2} \tag{5.32}$$

$$x^{\frac{1}{3}} = 2^{\frac{1}{2}} \tag{5.33}$$

$$x = (2^{\frac{1}{2}})^3 \tag{5.34}$$

$$= \pm 2^{\frac{3}{2}} = 2\sqrt{2} \tag{5.35}$$

5.1.4.2   part ii

Remember that:

$$\log_b a = \frac{\log_d a}{\log_d b} \tag{5.36}$$

Therefore:

$$(\log_8 16)^{\frac{1}{2}} = \left(\frac{\log_2 16}{\log_2 8}\right)^{\frac{1}{2}} \tag{5.37}$$

$$= \left(\frac{4}{3}\right)^{\frac{1}{2}} \tag{5.38}$$

$$= \frac{2}{\sqrt{3}} \tag{5.39}$$

(Remember that in words: $\log_2 16$ means 2 to the power of something gives me 16 i.e. if $c = \log_b a$ then $a = b^c$)

5.1.5   Question 5

Substitute $x = x^2$ so

$$y^2 - 13y + 36 = 0 \tag{5.40}$$

Now use the quadratic formula to solve:

$$y = \frac{13 \pm \sqrt{169 - 4 \times 1 \times 36}}{2} \tag{5.41}$$

$$= \frac{13 \pm \sqrt{169 - 144}}{2} \tag{5.42}$$

$$= \frac{13 \pm 5}{2} \tag{5.43}$$

$$= 4 \text{ or } 9 \tag{5.44}$$

Now $y = x^2$ therefore, $x = \pm\sqrt{y}$ so $x = \pm\sqrt{4}$ and $\pm\sqrt{9}$ which is ± 2 and ± 3.

5.1.6 Question 6

Notice that the right hand side is a geometric progression. The sum is given by the usual equation

$$\Sigma_\infty = \frac{a}{1-r} \tag{5.45}$$

a, the first term is 1 and the common ratio, r, is $1/x$ so

$$x + 2 < \frac{1}{1 - \frac{1}{x}} \tag{5.46}$$

Multiplying the right hand side by x/x

$$
\begin{array}{rcll}
x + 2 & < & \dfrac{x}{x-1} & (5.47) \\[2mm]
(x+2)(x-1) & < & x & (5.48) \\[2mm]
x^2 + x - 2 & < & x & (5.49) \\[2mm]
x^2 & < & 2 & (5.50) \\[2mm]
x < \pm\sqrt{2} & & & (5.51)
\end{array}
$$

But the question states $x > 0$ therefore $x < \sqrt{2}$. However this isn't quite the whole story. Consider a graph of

$$\frac{1}{1 - \frac{1}{x}} \tag{5.52}$$

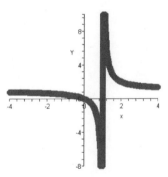

or the presence of a singularity when $x = 1$. Thus the sum of the geometric progression is only greater than $x + 2$ between 1 and $\sqrt{2}$ for positive x, so

$$1 < x < \sqrt{2} \tag{5.53}$$

However, if x is less than 1, the sum to infinity does not converge, but these values of x do satisfy the inequality. Therefore:

$$0 < x < \sqrt{2} \tag{5.54}$$

5.1.7 Question 7

5.1.7.1 part i

Follow the hint in the question - draw or at least think of a tree diagram.

The combinations given a sum of 10 or more are

$$4 \ + \ 6 \tag{5.55}$$

$$5 \ + \ 5 \tag{5.56}$$

$$5 \ + \ 6 \tag{5.57}$$

$$6 \ + \ 4 \tag{5.58}$$

$$6 \ + \ 5 \tag{5.59}$$

$$6 \ + \ 6 \tag{5.60}$$

Each of these has a probability of $1/6 \times 1/6 = 1/36$. Since there are six combinations this gives $6/36 = 1/6$.

5.1.7.2 part ii

Use the list from the previous question and calculate the totals:

$$4 \; + \; 6 = 10 \tag{5.61}$$

$$5 \; + \; 5 = 10 \tag{5.62}$$

$$5 \; + \; 6 = 11 \tag{5.63}$$

$$6 \; + \; 4 = 10 \tag{5.64}$$

$$6 \; + \; 5 = 11 \tag{5.65}$$

$$6 \; + \; 6 = 12 \tag{5.66}$$

If the total is 10, then on the third die a 5 or 6 is needed. Probability is

$$\frac{3}{6} \times \frac{2}{6} = \frac{6}{36} \tag{5.67}$$

Remember that the 10 or more on the first two dice is given so we don't need to take the probability for this into account. You just multiply the probability of getting a total of 10 (3/6) by the probability of getting a 5 or 6 2/6.

If the total is 11, then on the third die a 4, 5 or 6 is needed. Probability is

$$\frac{2}{6} \times \frac{3}{6} = \frac{6}{36} \tag{5.68}$$

Lastly, if the total is 12, then on the third die a 3,4,5 or 6 is needed. Probability is

$$\frac{1}{6} \times \frac{4}{6} = \frac{4}{36} \tag{5.69}$$

The total probability is given by adding:

$$\frac{6+6+4}{36} = \frac{16}{36} = \frac{4}{9} \tag{5.70}$$

5.1.8 Question 8

Start with the simple graph of $\sin x$ and modify it.

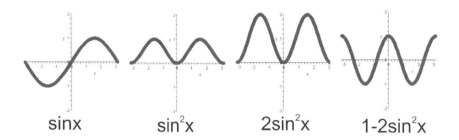

sinx   sin²x   2sin²x   1-2sin²x

Alternatively, remember the trig identity:

$$2\sin^2 x = 1 - \cos 2x \tag{5.71}$$

$$\cos 2x = 1 - 2\sin^2 x \tag{5.72}$$

and plot a graph of $\cos 2x$.

5.1.9 Question 9

As the question has given the equation of the line and has asked for an area, you should immediately be thinking about integrating. For this you need the limits in addition to the equation. The lower limit is obviously zero. To find the upper limit solve the equation for $y = 0$.

$$y = \frac{(x^2 - 4x)}{\sqrt{x}} \tag{5.73}$$

$$0 = \frac{(x^2 - 4x)}{\sqrt{x}} \tag{5.74}$$

$$\tag{5.75}$$

Notice that this is solved whenever the numerator is zero. So

$$0 = (x^2 - 4x) \tag{5.76}$$

$$4x = x^2 \tag{5.77}$$

$$4 = x \tag{5.78}$$

Now integrate by parts

$$\int u\,dv = uv - \int v\,du \tag{5.79}$$

$$dv = x^{-\frac{1}{2}} \tag{5.80}$$

$$v = 2x^{\frac{1}{2}} \tag{5.81}$$

$$u = x^2 - 4x \tag{5.82}$$

$$du = 2x - 4 \tag{5.83}$$

$$\int u\,dv = (x^2 - 4x)2x^{\frac{1}{2}} - \int 2x^{\frac{1}{2}}(2x - 4)dx \tag{5.84}$$

$$= (x^2 - 4x)2x^{\frac{1}{2}} - \int 4x^{\frac{3}{2}} - 8x^{\frac{1}{2}}dx \tag{5.85}$$

$$= \left[(x^2 - 4x)2x^{\frac{1}{2}} - \left[\frac{2}{5} \times x^{\frac{5}{2}} - \frac{2}{3} \times 8x^{\frac{3}{2}}\right]\right]_{x=0}^{x=4} \tag{5.86}$$

$$= -\left[\frac{2}{5} \times 4 \times 4^{\frac{5}{2}} - \frac{2}{3} \times 8 \times 4^{\frac{3}{2}}\right] \tag{5.87}$$

$$= -\left[\frac{2}{5} \times 4 \times 4 \times 4 \times 2 - \frac{2}{3} \times 8 \times 4 \times 2\right] \tag{5.88}$$

$$= -\left[\frac{256}{5} - \frac{128}{3}\right] \tag{5.89}$$

$$= -\left[\frac{768 - 640}{15}\right] \tag{5.90}$$

$$= -\frac{128}{15} = -8\frac{8}{15} \tag{5.91}$$

Note that I used $4^{5/2} = 4 \times 4 \times 4^{1/2} = 4 \times 4 \times 2 = 32$. Alteratively use the following method after finding the integration limits.

$$A = \int_0^4 \frac{x^2 - 4x}{\sqrt{x}}dx \tag{5.92}$$

$$= \int_0^4 x^{\frac{3}{2}} - 4x^{\frac{1}{2}}dx \tag{5.93}$$

$$= \left[\frac{2x^{\frac{5}{2}}}{5} - \frac{8x^{\frac{3}{2}}}{3}\right]_0^4 \tag{5.94}$$

$$= \frac{2 \times 4^{\frac{5}{2}}}{5} - \frac{8 \times 4^{\frac{3}{2}}}{3} \tag{5.95}$$

$$= \frac{2 \times 2^5}{5} - \frac{8 \times 2^3}{3} \tag{5.96}$$

$$= \frac{64}{5} - \frac{64}{3} \tag{5.97}$$

$$= \frac{192 - 320}{15} \tag{5.98}$$

$$= -\frac{128}{15} \tag{5.99}$$

5.1.10 Question 10

Notice that the given triangle is equilateral - i.e. all three internal angles are 60° and all sides are the same length. Do this question in four parts - A, B, C, D. For part A, triangle A has an angle of 30° at the top (since it's half of 60°) and one side is given by r. This is true since any straight line which touches a circle will be a tangent at that point, and so a line drawn radially out from the centre of the circle will be of length r and perpendicular to the tangent. So side A is

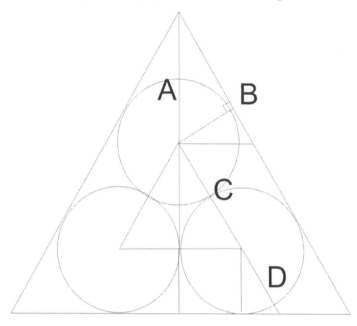

$$\sin\theta = \frac{\text{opp}}{\text{hyp}} \tag{5.100}$$

$$\sin 30 = \frac{r}{A} \tag{5.101}$$

$$\frac{1}{2} = \frac{r}{A} \tag{5.102}$$

$$A = 2r \tag{5.103}$$

Now length B will be given by the hypotenuse of the triangle with the angle in the bottom right of 60° and the opposite side of length 2r.

$$\sin 60 = \frac{2r}{B} \tag{5.104}$$

$$\frac{\sqrt{3}}{2} = \frac{2r}{B} \tag{5.105}$$

$$B = \frac{4r}{\sqrt{3}} \tag{5.106}$$

For part C, right angled triangle C has a hypotenuse of length 2r as it joins the centres of the circles along their radii. This is parallel, so the same length as the right hand side.

Length D is given by another right angle triangle with bottom right angle of 60° and an opposite of length r.

$$\sin 60 \quad = \quad \frac{r}{D} \tag{5.107}$$

$$\frac{\sqrt{3}}{2} = \frac{r}{D} \tag{5.108}$$

$$D \quad = \quad \frac{2r}{\sqrt{3}} \tag{5.109}$$

So the length of the side of the given triangle is

$$B + C + D \quad = \quad \frac{4r}{\sqrt{3}} + 2r + \frac{2r}{\sqrt{3}} \tag{5.110}$$

$$= \quad \frac{4r + 2\sqrt{3}r + 2r}{\sqrt{3}} \tag{5.111}$$

$$= \quad \frac{(6 + 2\sqrt{3})r}{\sqrt{3}} \tag{5.112}$$

The area of the triangle is given by

$$Area \quad = \quad \frac{1}{2}ab\sin C \tag{5.113}$$

$$= \quad \frac{1}{2}\left[\frac{(6 + 2\sqrt{3})r}{\sqrt{3}}\right]^2 \sin 60 \tag{5.114}$$

$$= \quad \frac{1}{2}\left[\frac{(6 + 2\sqrt{3})r}{\sqrt{3}}\right]^2 \frac{\sqrt{3}}{2} \tag{5.115}$$

$$= \quad \frac{1}{2} \times \frac{\sqrt{3}}{2} \times \frac{r^2}{3}(6 + 2\sqrt{3})^2 \tag{5.116}$$

$$= \quad \frac{r^2}{4\sqrt{3}}(36 + 24\sqrt{3} + 12) \tag{5.117}$$

$$= \quad \frac{r^2}{4\sqrt{3}}(48 + 24\sqrt{3}) \tag{5.118}$$

$$= \quad r^2\left[\frac{48 + 24\sqrt{3}}{4\sqrt{3}}\right] \tag{5.119}$$

$$= \quad r^2\left[\frac{12 + 6\sqrt{3}}{\sqrt{3}}\right] \tag{5.120}$$

$$= \quad 6r^2\left[\frac{2 + \sqrt{3}}{\sqrt{3}}\right] \tag{5.121}$$

Now for the ratio with the area of the circles divide $3\pi r^2$ by the area of the triangle.

$$\frac{3\pi r^2}{6r^2\left[\frac{2+\sqrt{3}}{\sqrt{3}}\right]} = \frac{3\pi}{6\left[\frac{2+\sqrt{3}}{\sqrt{3}}\right]} \tag{5.122}$$

$$= \frac{\pi}{2\left[\frac{2+\sqrt{3}}{\sqrt{3}}\right]} \tag{5.123}$$

$$= \frac{\pi}{\frac{4}{\sqrt{3}}+2} \tag{5.124}$$

5.1.11 Question 11

For an arithmetic progression there must be the same difference between all terms. So

$$a - \frac{a}{b} = \frac{a}{b} - -\frac{a}{b} \tag{5.125}$$

$$a - \frac{a}{b} = \frac{2a}{b} \tag{5.126}$$

$$a = \frac{3a}{b} \tag{5.127}$$

$$b = 3 \tag{5.128}$$

To confirm this gives a arithmetic progression:

$$-a, -\frac{a}{3}, \frac{a}{3}, a \tag{5.129}$$

with a common difference of $\frac{2}{3}$.

5.1.12 Question 12

Express as a fraction and multiply out the brackets. It might look tedious, but its simple maths - you'll easily get the correct answer as long as you're careful:

$$2.1^5 = \left(2+\frac{1}{10}\right)\left(2+\frac{1}{10}\right)\left(2+\frac{1}{10}\right)^3 \tag{5.130}$$

$$= \left[4+\frac{4}{10}+\frac{1}{100}\right]\left(2+\frac{1}{10}\right)\left(2+\frac{1}{10}\right)^2 \tag{5.131}$$

$$= \left[8+\frac{4}{10}+\frac{8}{10}+\frac{4}{10}+\frac{2}{100}+\frac{1}{1000}\right]\left[4+\frac{4}{10}+\frac{1}{100}\right] \tag{5.132}$$

Multiplying out these two brackets gives:

$$= \quad 32 + \frac{32}{10} + \frac{8}{100} + \frac{16}{10} + \frac{16}{100} + \frac{4}{1000} + \frac{32}{10} + \frac{32}{100} + \frac{8}{1000} \tag{5.133}$$

$$+ \quad \frac{16}{100} + \frac{16}{1000} + \frac{4}{10000} + \frac{8}{100} + \frac{8}{1000} \tag{5.134}$$

$$+ \quad \frac{2}{10000} + \frac{4}{1000} + \frac{4}{10000} + \frac{1}{100000} \tag{5.135}$$

$$= \quad 32 + \frac{32 + 16 + 32}{10} + \frac{8 + 16 + 32 + 16 + 8}{100} \tag{5.136}$$

$$+ \quad \frac{4 + 8 + 16 + 8 + 4}{1000} + \frac{4 + 2 + 4}{10000} \tag{5.137}$$

$$= \quad 32 + 8 + 0.8 + 0.04 + 0.001 \tag{5.138}$$

$$= \quad 40.841 \tag{5.139}$$

$$= \quad 40.8 \tag{5.140}$$

5.2 Part B - Physics

5.2.1 Question 13

Use the equation $E = mc^2$ as this relates mass and energy (and the value of c is a useful hint given in the question).

$$E \quad = \quad mc^2 \tag{5.141}$$

$$3.8 \times 10^{26} \quad = \quad m \times \left(3 \times 10^8\right)^2 \tag{5.142}$$

$$= \quad m \times 9 \times 10^{16} \tag{5.143}$$

$$\frac{3.8 \times 10^{26}}{9 \times 10^{16}} \quad = \quad m \tag{5.144}$$

$$\left(\frac{3.8}{9}\right) \times 10^{10} \quad = \quad m \tag{5.145}$$

$$\approx \quad \frac{4}{10} \times 10^{10} = 0.4 \times 10^{10} = 4 \times 10^9 \tag{5.146}$$

Therefore the answer is A. To check the units remember $1W = 1J/s$ so if the left hand side is its usual units but additionally per second, the right hand side also needs to be its usual units but per second as well.

5.2.2 Question 14

The batteries in parallel will give the same maximum voltage (as the voltages can't add), but a higher maximum current as there are more batteries. Therefore the answer is C.

5.2.3 Question 15

NOTE: there is a mistake in the question, it should say: the Sun has an angular diameter of 9.3mrad as seen from the surface of Saturn. A lunar eclipse of Titan by Saturn, involves Saturn coming between the Sun and Titan - this is obviously possible. A solar eclipse involves Titan coming between the Sun and Saturn. A partial eclipse, when the bodies' paths pass very near each other and only partially cover each other, is again obviously possible. An annular eclipse is also possible as this is where their paths cross perfectly but they appear different sizes. The only one which can't occur is C a total solar eclipse due to Titan as Titan and the Sun appear different sizes. The Earth and Moon are unique in the solar system, in that the Moon is exactly the correct size so that a total solar eclipse can occur.

5.2.4 Question 16

When in the boat the anchor displaces its weight in water. When in the lake the anchor displaces its volume in water. If you assume the anchor is more dense than water it will displace more water when it is in the boat so if it dropped into the lake the water level drops slightly. Therefore the answer is C.

5.2.5 Question 17

Here you need to compare the gravitational potential energy lost by the water as it drops to the energy gained as its temperature increases. The hints given in the question are the fact that the height is given (suggests gravitational potential energy) and the specific heat capacity of water which suggests $E = mc\Delta T$.

$$mc\Delta T = mgh \tag{5.147}$$
$$c\Delta T = gh \tag{5.148}$$
$$\Delta T = \frac{gh}{c} \tag{5.149}$$
$$= \frac{10 \times 105}{4200} \tag{5.150}$$
$$= \frac{1050}{4200} \tag{5.151}$$
$$= 0.25°C \tag{5.152}$$

Therefore the answer is B. Note that the standard until for c is $\text{Jkg}^{-1}\text{K}^{-1}$ so you must use 4200 and also $1\text{K} = 1°C$.

5.2.6   Question 18

This question is a simple exercise in substituting numbers into an equation. Remember to use the correct units 16kV is 16,000V.

$$t = d\sqrt{\frac{m}{2qU}} \tag{5.153}$$

$$\frac{t}{d} = \sqrt{\frac{m}{2qU}} \tag{5.154}$$

$$\frac{t^2}{d^2} = \frac{m}{2qU} \tag{5.155}$$

$$\frac{2qUt^2}{d^2} = m \tag{5.156}$$

$$m = \frac{2 \times 1.6 \times 10^{-19} \times 16 \times 10^3 \times (30 \times 10^{-6})^2}{1.5^2} \tag{5.157}$$

$$= \frac{2 \times 1.6 \times 10^{-19} \times 16 \times 10^3 \times 900 \times 10^{-12}}{1.5^2} \tag{5.158}$$

$$= \frac{32 \times 1.6 \times 900 \times 10^{-19} \times 10^3 \times 10^{-12}}{2.25} \tag{5.159}$$

$$= \frac{32 \times 1440 \times 10^{-28}}{2.25} \tag{5.160}$$

$$= \frac{3.2 \times 10^1 \times 1.44 \times 10^3 \times 10^{-28}}{2.25} \tag{5.161}$$

$$= \frac{3.2 \times 1.44}{2.25} \times 10^{-24} \tag{5.162}$$

$$\approx \frac{3 \times 1.5}{2} \times 10^{-24} = 2 \times 10^{-24} \text{kg} \tag{5.163}$$

Therefore the answer is D.

5.2.7   Question 19

To find out the sort of quantity you need to know its units. So rearrange the given equation to make K the subject.

$$F = Kv^2 A \tag{5.164}$$

$$\frac{F}{v^2 A} = K \tag{5.165}$$

Now substitute in the units for the quantities on the right hand side. Remember force can be measured in N or kgms^{-2} (F=ma). So

$$K = \frac{\text{kgms}^{-2}}{\text{m}^2\text{s}^{-2}\text{m}^2} \tag{5.166}$$

$$= \frac{\text{kgms}^{-2}}{\text{m}^4\text{s}^{-2}} \tag{5.167}$$

$$= \frac{\text{kg}}{\text{m}^3} \text{ or kgm}^{-3} \tag{5.168}$$

Therefore K has the units of a density and the answer is D.

5.2.8 Question 20

The battery provides DC. Initially the current will increase as one resistor has been removed. But the steady state for direct current in a capacitor is for no current to flow. A current flows initially to charge the capacitor but then drops. The answer is C.

5.2.9 Question 21

The light will be refracted by the prism. It does not matter that it is coloured light, rather than white light. Consider what happens when light goes into the prism from a less to more dense material it will bend towards the normal - i.e. downwards slightly. As it then travels from the prism back into the air it is traveling from a more to less dense material and it bends away from the normal. This is again downwards as the direction of the normals are different on each side of the prism. In total the light bends down and the answer is B.

5.2.10 Question 22

The Moon can be considered in circular motion around the Earth. Therefore you need circular motion equations.

$$a = \frac{v^2}{r} \tag{5.169}$$

$$v = \frac{2\pi r}{T} \tag{5.170}$$

$$a = \left[\frac{2\pi r}{T}\right]^2 \frac{1}{r} \tag{5.171}$$

$$= \frac{4\pi^2 r}{T^2} \tag{5.172}$$

$$= \frac{4\pi^2 \times 4 \times 10^8}{(2.4 \times 10^6)^2} \tag{5.173}$$

$$= \frac{16\pi^2 \times 10^8}{2.4^2 \times 10^{12}} \tag{5.174}$$

$$= \frac{16\pi^2}{2.4^2} \times 10^{-4} \tag{5.175}$$

$$= \frac{1.6\pi^2}{2.4^2} \times 10^{-3} \tag{5.176}$$

$$\tag{5.177}$$

Now

$$2.4^2 = \left(2 + \frac{4}{10}\right)\left(2 + \frac{4}{10}\right) \tag{5.178}$$

$$= 4 + \frac{8}{10} + \frac{8}{10} + \frac{16}{100} \tag{5.179}$$

$$= 4 + 1.6 + 0.16 \tag{5.180}$$

$$= 5.76 \tag{5.181}$$

and

$$\pi^2 \approx 3.1^2 \tag{5.182}$$

$$3.1^2 = \left(3 + \frac{1}{10}\right)\left(3 + \frac{1}{10}\right) \tag{5.183}$$

$$= 9 + \frac{6}{10} + \frac{1}{100} \tag{5.184}$$

$$= 9.61 \tag{5.185}$$

So

$$a = \frac{1.6 \times 9.61}{5.76} \times 10^{-3} \tag{5.186}$$

$$= \frac{(1 + 0.5 + 0.1) \times 9.61}{5.76} \times 10^{-3} \tag{5.187}$$

$$= \frac{9.61 + 4.805 + 0.961}{5.76} \times 10^{-3} \tag{5.188}$$

$$= \frac{15.376}{5.76} \times 10^{-3} \tag{5.189}$$

$$\approx 3 \times 10^{-3} \text{ms}^{-2} \tag{5.190}$$

Therefore the answer is A.

5.2.11 Question 23

Simply rearrange the equation and substitute number in.

$$P = AkT^2 \tag{5.191}$$

$$\frac{P}{kT^2} = A \tag{5.192}$$

$$\frac{75}{6 \times 10^{-8} \times 5000^4} = A \tag{5.193}$$

$$\frac{75}{6 \times 10^{-8} \times 5^4 \times (10^3)^4} = A \tag{5.194}$$

$$\frac{75}{6 \times 10^{-8} \times 625 \times 10^{12}} = A \tag{5.195}$$

$$\frac{7.5 \times 10^1}{3750 \times 10^4} = A \tag{5.196}$$

$$\frac{7.5 \times 10^1}{3.75 \times 10^3 \times 10^4} = A \tag{5.197}$$

$$2 \times 10^{-6} m^2 = A \tag{5.198}$$

5.2.12 Question 24

Represent the length of each vessel by the letters p,q,r. From the question you know - remember the hint from the question: surface area is proportional to length^2 and volume is proportional to length^3

$$q + r = 2p \tag{5.199}$$

$$q^2 = 2p^2 + r^2 \tag{5.200}$$

Rearranging and substituting:

$$q = 2p - r \tag{5.201}$$

$$q^2 = 4p^2 - 4pr + r^2 = 2p^2 + r^2 \tag{5.202}$$

$$4p^2 - 4pr = 2p^2 \tag{5.203}$$

$$2p^2 - 4pr = 0 \tag{5.204}$$

$$2p - 4r = 0 \tag{5.205}$$

$$p = 2r \tag{5.206}$$

Substituting this back in:

$$q = 2p - r \tag{5.207}$$

$$= 4r - r \tag{5.208}$$

$$= 3r \tag{5.209}$$

Considering the crew:

$$p^2 = 4r^2 \tag{5.210}$$

$$q^2 = 9r^2 \tag{5.211}$$

Considering the cargo capacity

$$p^3 = 8r^3 \tag{5.212}$$

$$q^3 = 27r^3 \tag{5.213}$$

Considering the cargo capacity of the fully loaded quizzer, where a is the number of pangs and b is the number of roodles:

$$27r^3 = a8r^3 + br^3 \tag{5.214}$$

$$27 = 8a + b \tag{5.215}$$

Consider the total number of crew needed for these pangs and roodles:

$$4ar^2 + br^2 \tag{5.216}$$

$$4a + b \tag{5.217}$$

This need to be minimised. Note a and b can't be negative. So using the equation $27 = 8a + b$ we find that a can either be 0 (b=27), 1 (b=19), 2(b=11), 3(b=3) or 4(b=0). The minimum value of crew is be given by minimising $4a + b$ - thus a=3 and b=3.

5.2.13 Question 25

Label the resistors as follows

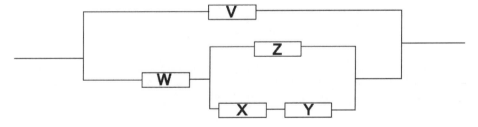

Now calculate resistances using

$$\frac{1}{R_T} = \frac{1}{R_1} + \frac{1}{R_2} \tag{5.218}$$

$$R_T = \frac{R_1 R_2}{R_1 + R_2} \tag{5.219}$$

$$X + Y \quad = \quad 2000\Omega \tag{5.220}$$

$$X + Y + Z \quad = \quad \frac{1000 \times 2000}{1000 + 2000} \tag{5.221}$$

$$= \quad \frac{2 \times 10^6}{3 \times 10^3} \tag{5.222}$$

$$= \quad \frac{2}{3} \times 10^3 \Omega \tag{5.223}$$

$$W + X + Y + Z \quad = \quad \frac{2}{3} \times 10^3 + 1000 = \frac{5}{3} \times 10^3 \Omega \tag{5.224}$$

$$V + W + X + Y + Z \quad = \quad \frac{1 \times \frac{5}{3} \times 10^6}{\frac{8}{3} \times 10^3} \tag{5.225}$$

$$= \quad \frac{\frac{5}{3}}{\frac{8}{3}} \times 10^3 \tag{5.226}$$

$$= \quad \frac{5}{8} \times 10^3 \tag{5.227}$$

$$= \quad 625\Omega \tag{5.228}$$

If a 6V battery is connected:

$$V_{battery} \quad = \quad \frac{125}{625 + 125} \times 6 \tag{5.229}$$

$$= \quad \frac{1}{6} \times 6 = 1V \tag{5.230}$$

$$V_{VWXYZ} \quad = \quad \frac{625}{625 + 125} \times 6 \tag{5.231}$$

$$= \quad 5V \tag{5.232}$$

Now continue will each stage of resistors. As resistor V is in parallel with resistors WXYZ, there will be 5V across each. Now considering the W and XYZ resistors in series:

$$V_W \quad = \quad \frac{1000}{1000 + 2/3 \times 10^3} \times 5V \tag{5.233}$$

$$= \quad \frac{3/3}{5/3} \times 5V \tag{5.234}$$

$$= \quad \frac{3}{5} \times 5V \tag{5.235}$$

$$= \quad 3V \tag{5.236}$$

Therefore there must by 2V across XYZ. Since Z is in parallel with XY, there will be 2V across each. So is there is 2V across XY with resistance 2000Ω using $V = IR$ there will be a current of

$$I \quad = \quad \frac{V}{R} \tag{5.237}$$

$$= \quad \frac{2}{2000} \tag{5.238}$$

$$= \quad 1 \times 10^{-3} = 1\text{mA} \tag{5.239}$$

5.2.14 Question 26

Firstly remember that perpendicular components of motion are independent and that a particle accelerated through a potential difference gains an energy of eV. So:

$$eV = \frac{1}{2}mv^2 \tag{5.240}$$

$$\frac{2eV}{m} = v^2 \tag{5.241}$$

$$\frac{2 \times 1.6 \times 10^{-19} \times 50}{10^{-30}} = v^2 \tag{5.242}$$

$$1.6 \times 10^{13} = v^2 \tag{5.243}$$

$$16 \times 10^{12} = v^2 \tag{5.244}$$

$$4 \times 10^6 = v \tag{5.245}$$

This gives us the final velocity when the electron reaches the second plate, but the average velocity over its journey is half this. Using $v = d/t$

$$t = \frac{d}{v} = \frac{0.4}{2 \times 10^6} \tag{5.246}$$

$$= 0.2 \times 10^{-6}\text{s} \tag{5.247}$$

Now note down what you know for the vertical component of the motion:

$$u = 0 \tag{5.248}$$

$$a = 10 \tag{5.249}$$

$$t = 0.2 \times 10^{-6} \tag{5.250}$$

$$s = ? \tag{5.251}$$

Therefore:

$$s = ut + \frac{1}{2}at^2 \tag{5.252}$$

$$= \frac{1}{2} \times 10 \times (0.2 \times 10^{-6})^2 \tag{5.253}$$

$$= 5 \times 0.04 \times 10^{-12} \tag{5.254}$$

$$= 0.2 \times 10^{-12}\text{m} \tag{5.255}$$

$$= 2 \times 10^{-13}\text{m} \tag{5.256}$$

5.2.15   Question 27

5.2.15.1   part a

$$E = \frac{1}{2}mv^2 \tag{5.257}$$

5.2.15.2   part b

$$v = \frac{s}{t} \tag{5.258}$$

$$t = \frac{s}{v} \tag{5.259}$$

$$\text{Power} = \frac{\text{Energy}}{\text{Time}} \tag{5.260}$$

$$= \frac{mv^2v}{2s} \tag{5.261}$$

$$= \frac{mv^3}{2s} \tag{5.262}$$

5.2.15.3   part c

$$\text{Energy used for distance d} = \text{Power} \times \text{Time to travel distance d} \tag{5.263}$$

$$E = \frac{mv^3}{2s} \times \frac{d}{v} \tag{5.264}$$

$$= \frac{mv^2d}{2s} \tag{5.265}$$

5.2.15.4   part d

$$E = \frac{mv^2d}{2s} \tag{5.266}$$

$$= \frac{10^3 \times 10^2 \times 10^3}{2 \times 100} \tag{5.267}$$

$$= 0.5 \times 10^6 \text{J} \tag{5.268}$$

If v doubles to 20ms^{-1} then $20^2 = 400$ rather than 100 so energy is multiplied by 4.

5.2.15.5   part e

$$\text{Volume} = \text{Area} \times \text{Distance traveled} \tag{5.269}$$

$$V = Avt \tag{5.270}$$

$$\text{Density} = \frac{\text{Mass}}{\text{Volume}} \tag{5.271}$$

$$m = DV \tag{5.272}$$

$$= DAvt \tag{5.273}$$

Now

$$KE = \frac{1}{2}mv^2 \tag{5.274}$$

$$= \frac{1}{2}DAvtv^2 \tag{5.275}$$

$$= \frac{1}{2}DAv^3t \tag{5.276}$$

$$\text{Power} = \frac{\text{Energy}}{\text{Time}} \tag{5.277}$$

$$= \frac{1}{2}DAv^3 \tag{5.278}$$

5.2.15.6   part f

Energy lost due to air resistance is given by:

$$\text{Energy} = \text{Power} \times \text{Time} \tag{5.279}$$

$$= \frac{1}{2}DAv^3t \tag{5.280}$$

$$= \frac{1}{2}DAv^3 \times \frac{d}{v} \tag{5.281}$$

$$= \frac{DAv^2d}{2} \tag{5.282}$$

$$= \frac{1 \times 1 \times 10^2 \times 10^3}{2} \tag{5.283}$$

$$= 0.5 \times 10^5 \text{J} \tag{5.284}$$

Total energy used is that due to air resistance as well as driving the car therefore: $0.55 \times 10^6 J$.

5.2.15.7 part g

Equating the two previous equations:

$$\frac{mv^2d}{2s} = \frac{DAv^2d}{2} \tag{5.285}$$

$$\frac{m}{s} = DA \tag{5.286}$$

$$s = \frac{m}{DA} \tag{5.287}$$

$$= \frac{1000}{1 \times 1} \tag{5.288}$$

$$= 1\text{km} \tag{5.289}$$

5.2.15.8 part h

In cities: cars make frequent stops so more energy is lost through brakes. Therefore they don't need to be aerodynamic, but need to be light. On motorways: cars make infrequent stops so more energy is lost due to air resistance. Therefore cars need to be aerodynamic to be efficient.

Chapter 6

Oxford Physics Aptitude Test Specimen May 2009 Answers

6.1 Part A - Maths

6.1.1 Question 1

$$\sqrt{(5p - 4q)^2 - (4p - 5q)^2} \tag{6.1}$$

Start by multiplying out the brackets, do not introduce $\sqrt{3}$ and $\sqrt{2}$ yet as this will overcomplicate the algebra

$$\sqrt{25p^2 - 40pq + 16q^2 - 16p^2 + 40pq - 25q^2} \tag{6.2}$$

Cancel out $-40pq$ and $+40pq$ and simplify p^2 and q^2 factors

$$\sqrt{9p^2 - 9q^2} \tag{6.3}$$

Take a factor of 9 out

$$\sqrt{9(p^2 - q^2)} = \sqrt{9}\sqrt{p^2 - q^2} = 3\sqrt{(p^2 - q^2)} \tag{6.4}$$

Now add in values for $p = 3$ and $q = 2$

$$3\sqrt{3 - 2} = \pm 3 \tag{6.5}$$

6.1.2 Question 2

The question asks for the set of real numbers for which the equation has real, distinct roots. The first thing you should be thinking here is to find the roots using the quadratic formula

$$x = \frac{-b \pm \sqrt{b^2 - 4ac}}{2a} \tag{6.6}$$

So...

$$x = \frac{-(\lambda - 3) \pm \sqrt{(\lambda - 3)^2 - 4 \times 1 \times \lambda}}{2} \tag{6.7}$$

Multiplying out the $(\lambda - 3)^2$ bracket and applying the minus sign at the start

$$x = \frac{3 - \lambda \pm \sqrt{\lambda^2 - 6\lambda + 9 - 4\lambda}}{2} \tag{6.8}$$

$$= \frac{3 - \lambda \pm \sqrt{\lambda^2 - 10\lambda + 9}}{2} \tag{6.9}$$

Now consider in detail what the question requires. "Real" implies that the number contained within the square root must not be negative (otherwise this would introduce imaginary numbers). "Distinct" implies that the number contained within the square root must not be zero, as this would give two roots which were the same: $(-b \pm 0)/2a$. To find out what values λ can take we apply the quadratic formula again to the contents of the square root i.e. to

$$\lambda^2 - 10\lambda + 9 = 0 \tag{6.10}$$

So

$$\lambda = \frac{10 \pm \sqrt{(-10)^2 - 4 \times 1 \times 9}}{2} \tag{6.11}$$

$$= \frac{10 \pm 8}{2} \tag{6.12}$$

$$\tag{6.13}$$

This has solutions of 1 and 9. These are boundary values. We now need to identify which side of these numbers (1 and 9) allows our equation for λ to have a positive value. Considering the "u" shape of a quadratic with a positive square term (as opposed to the "n" shape of a quadratic with a negative square term), the quadratic for lambda will be greater than zero if lambda is away from the middle i.e. less than 1 or greater than 9. So

$$\lambda < 1 \tag{6.14}$$

and

$$\lambda > 9 \qquad (6.15)$$

6.1.3 Question 3

6.1.3.1 part i

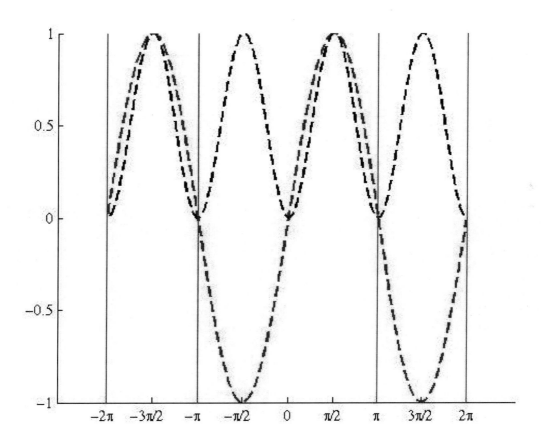

6.1.3.2 part ii

Here you need to think in detail about the values $\sin x$ and $\tan x$ can take. Remember that

$$\sin x \quad = \quad \frac{opposite}{hypotenuse} \qquad (6.16)$$

$$\tan x \quad = \quad \frac{opposite}{adjacent} \qquad (6.17)$$

Now if $0 < x < \pi/2$ you are just considering the angles allowed in a triangle. You also know that the hypotenuse of a triangle must be the longest side. Looking closely at the formulae for sin and tan shows that the numerator is same. If the denominator is larger (as is the case for sin), the fraction is smaller. Therefore $\sin x$ is smaller than $\tan x$

6.1.3.3   part iii

Firstly recognise that $\cos^4 \theta = (\cos^2 \theta)^2$ so that

$$\cos^4 \theta = \frac{1}{4}(1 + \cos 2\theta)^2 \tag{6.18}$$

$$4 \cos^4 \theta = 1 + 2\cos 2\theta + \cos^2 2\theta \tag{6.19}$$

Now reapply the given equality to find an equality for $\cos^2 2\theta$

$$\cos^2 2\theta = \frac{1}{2}(1 + \cos 4\theta) \tag{6.20}$$

Substitute this into the previous equation

$$\cos^4 \theta = \frac{1}{4}\left(1 + 2\cos 2\theta + \frac{1}{2}(1 + \cos 4\theta)\right) \tag{6.21}$$

$$= \frac{1}{4} + \frac{1}{2}\cos 2\theta + \frac{1}{8} + \frac{1}{8}\cos 4\theta \tag{6.22}$$

$$= \frac{3}{8} + \frac{1}{2}\cos 2\theta + \frac{1}{8}\cos 4\theta \tag{6.23}$$

$$= \frac{1}{8}(3 + 4\cos 2\theta + \cos 4\theta) \tag{6.24}$$

6.1.4   Question 4

First start with a quick sketch to check orientation and shape of the triangle.

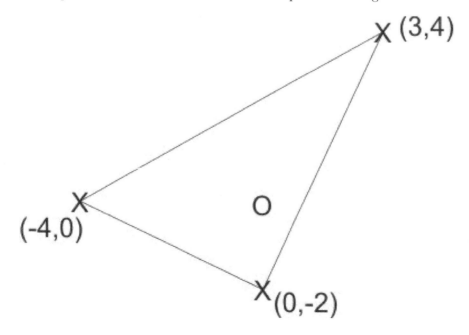

Three points, one of which is not on the straight line joining the other two defines a triangle. A right angle triangle has an angle of 90° between two of the sides. This can be shown by calculating the angles between sides.

A more elegant way is to remember than the gradients of two perpendicular lines multiply to -1. So

$$m_1 = \frac{y_2 - y_1}{x_2 - x_1} = \frac{4 - (-2)}{3 - 0} = 2 \tag{6.25}$$

and

$$m_2 = \frac{y_3 - y_1}{x_3 - x_1} = \frac{0 - (-2)}{-4 - 0} = -\frac{1}{2} \tag{6.26}$$

$$m_1 \times m_2 = 2 \times -\frac{1}{2} = -1 \tag{6.27}$$

Therefore these lines are perpendicular and make up a triangle.

The area is given by the usual equation $A = 0.5 \times base \times height$ so we need to find the lengths of the sides using Pythagoras. Staring with the bottom right edge

$$a = \sqrt{6^2 + 3^2} = \sqrt{45} \tag{6.28}$$

and the bottom left edge

$$a = \sqrt{4^2 + 2^2} = \sqrt{20} \tag{6.29}$$

Therefore

$$Area = \frac{1}{2} \times \sqrt{45} \times \sqrt{20} = \frac{1}{2}\sqrt{45 \times 20} = \frac{1}{2}\sqrt{900} = \frac{1}{2} \times 30 = 15 \tag{6.30}$$

6.1.5 Question 5

For this question you need to remember the definition of logs

$$a = b^c \tag{6.31}$$

$$c = \log_c a \tag{6.32}$$

6.1.5.1 part 1

$$x = 2^2 = 4 \tag{6.33}$$

6.1.5.2 part ii

$$2 = x^2 \tag{6.34}$$

$$x = \sqrt{2} \tag{6.35}$$

6.1.5.3 part iii

$$2 = 2^x \tag{6.36}$$

$$x = 1 \tag{6.37}$$

6.1.6 Question 6

This could be attempted using a Binomial expansion on $(2+0.002)^6$, but an easier method is multiply the bracket out in stages.

$$(2.002)^6 = (2.002^3)^2 \tag{6.38}$$

$$= \left(\left(2+\frac{2}{1000}\right)^3\right)^2 \tag{6.39}$$

$$= \left(2^3 + 3\times2^2\times\frac{2}{10^3} + 3\times2\times\frac{2^2}{10^6} + \frac{2^3}{10^9}\right)^2 \tag{6.40}$$

We can ignore the $2^3/10^9$ part as it won't affect the 4th decimal place. So

$$= \left(8 + \frac{24}{10^3} + \frac{24}{10^6}\right)^2 \tag{6.41}$$

$$= 8^2 + \frac{24^2}{10^6} + \frac{24^2}{10^{12}} + \frac{2\times8\times24}{10^3} + \frac{2\times8\times24}{10^6} + \frac{2\times24\times24}{10^9} \tag{6.42}$$

We can now ignore the $24^2/10^{12}$ and $2\times24\times24/10^9$ part as these will not affect the 4th decimal place. So

$$= 64 + \frac{576}{10^6} + \frac{384}{10^3} + \frac{384}{10^6} \tag{6.43}$$

$$= 64 + \frac{384}{10^3} + \frac{960}{10^6} \tag{6.44}$$

$$= 64 + 0.384 + 0.00096 \tag{6.45}$$

$$= 64.38496 \tag{6.46}$$

$$= 64.3850 \tag{6.47}$$

6.1.7 Question 7

You may find it useful to draw a diagram. After first bounce, ball will have traveled a distance of h, on second bounce, ball will have traveled up to $h/3$ and back down again: so a total of $h + 2h/3$. On the third bounce the ball will have traveled an additional distance of $2h/3^2$ and so on. So ignoring the first term of h, there is a geometric series. The sum to infinity is given be

$$\Sigma\infty = \frac{a}{1-r} \tag{6.48}$$

where a is the first term and r is the common ratio. Be careful to include the correct first term here - it's the first term of the geometric series $2h/3$ and not the overall first term h. If H is the total distance traveled

$$H = h + \frac{\frac{2h}{3}}{1 - \frac{1}{3}} = h + \frac{2h}{3}\frac{3}{2} = 2h \tag{6.49}$$

6.1.8 Question 8

6.1.8.1 part i

The $|x|$ or modulus of x means we always take a positive value for x. To sketch the graph between -1 and 1, evaluate y at some critical points - say x=-1,0,1. This gives y=3,1,3.

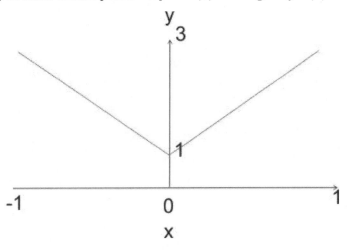

6.1.8.2 part ii

The area can be calculated by dividing the area into a rectangle and two triangles (note height is 2).

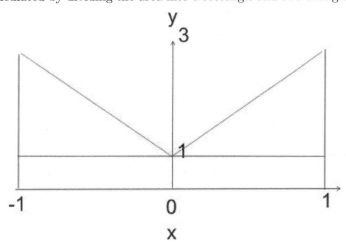

$$Area \quad = \quad 2 \times Triangle + Rectangle \tag{6.50}$$

$$Area \quad = \quad 2 \times \left(\frac{1}{2} \times 1 \times 2\right) + 2 \times 1 \tag{6.51}$$

$$= \quad 4 \tag{6.52}$$

6.1.9 Question 9

With these type of probability questions, the simplest and safest way is to draw, or at least imagine a tree diagram. This doesn't need to be perfectly neat and tidy (unless a tree diagram is specifically asked for). In this case each branch has probability 1/6

6.1.9.1 part i

We can easily see the combinations which add to 6 are (1,5),(2,4),(3,3),(4,2) and (5,1) each with probability $1/6 \times 1/6 = 1/36$. The probability of getting a total of 6 between the two dice is 5/36.

6.1.9.2 part ii

Again you should refer to a tree diagram and remember that we multiply along branches and add between them. So if we get 1 on the first die (with probability 1/6) the probability that the second die shows a number greater than 1 is 5/6. If 2 is thrown first (with probability 1/6) then the second die shows a number greater than 2 with probability 4/6 etc. So

$$p = \frac{1}{6}\frac{5}{6} + \frac{1}{6}\frac{4}{6} + \frac{1}{6}\frac{3}{6} + \frac{1}{6}\frac{2}{6} + \frac{1}{6}\frac{1}{6} \tag{6.53}$$

$$= \frac{5+4+3+2+1}{36} \tag{6.54}$$

$$= \frac{15}{36} \tag{6.55}$$

$$= \frac{5}{12} \tag{6.56}$$

6.1.10 Question 10

A geometric progression has the form

$$a, ar, ar^2, ar^3, ar^4, ... \tag{6.57}$$

and an arithmetic progression has the form

$$b, b+c, b+2c, b+3c, b+4c, ... \tag{6.58}$$

If they have the same first term then a=b. If the second and third terms of the geometric progression are equal to the third and fourth terms of the arithmetic progression respectively

$$ar = a + 2c \tag{6.59}$$

$$ar^2 = a + 3c \tag{6.60}$$

6.1.10.1   part i

To find the common ratio we need to eliminate either a or c from these two equations. Choose c, so

$$\frac{ar - a}{2} = c \tag{6.61}$$

$$\frac{ar^2}{3} = c \tag{6.62}$$

$$\frac{ar - a}{2} = \frac{ar^2 - a}{3} \tag{6.63}$$

$$3ar - 3a = 2ar^2 - 2a \tag{6.64}$$

$$3ar = 2ar^2 + a \tag{6.65}$$

$$3r = 2r^2 + 1 \tag{6.66}$$

$$2r^2 - 3r + 1 = = 0 \tag{6.67}$$

Now, apply the quadratic formula to solve for r

$$r = \frac{3 \pm \sqrt{9^2 - 8}}{4} \tag{6.68}$$

$$r = \frac{3 \pm 1}{4} \tag{6.69}$$

$$r = 1 \text{or} \frac{1}{2} \tag{6.70}$$

As the question says the second and third terms of the geometric progression are distinct, r must equal 1/2 and not 1.

6.1.10.2   part ii

The fifth term of the arithmetic progression is $a + 4c$. So eliminate r from the original two equations by making it the subject. Firstly divide them

$$\frac{ar^2}{ar} = \frac{a + 3c}{a + 2c} \tag{6.71}$$

$$r = \frac{a + 3c}{a + 2c} \tag{6.72}$$

Rearranging the first equation gives

$$r = \frac{a + 2c}{a} \tag{6.73}$$

Putting these together to eliminate r gives

$$\frac{a+3c}{a+2c} = \frac{a+2c}{a} \tag{6.74}$$

$$a(a+3c) = (a+2c)^2 \tag{6.75}$$

$$a^2 + 3ac = a^2 + 4ac + 4c^2 \tag{6.76}$$

$$0 = ac + 4c^2 \tag{6.77}$$

$$0 = a + 4c \tag{6.78}$$

6.1.11 Question 11

To find the maximum and minimum values of a cubic equation within a certain interval you should be thinking about differentiating the equation given and setting it equal to zero to find the turning points.

$$y = x^3 - 12x + 2 \tag{6.79}$$

$$\frac{\delta y}{\delta x} = 3x^2 - 12 = 0 \tag{6.80}$$

$$3x^2 = 12 \tag{6.81}$$

$$x^2 = 4 \tag{6.82}$$

$$x = \pm 2 \tag{6.83}$$

Now consider drawing a sketch. The graph has the usual cubic form with a positive gradient as the x^3 term is positive. Calculate y at a number of 'critical' points - the turning points, the limits of the region we are considering and zero: x=-3,-2,0,2,5. This gives y=10,17,1,-15,66 respectively.

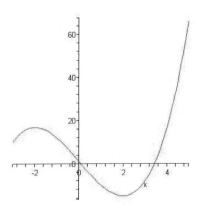

From the sketch is can be clearly seen that the minimum value of x is -15 and the maximum is 66.

6.2 Part B

6.2.1 Question 12

With the detector 6cm from the source, no α will be detected since its range in air is $\approx$ 5cm.

The aluminium plate decreases the counts from 74 to 45 per min therefore this must block something. This must be β.

When the source is removed and the count rate stays the same it shows there was nothing getting through the aluminium - the count rate of 45 per min is the background.

If there is no plate and the source is 2cm away, the count rate increases to 5000 per min - this suggests that there is α present. So the answer is C: alpha and beta

6.2.2 Question 13

If the left engine stops, the forces forwards produced by the two engines will be imbalanced. There will still be the same force on the right, but no forwards force on the left. Therefore the place turns to the left.

If one engine stops, there will be less force pushing it forwards which will reduced its speed. As a result of the speed decreasing, the lift generated by the wings will be less and the plane will fall. So the answer is C, it turns left, falls and slows.

6.2.3 Question 14

Terminal velocity is the constant speed reached when the forces of air resistance (upthrust) and weight are equal in size (but opposite in direction). The answer is A.

6.2.4 Question 15

The answer is A: 1/2 your height. This can be seen by drawing a simple ray diagram. Remember: angle of incidence equals angle of reflection.

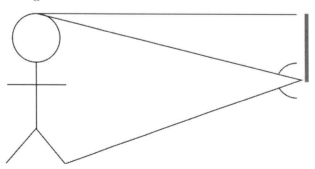

6.2.5   Question 16

All dimensions expand by 1% therefore the radius and circumference of both the hole and the disk expand. The answer is A.

6.2.6   Question 17

The simplest way to answer this question is to use the equation for the heat capacity of the water:

$$E = mc\Delta T \tag{6.84}$$

Where E is the energy, m is the mass, c is the specific heat capacity and ΔT is the change in temperature.

$$\text{Energy of 10kg at } 15°C \quad + \quad \text{Energy of additional water at } 50°C \tag{6.85}$$
$$= \quad \text{Energy of total water at } 37°C \tag{6.86}$$
$$\tag{6.87}$$

Substituting for $E = mc\Delta T$, we can neglect the c term as it is common to all terms on both sides.

$$10 \times 15 + x \times 50 \quad = \quad (10 + x) \times 37 \tag{6.88}$$
$$150 + 50x \quad = \quad 370 + 37x \tag{6.89}$$
$$13x \quad = \quad 220 \tag{6.90}$$
$$x \quad = \quad \frac{220}{13} \approx 17 \tag{6.91}$$

The answer is C: 17kg. Alternatively base yourself at 37°C:

$$10 \times 22 \quad = \quad m \times 13 \tag{6.92}$$
$$m \quad = \quad \frac{220}{13} \tag{6.93}$$

6.2.7   Question 18

Acceleration will be $10ms^{-2}$ as the acceleration will always be equal to g. The answer is C.

6.2.8   Question 19

Recall the equation $V = IR$. Two bulbs will have twice as much resistance, the voltage will be the same, so the current will be half. The answer is A: less current to the series combination.

6.2.9 Question 20

From Earth: A lunar eclipse occurs when the Moon passes behind the Earth such that the Earth blocks the Suns rays from striking the Moon. A solar eclipse occurs when the Moon passes between the Sun and the Earth, and the Moon fully or partially covers the Sun as viewed from some location on Earth.

From the Moon a solar eclipse will occur when the Earth passes between the Sun and the Moon, Thus, on Earth a lunar eclipse will occur. The answer is B.

6.2.10 Question 21

Your image appears behind the mirror - the same distance behind the mirror as you are in front of it. Therefore, if you move 5m towards the mirror, your image also gets 5m closer to you - giving a total of 10m. The answer is C.

6.2.11 Question 22

Remember: angle of incidence equals angle of reflection.

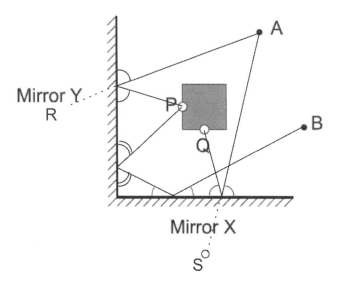

6.2.12 Question 23

Demote the slepton by s and the antisleption by $\bar{s}$; the hozon by h and the elephoton by e. From the question write some equations for the charge

$$q_s + q_s + q_h = 0 \tag{6.94}$$

$$q_s + q_s + q_s + q_h + q_e = 1 \tag{6.95}$$

$$q_{\bar{s}} + q_e = -2 \tag{6.96}$$

and mass

$$m_s + m_h + m_e = 6m_e \tag{6.97}$$

$$m_{\bar{s}} + m_e = 3m_e \tag{6.98}$$

Since $m_{\bar{s}} = m_s$

$$m_{\bar{s}} + m_e = 3m_e \tag{6.99}$$

$$m_{\bar{s}} = 2m_e \tag{6.100}$$

$$m_s = 2m_e \tag{6.101}$$

Substituting $m_s = 2m_e$ into $m_s + m_h + m_e = 6m_e$ gives

$$m_s + m_h + m_e = 6m_e \tag{6.102}$$

$$2m_e + m_h + m_e = 6m_e \tag{6.103}$$

$$m_h = 3m_e \tag{6.104}$$

Moving onto the charge the above equations can be simplified. Since $q_s + q_s + q_h = 0$ and $q_s + q_s + q_s + q_h + q_e = 1$, $q_s + q_e = 1$. Also $q_{\bar{s}} = -q_s$ so $-q_s + q_e = -2$. Rearranging and substituting

$$-q_s + q_e = -2 \tag{6.105}$$

$$-(1 - q_e) + q_e = -2 \tag{6.106}$$

$$-1 + q_e + q_e = -2 \tag{6.107}$$

$$-1 + 2q_e = -2 \tag{6.108}$$

$$2q_e = -1 \tag{6.109}$$

$$q_e = -\frac{1}{2} \tag{6.110}$$

Again substituting

$$q_s + q_e = 1 \qquad (6.111)$$

$$q_s - \frac{1}{2} = 1 \qquad (6.112)$$

$$q_s = \frac{3}{2} \qquad (6.113)$$

and

$$q_s + q_s + q_h = 0 \qquad (6.114)$$

$$\frac{3}{2} + \frac{3}{2} + q_h = 0 \qquad (6.115)$$

$$q_h = -3 \qquad (6.116)$$

6.2.13   Question 24

6.2.13.1   part a

As a finite current flows when the battery is connected between A and B this must be the resistor. When the battery is connected one way round across B and C no current flows, then the battery is the other way around a very large current flows. This is characteristic of a diode. By process of elimination, the capacitor must be between A and C. You just need to get the diode around the correct way. Remember current is a flow of electrons, but circuits are drawn according to conventional flow - from positive to negative. The diode symbol has an arrow which points in the direction of conventional flow and so should point from B to C.

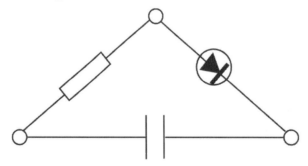

6.2.13.2   Part B - Physics

$$V = IR \qquad (6.117)$$

$$9 = \frac{3}{1000} \times R \qquad (6.118)$$

$$9 \times \frac{1000}{3} = R \qquad (6.119)$$

$$3000\Omega = R \qquad (6.120)$$

6.2.13.3   part c

If the battery is connected across the resistor the other way around a current of 3mA will flow through the resistor. Note in a steady state the capacitor doesn't let DC current through as it is effectively an insulator. A further way to look at it is consider that you have a resistor and capacitor in parallel with the battery. The reactance of a capacitor is given by $X_c = 1/2\pi f C$ where f is the frequency. As the frequency tends to zero (for DC), then X_c goes to infinity. Kirchhoff's laws tell us that no current will flow through this branch of the circuit.

6.2.13.4   part d

Similar to part c: 3mA current will flow. The only additional complication is that you need to consider the diode. In this configuration with C- and A+ the diode passes current and can effectively be thought of as a simple wire. (Compare with the information given in the question which says a large current flows when C- and B+.)

6.2.14   Question 25

6.2.14.1   part a

$$
\begin{align}
\text{GPE} &= mgh \tag{6.121}\\
&= (700 + 600) \times 10 \times 9 \tag{6.122}\\
&= 13000 \times 9 \tag{6.123}\\
&= 130000 - 13000 \tag{6.124}\\
&= 117000 J \tag{6.125}\\
&= 120 kJ \tag{6.126}
\end{align}
$$

$$
\begin{align}
\text{Power} &= \frac{\text{Energy}}{\text{Time}} \tag{6.127}\\
&= \frac{117}{30} \tag{6.128}\\
&= 3\frac{27}{30} \tag{6.129}\\
&= 3\frac{9}{10} \tag{6.130}\\
&= 3.9 kW \tag{6.131}
\end{align}
$$

6.2.14.2   part b

Since the weight is hung from two places, the tension in the wire will be 10,000N. Which effectively acts as a 1000kg counter weight from which you subtract the weight of the lift:

$$1000 - 700 = 300kg \tag{6.132}$$

6.2.14.3   part c

$$
\begin{aligned}
\text{Speed} &= \frac{\text{Distance}}{\text{Time}} \tag{6.133} \\
&= \frac{9m}{30s} \tag{6.134} \\
&= \frac{3}{20} \tag{6.135} \\
&= 0.3ms^{-1} \tag{6.136}
\end{aligned}
$$

The kinetic energy of the lift and passengers is

$$
\begin{aligned}
\text{KE} &= \frac{1}{2}mv^2 \tag{6.137} \\
&= \frac{1}{2} \times 1000 \times 0.3^2 \tag{6.138} \\
&= 1000 \times 0.09 \tag{6.139} \\
&= 45J \tag{6.140}
\end{aligned}
$$

Since the counterweight moves half the distance its speed is half so $0.15ms^{-1}$. Its weight is double that of the lift. If the mass is double, but the speed is half, then because of the square factor the final kinetic energy is half or $45/2 = 22.5J$. Thus the total kinetic energy is 67.5J.

6.2.14.4   part d

Consider the distance traveled by the lift in each of the three stages: acceleration, constant speed, deceleration.

$$
\begin{aligned}
s_{acceleration} &= ut + \frac{1}{2}at^2 = \frac{1}{2} \times a \times 100 = 50a \tag{6.141} \\
s_{constant} &= \left(\frac{u+v}{2}\right)t = 10v \tag{6.142} \\
s_{deceleration} &= ut + \frac{1}{2}at^2 = 50a \tag{6.143}
\end{aligned}
$$

and

$$v = u + at = 10a \tag{6.144}$$

Remember that the total distance is 9m so

$$50a + 10v + 50a = 9 \tag{6.145}$$

$$100a + 10v = 9 \tag{6.146}$$

$$100a + 10 \times 10a = 9 \tag{6.147}$$

$$200a = 9 \tag{6.148}$$

$$a = \frac{9}{200}ms^{-2} = 0.045ms^{-2} \tag{6.149}$$

Since

$$v = 10a \tag{6.150}$$

$$v = 10 \times 0.045 \tag{6.151}$$

$$v = 0.45ms^{-1} \tag{6.152}$$

6.2.14.5 part e

From part d:

$$a = 0.045ms^{-2} \tag{6.153}$$

Normally weight is $68 \times 10 = 680N$. When the lift is accelerating upwards change in acceleration is $0.045ms^{-2}$ (from part d). So change in weight is $68 \times 0.045 = 3.06N$. Finally when the lift is traveling at a constant speed the acceleration is just gravity so the answer is the same as part a: 680N.

Chapter 7

Oxford Physics Aptitude Test 2010 Answers

7.1 Part A - Maths

7.1.1 Question 1

7.1.1.1 part i

$$\sin 3x = \sqrt{3}\cos 3x \tag{7.1}$$

$$\frac{\sin 3x}{\cos 3x} = \sqrt{3} \tag{7.2}$$

Using the trig identities you should know:

$$\frac{\sin 3x}{\cos 3x} = \tan 3x \tag{7.3}$$

$$\tan 3x = \sqrt{3} \tag{7.4}$$

$$3x = \frac{\pi}{3} \tag{7.5}$$

$$x = \frac{\pi}{9} \tag{7.6}$$

tan has a period of/repeats very π so $\tan 3x$ repeats every $x = \frac{\pi}{3}$ so

$$x = \frac{\pi}{9}, \frac{4\pi}{9}, \frac{7\pi}{9} \tag{7.7}$$

7.1.1.2 part ii

Remember the identity

$$\sin^2 x + \cos^2 x = 1 \tag{7.8}$$

Rearrange to make the $\cos^2$ part the subject

$$\cos^2 x = 1 - \sin^2 x \tag{7.9}$$

and substitute this into the equation in the question

$$\cos^2 x - \sin x + 1 = 0 \tag{7.10}$$

$$1 - \sin^2 x - \sin x + 1 = 0 \tag{7.11}$$

$$0 = \sin^2 x + \sin x - 2 \tag{7.12}$$

Substitute $y = \sin x$ and solve as a quadratic

$$0 - y^2 + y - 2 \tag{7.13}$$

$$0 = (y + 2)(y - 1) \tag{7.14}$$

Therefore $y = -2$ and $y = 1$. Since $\sin x$ ranges between 1 and -1 we can neglect the $y = -2$ solution. Reversing the substitution $y = \sin x$ gives $\sin x = 1$. Meaning that $x = \frac{\pi}{2}$.

7.1.2 Question 2

The general equation for a circle is

$$(x - h)^2 + (y - h)^2 = r^2 \tag{7.15}$$

Where the coordinates of the centre are $(+h, +k)$ and the radius is r. Given the equation in the question the centre of the large circle must be at $(1, 1)$ and the radius is 1. So the centre of small circle is $\left(\frac{3}{2}, \frac{3}{2}\right)$ and the radius is $\frac{1}{2}$. Thus the equation of the small circle is

$$\left(x - \frac{3}{2}\right)^2 + \left(y - \frac{3}{2}\right)^2 = \frac{1}{4} \tag{7.16}$$

7.1.3 Question 3

To show that $x = -1$ is a root, substitute this into the equation:

$$-1 + 2x1 + 5 - 6 = 0 \tag{7.17}$$

$$7 + 7 = 0 \tag{7.18}$$

which is true. Next, to find the other roots the easiest and quickest is to factorise the equation. You already know one bracket: $(x + 1)$ which is given by the fact that -1 is a root.

$$(x + 1)(x^2 + x - 6) = 0 \tag{7.19}$$

This can be deduced in a straight forward manner by attempting to multiply out the basic form:

$$(x + 1)(ax^2 + bx + c) = 0 \tag{7.20}$$

noticing that the coefficient of x^3 must come from the coefficient of x in the $(x+1)$ bracket multiplied by a. Further notice that the number -6 in the original equation must come from the number one in the $(x + 1)$ bracket multiplied by c. The solution so far gives us that:

$$
\begin{aligned}
x^3 + 2x^2 - 5x - 6 &= (x + 1)(x^2 + x - 6) \tag{7.21}\\
&= (x + 1)(x + 3)(x - 2) \tag{7.22}
\end{aligned}
$$

Where the $(x+3)$ and $(x-2)$ brackets are found in the usual way for a quadratic (find two numbers that multiply to 6 and add or subtract to 1). The roots are found by setting the brackets equal to zero and rearranging i.e. $x + 3 = 0$ so $x = -3$ similarly $x = -1$ and $x = 2$.

7.1.4   Question 4

First find the gradient:

$$
\begin{aligned}
m &= \frac{y_2 - y_1}{x_2 - x_1} \tag{7.23}\\
&= \frac{5 - 3}{1 - 2} \tag{7.24}\\
&= -2 \tag{7.25}
\end{aligned}
$$

The equation of a straight line is

$$
\begin{aligned}
y &= mx + c \tag{7.26}\\
y &= -2x + c \tag{7.27}\\
& \tag{7.28}
\end{aligned}
$$

Substitute in one of the given points to find c:

$$3 = -2 \times 2 + c \tag{7.29}$$

$$c = 7 \tag{7.30}$$

$$y = -2x + 7 \tag{7.31}$$

7.1.5   Question 5

The area of a segment of a circle is the area of the sector minus the area of the corresponding triangle.

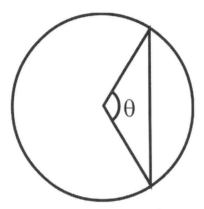

$$Area_{segment} = Area_{sector} - Area_{triangle} \tag{7.32}$$

$$= Area_{circle} \times Angle - \frac{1}{2}r^2 \sin\theta \tag{7.33}$$

$$= \pi r^2 \times \frac{\theta}{2\pi} - \frac{1}{2}r^2 \sin\theta \tag{7.34}$$

$$= \frac{r^2\theta}{2} - \frac{r^2 \sin\theta}{2} \tag{7.35}$$

$$\tag{7.36}$$

Now find the angle $\frac{\theta}{2}$.

$$\cos\frac{\theta}{2} = \frac{\frac{r}{2}}{r} \qquad (7.37)$$

$$\cos\frac{\theta}{2} = \frac{1}{2} \qquad (7.38)$$

$$\frac{\theta}{2} = \frac{\pi}{3} \qquad (7.39)$$

$$\theta = \frac{2\pi}{3} \qquad (7.40)$$

Now substitute this into the previous equation for the area of a segment:

$$Area_{segment} = \frac{r^2\theta}{2} - \frac{r^2\sin\theta}{2} \qquad (7.41)$$

$$= \frac{2r^2\pi}{2\times 3} - \frac{r^2}{2}\sin\frac{2\pi}{3} \qquad (7.42)$$

$$= \frac{r^2\pi}{3} - \frac{r^2\sqrt{3}}{2\times 2} \qquad (7.43)$$

$$= r^2\left(\frac{\pi}{3} - \frac{\sqrt{3}}{4}\right) \qquad (7.44)$$

7.1.6 Question 6

Largest enclosed area occurs if the shape is a square (i.e. a special case of a rectangle). So each side will have length $L/4$ meaning the areas will be:

$$\frac{L}{4}\times\frac{L}{4} = \frac{L^2}{16} \qquad (7.45)$$

7.1.7 Question 7

7.1.7.1 part i

Using your knowledge of logs:

$$x = b^y \qquad (7.46)$$

$$y = \log_b x \qquad (7.47)$$

So

$$9 = 3^{\log_3 9} \qquad (7.48)$$

$$3^2 = 3^{\log_3 9} \qquad (7.49)$$

$$2 = \log_3 9 \qquad (7.50)$$

7.1.7.2 part ii

Remembering that

$$\log a^b = b \log a \tag{7.51}$$

$$\log 4 + \log 16 - \log 2 = \log 2^2 + \log 2^4 - \log 2 \tag{7.52}$$
$$= 2 \log 2 + 4 \log 2 - \log 2 \tag{7.53}$$
$$= 5 \log 2 \tag{7.54}$$

7.1.8 Question 8

7.1.8.1 part i

One way is to split up one of the 16.1 i.e.

$$16.1 \times 16.1 = 16.1 \times 10 + 16.1 \times 6 + 16.1 \times 0.1 \tag{7.55}$$
$$= 161 + 96.6 + 1.61 \tag{7.56}$$
$$= 259.21 \tag{7.57}$$

Note that multiplying by 6 is equivalent to multiplying by 10, dividing by 2 and then adding on the original number once.

7.1.8.2 part ii

Split up in a similar way:

$$10.11 \times 3.2 = 10.11 \times 3 + 10.11 \times 0.2 \tag{7.58}$$
$$= 30.33 + 2 \times 1.011 \tag{7.59}$$
$$= 30.33 + 2.022 \tag{7.60}$$
$$= 32.352 \tag{7.61}$$

7.1.9 Question 9

Draw and fill in the table:

1	2	3	4	5	6	7
x^3			x			x^2
$x - 3a$	$x - 2a$	$x - a$	x	$x + a$	$x + 2a$	$x + 3a$

Now lets equate

$$\frac{x^3}{x^2} = x \quad = \quad \frac{x - 3a}{x + 3a} \tag{7.62}$$

$$x(x + 3a) \quad = \quad x - 3a \tag{7.63}$$

$$x^2 + 3xa \quad = \quad x - 3a \tag{7.64}$$

$$x + 3a + 3xa \quad = \quad x - 3a \tag{7.65}$$

$$3a + 3xa \quad = \quad -3a \tag{7.66}$$

$$6a \quad = \quad -3xa \tag{7.67}$$

$$6 \quad = \quad -3x \tag{7.68}$$

$$-2 \quad = \quad x \tag{7.69}$$

Finally

$$x^2 \quad = \quad x + 3a \tag{7.70}$$

$$4 \quad = \quad -2 + 3a \tag{7.71}$$

$$6 \quad = \quad 3a \tag{7.72}$$

$$2 \quad = \quad a \tag{7.73}$$

7.1.10   Question 10

Draw a probability table

Score		Probability	
1		$\frac{1}{6}$	
2		$\frac{1}{6}$	
3		$\frac{1}{6}$	
4		$\frac{1}{6}$	
5		$\frac{1}{6}$	
6	7	$\frac{1}{6} \times \frac{1}{6} = \frac{1}{36}$	
	8	$\frac{1}{6} \times \frac{1}{6} = \frac{1}{36}$	
	9	$\frac{1}{6} \times \frac{1}{6} = \frac{1}{36}$	
	10	$\frac{1}{6} \times \frac{1}{6} = \frac{1}{36}$	
	11	$\frac{1}{6} \times \frac{1}{6} = \frac{1}{36}$	
	12	$\frac{1}{6} \times \frac{1}{6} = \frac{1}{36}$	

So to get an even score add the probabilities for 2, 4, 8, 10 and 12 (note a score of 6 is not possible):

$$\frac{1}{6} + \frac{1}{6} + \frac{1}{36} + \frac{1}{36} + \frac{1}{36} \tag{7.74}$$

$$\frac{2}{6} + \frac{3}{36} \tag{7.75}$$

$$\frac{15}{36} = \frac{5}{12} \tag{7.76}$$

7.1.11   Question 11

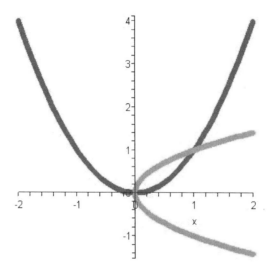

The first intercept is at $(0,0)$ and the second can be found from:

$$x = y^2 \tag{7.77}$$

$$x^2 = y^4 \tag{7.78}$$

but

$$y = x^2 \tag{7.79}$$

$$y = y^4 \tag{7.80}$$

$$y = 1 \tag{7.81}$$

so

$$x = y^2 \tag{7.82}$$

$$x = 1 \tag{7.83}$$

118

So the second intercept is $(1, 1)$. To find the area between the curves, integrate to find the area under the $x = y^2$ line and then subtract the area under the $y = x^2$ line.

$$\int_0^1 x^{\frac{1}{2}} - \int_0^1 x^2 = \left[\frac{2x^{\frac{3}{2}}}{3} + c\right]_0^1 - \left[\frac{x^3}{3} + c\right]_0^1 \tag{7.84}$$

$$= \frac{2}{3} - \frac{1}{3} \tag{7.85}$$

$$= \frac{1}{3} \tag{7.86}$$

7.2   Part B - Physics

7.2.1   Question 12

If isotope A has a half life of 8,000 years, after 16,000 years it will have had two half lives and reduced to a quarter (0.25) of its original amount. Isotope B has a half life of 16,000 years so will have reduced to half (0.5) of its original amount after 16,000 years. So the ratio of A:B is 0.25:0.5 or 1:2 which is answer B.

7.2.2   Question 13

There are two resistors in series so you have a potential divider. So you can use the potential divider equation

$$V_{out} = \frac{V_{in}R_1}{R_1 + R_2} \tag{7.87}$$

where the V_{out} is measured across resistor R_1. So

$$V_{across\ R_1} = \frac{VR_1}{R_1 + R_2} \tag{7.88}$$

Substituting this into the equation for power gives

$$P = \frac{V^2}{R} \tag{7.89}$$

$$P = \frac{V^2R_1^2}{(R_1 + R_2)^2} \times \frac{1}{R_1} \tag{7.90}$$

$$P = \frac{V^2R_1}{(R_1 + R_2)^2} \tag{7.91}$$

$$\tag{7.92}$$

Thus the answer is A.

7.2.3 Question 14

If the builder has lifted one end of the plank the plank will pivot about its one end. This means that the moments (around the end of the plank that sits on the floor) must balance. Remember that

$$Moment = Force \times distance \tag{7.93}$$

So:

$$
\begin{aligned}
Total\,Moment\,Clockwise &= Total\,Moment\,Anticlockwise \tag{7.94}\\
2m \times F &= 1000N \times 0.5m \tag{7.95}\\
F &= 250N \tag{7.96}
\end{aligned}
$$

So the answer is C.

7.2.4 Question 15

Draw a simple sketch:

If the plane is traveling at 141km/h NW you can notice that $1.41 = \sqrt{2}$. If the wind is coming from the north at 100km/h then using Pythagoras ($1^2 + 1^2 = 1.41^2$ or $1 + 1 = 2$)the other side of the triangle must be 100km/h. So the plane is traveling 100km/hr west and the answer is B.

7.2.5 Question 16

Use the equation

$$c = f\lambda \tag{7.97}$$

Note that $1,000kHz = 1,000,000Hz$ so

$$\lambda = \frac{c}{f} \tag{7.98}$$

$$= \frac{3 \times 10^8}{1 \times 10^6} \tag{7.99}$$

$$= 300m \tag{7.100}$$

So the answer is A.

7.2.6 Question 17

Draw a diagram:

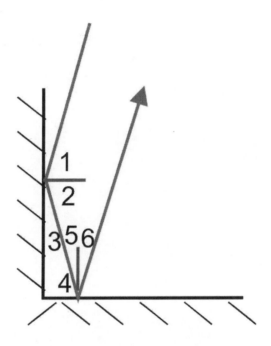

To turn back 180° the interior angles need (labeled 1,2,5,6) to add to 180. Noticing that the mirrors are at 90° and therefore the normals (in red) must also be at 90° to each other and that the angle to reflection must equal the angle of reflection it can be seen that

$$angle\ 2 + angle\ 5 = 90 \tag{7.101}$$

and that

$$angle\ 1 = angle\ 2 \tag{7.102}$$

$$angle\ 5 = angle\ 6 \tag{7.103}$$

Therefore the total is 180° and the answer is B.

7.2.7 Question 18

Use the equation

$$Q = CV \tag{7.104}$$
$$= 3 \times 10^{-9} \times 10 \tag{7.105}$$
$$= 3 \times 10^{-8}\, C \tag{7.106}$$

So the answer is C.

7.2.8 Question 19

Use the equation

$$F = kx \tag{7.107}$$
$$x = \frac{F}{k} \tag{7.108}$$
$$= \frac{800}{80000} \tag{7.109}$$
$$= 0.01m \tag{7.110}$$
$$= 10mm \tag{7.111}$$

Therefore the answer is B.

7.2.9 Question 20

Consider Kepler's Second Law which says that equal areas are swept out in equal times by a line joining the comet and the sun. The area of a sector of a circle is given by $r\delta c$ where δc is the distance along the circumference. Considering just one second of motion at the slowest and fastest points

$$4 \times 10^{10} \times 50 = 10 \times 10^{10} \times v \tag{7.112}$$
$$v = 20km/s \tag{7.113}$$

So the answer is C.

7.2.10 Question 21

Light going from the fish out of the water will bend away from the normal as it is traveling from a more to a less dense material. This will mean the fish is actually deeper in the water than it appears.

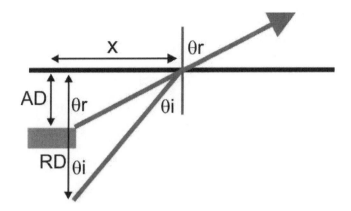

Start by considering Snell's Law

$$n_1 \sin \theta_1 = n_2 \sin \theta_2 \tag{7.114}$$

Defining RD as the real depth, AD as the actual depth and x as the distance from where the light leaves the water and a point directly above the fish on the surface of the water:

$$\tan \theta_r = \frac{x}{AD} \tag{7.115}$$

$$\tan \theta_i = \frac{x}{RD} \tag{7.116}$$

$$\tag{7.117}$$

Using the fact that for small angles

$$\tan \theta \approx \sin \theta \tag{7.118}$$

Then

$$n_i \sin \theta_i = n_r \sin \theta_r \tag{7.119}$$

$$1.33 \frac{x}{RD} = \frac{x}{AD} \tag{7.120}$$

$$\frac{1.33}{RD} = \frac{1}{0.75} \tag{7.121}$$

$$1.33 \times 0.75 = RD \tag{7.122}$$

$$RD = 1m \tag{7.123}$$

7.2.11   Question 22

Write some equations from the details given in the question.

$$l_r = l_b + l_g \tag{7.124}$$

$$l_g^2 = 4l_b^2 \tag{7.125}$$

$$m_b = 3 \propto l_b^3 \tag{7.126}$$

Where l is the length, m is the mass and the subscripts refer to the first letter of the colours. Rearranging (taking the square root) the second equation gives:

$$l_g = 2l_b \tag{7.127}$$

Substituting this into the first equations gives:

$$l_r = 3l_b \tag{7.128}$$

Now since mass depends on length we cube the previous two equations:

$$l_g^3 = 8l_b^3 \tag{7.129}$$
$$l_r^3 = 27l_b^3 \tag{7.130}$$

so using

$$m_b = 3 \propto l_b^3 \tag{7.131}$$

gives

$$m_g = 24g \tag{7.132}$$
$$m_r = 81g \tag{7.133}$$

Finally, remembering that

$$mass = density \times volume \tag{7.134}$$
$$m_g = 24 \tag{7.135}$$
$$= density \times 32 \tag{7.136}$$
$$density = \frac{24}{32} \tag{7.137}$$
$$= 0.75 \; that \; of \; water \tag{7.138}$$
$$= 750 kgm^{-3} \tag{7.139}$$

7.2.12   Question 23

Use the following equation to find the energy needed to heat the pan:

$$E = mc\Delta T \tag{7.140}$$
$$= 2 \times 490 \times 50 \tag{7.141}$$
$$= 49000J \tag{7.142}$$

The energy falling on the pan from the sun is given by:

$$1000 \times 0.07 = 70J/s \tag{7.143}$$

So the time required is:

$$\frac{49000}{70} = 700s \tag{7.144}$$

The second part of the question requires you to consider the energy lost by the pan compared to the energy gained by the water. So consider the energy above 20°:

$$
\begin{aligned}
Energy\ pan\ at\ 70° &= Energy\ pan\ at\ T + Energy\ water\ at\ T \tag{7.145} \\
49000 &= 4 \times 4200 \times \Delta T + 2 \times 490 \times \Delta T \tag{7.146} \\
49000 &= 16800\Delta T + 980\Delta T \tag{7.147} \\
49000 &= 17780\Delta T \tag{7.148} \\
\frac{49000}{17780} &= \Delta T \tag{7.149} \\
\frac{4900}{1778} &= \Delta T \tag{7.150} \\
3 &\approx \Delta T \tag{7.151}
\end{aligned}
$$

Therefore the final temperature of the water is 23°C.

7.2.13   Question 24

Draw a diagram and notice how the labeled angle is also 5mrad.

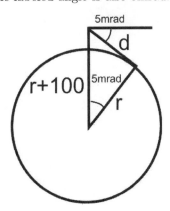

$$\cos\theta = \frac{adj}{hyp} \tag{7.152}$$

$$\cos\frac{5}{1000} = \frac{r}{r+100} \tag{7.153}$$

$$\cos\theta = 1 - \frac{x^2}{2} \tag{7.154}$$

$$1 - \frac{1}{2}\frac{5^2}{1000^2} = \frac{r}{r+100} \tag{7.155}$$

$$1 - \frac{12.5}{10^6} = \frac{r}{r+100} \tag{7.156}$$

$$\frac{10^6 - 12.5}{10^6} = \frac{r}{r+100} \tag{7.157}$$

$$10^6 r = 10^6 r + 10^8 - 12.5r - 1250 \tag{7.158}$$

$$0 = 10^8 - 12.5r - 1250 \tag{7.159}$$

$$r = \frac{10^8 - 1250}{12.5} \tag{7.160}$$

$$r = \frac{10^8}{12.5} - 100 \tag{7.161}$$

$$= 8 \times 10^6 - 100 \tag{7.162}$$

$$= 7,999,900m \tag{7.163}$$

For the second part simply use Pythagoras:

$$(r+100)^2 = r^2 + d^2 \tag{7.164}$$

$$r^2 + 200r + 10^4 = r^2 + d^2 \tag{7.165}$$

$$200r + 10^4 = d^2 \tag{7.166}$$

$$200(r+100) - 200 \times 100 + 10^4 = d^2 \tag{7.167}$$

$$200 \times 8 \times 10^6 - 10000 = d^2 \tag{7.168}$$

$$1600 \times 10^6 \approx d^2 \tag{7.169}$$

$$40,000m \approx d \tag{7.170}$$

An alternative method follows. Using the same diagram note that:

$$\theta = \frac{5}{1000} \tag{7.171}$$

$$\sin\theta \approx \theta \tag{7.172}$$

as long and θ is small and given in radians. So

$$\theta = \frac{d}{r+100} \tag{7.173}$$

and

$$d^2 + r^2 = (r + 100)^2 \tag{7.174}$$

Therefore:

$$\frac{d^2}{(r+100)^2} + \frac{r^2}{(r+100)^2} = 1 \tag{7.175}$$

$$\left(\frac{5}{1000}\right)^2 + \frac{r^2}{(r+100)^2} = 1 \tag{7.176}$$

$$\frac{r^2}{(r+100)^2} = 1 - \frac{25}{10^6} \tag{7.177}$$

$$= \frac{10^6 - 25}{10^6} \tag{7.178}$$

$$(10^6 - 25)(r^2 + 200r + 10^4) = 10^6 r^2 \tag{7.179}$$

$$200 \times 10^6 r + 10^{10} - 25r^2 - 5000r - 25 \times 10^4 = 0 \tag{7.180}$$

$$25r^2 - 2 \times 10^8 r + 10^{10} = 0 \tag{7.181}$$

Now applying the quadratic formula:

$$r = \frac{-b \pm \sqrt{b^2 - 4ac}}{2a} \tag{7.182}$$

$$\approx \frac{2 \times 10^8 \pm \sqrt{4 \times 10^{16}}}{50} \tag{7.183}$$

$$\approx \frac{4 \times 10^8}{50} \tag{7.184}$$

$$\approx 8 \times 10^6 m \tag{7.185}$$

Then to find d substitute back into

$$\theta = \frac{d}{r + 100} \tag{7.186}$$

$$\frac{5}{1000} \approx \frac{d}{8 \times 10^6} \tag{7.187}$$

$$d \approx \frac{40 \times 10^6}{1000} \tag{7.188}$$

$$d \approx 4 \times 10^4 m \tag{7.189}$$

7.2.14 Question 25

7.2.14.1 part i

The horizontal and vertical components can be treated separately. If the projectile is fired at $200m/s$ and the rail car is traveling at $100m/s$ the horizontal component of the projectile's speed must be

$100m/s$ so:

$$200\cos\theta = 100 \tag{7.190}$$
$$\cos\theta = \frac{1}{2} \tag{7.191}$$
$$\theta = 60° \tag{7.192}$$

7.2.14.2   part ii

The vertical component of the projectile speed is

$$200\sin\theta = 200\sin 60 \tag{7.193}$$
$$= 200\frac{\sqrt{3}}{2} \tag{7.194}$$
$$= 100\sqrt{3} \tag{7.195}$$

Now apply SUVAT vertically:

$$s = \tag{7.196}$$
$$u = 100\sqrt{3} \tag{7.197}$$
$$v = 0 \tag{7.198}$$
$$a = -10 \tag{7.199}$$
$$t = ? \tag{7.200}$$
$$v = u + at \tag{7.201}$$
$$t = \frac{v - u}{a} \tag{7.202}$$
$$t = \frac{100\sqrt{3}}{10} \tag{7.203}$$
$$t = 10\sqrt{3} \tag{7.204}$$
$$t = 17.32s \tag{7.205}$$

7.2.14.3   part iii

$$d = s \times t \tag{7.206}$$
$$= 100 \times 17.32 \times 2 \tag{7.207}$$
$$= 3464m \tag{7.208}$$

The factor of 2 is required to give the correct time. 17.32 seconds is the time to the maximum height, 2×17.32 is the time taken for the projectile to reach its maximum height and then to fall back to the ground again.

7.2.14.4 part iv

Apply SUVAT vertically again

$$s = ? \tag{7.209}$$

$$u = 100\sqrt{3} \tag{7.210}$$

$$v = 0 \tag{7.211}$$

$$a = -10 \tag{7.212}$$

$$t = 10\sqrt{3} = 17.32 \tag{7.213}$$

$$s = \frac{u+v}{2} \times t \tag{7.214}$$

$$= 50\sqrt{3} \times 10\sqrt{3} \tag{7.215}$$

$$= 50 \times 10 \times 3 \tag{7.216}$$

$$= 1500m \tag{7.217}$$

7.2.14.5 part v

For the car (only has a horizontal velocity so only horizontal kinetic energy):

$$KE_{car} = \frac{1}{2}mv^2 \tag{7.218}$$

$$= \frac{1}{2} \times 200 \times 100^2 \tag{7.219}$$

$$= 1,000,000J \tag{7.220}$$

For the projectile horizontally:

$$KE_{proj_hor} = \frac{1}{2} \times 10 \times 100^2 \tag{7.221}$$

$$= 50,000J \tag{7.222}$$

For the projectile vertically:

$$KE_{proj_vert} = \frac{1}{2} \times 10 \times (100\sqrt{3})^2 \tag{7.223}$$

$$= 5 \times 10000 \times 3 \tag{7.224}$$

$$= 150,000J \tag{7.225}$$

7.2.14.6   part vi

As the projectile travels upwards its vertical KE is converted into gravitational potential energy:

$$KE_{proj_v ert} = mgh \tag{7.226}$$
$$150,000 = 10 \times 10 \times h \tag{7.227}$$
$$h = 1500m \tag{7.228}$$

7.2.14.7   part vii

The velocity of the projectile has two components. The vertical component won't alter speed of car since it is perpendicular to the direction of motion of the car. The horizontal component of the projectile velocity is the same as that of the rail car. Considering momentum conservation for the collision:

$$m_p \times 100 + m_{rc} \times 100 = (m_p + m_{rc}) \times 100 \tag{7.229}$$

the velocity of the combination of the projectile and rail car will still be $100m/s$.

7.2.14.8   part viii

Simply add the kinetic energy of the rail car and the projectile when both are traveling at $100m/s$:

$$KE = \frac{1}{2} \times 200 \times 100^2 + \frac{1}{2} \times 10 \times 100^2 \tag{7.230}$$
$$= 1,000,000 + 50,000 \tag{7.231}$$
$$= 1,050,000J \tag{7.232}$$

Chapter 8

Oxford Physics Aptitude Test 2011 Answers

8.1 Part A - Maths

8.1.1 Question 1

$$\sin\theta - 2\cos^2\theta = -1 \tag{8.1}$$

Using the identity

$$\cos^2\theta = 1 - \sin^2\theta \tag{8.2}$$

then

$$\sin\theta - 2(1 - \sin^2\theta) = -1 \tag{8.3}$$

$$\sin\theta - 2 + 2\sin^2\theta = -1 \tag{8.4}$$

$$2\sin^2\theta + \sin\theta - 1 = 0 \tag{8.5}$$

$$\tag{8.6}$$

This is a quadratic in $\sin\theta$, and can be solved by factorising or using the quadratic formula to give

$$\sin\theta = -1 \tag{8.7}$$

$$\sin\theta = \frac{1}{2} \tag{8.8}$$

so

$$\theta = \frac{3\pi}{2} \tag{8.9}$$

$$\theta = \frac{\pi}{6} \tag{8.10}$$

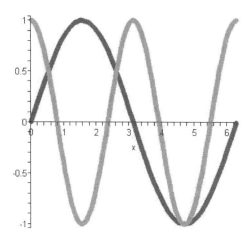

Using a sketch of $\sin\theta$ and $\cos 2\theta$ we can see that the other answer is $\pi - \frac{\pi}{6} = \frac{5\pi}{6}$.

8.1.2 Question 2

From the equation we can work out some features. The number 3 at the front tells us the sin wave oscillates about $y = 3$. The coefficient of 2 in front of the sin term tells us the amplitude is 2. Multiplying out the terms in the sin gives us

$$(x - 3)\frac{\pi}{3} = \frac{\pi x}{3} - \pi \tag{8.11}$$

The π term on the end tells us the sin wave is displaced by π. The sin wave repeats after 2π so

$$\frac{\pi x}{3} = 2\pi \tag{8.12}$$

$$x = 6 \tag{8.13}$$

Therefore the wave repeats every $x = 6$ units, so there are two wavelengths between zero and twelve.

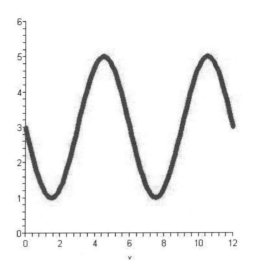

8.1.3 Question 3

8.1.3.1 part i

Consider the height, h, of the grey triangle:

$$\tan 60 = \frac{h}{x} \tag{8.14}$$

$$h = x \tan 60 \tag{8.15}$$

The area, A, of the grey triangle is:

$$A = \frac{1}{2} \times x \times h \tag{8.16}$$

$$= \frac{1}{2} x^2 \tan 60 \tag{8.17}$$

$$= \frac{\sqrt{3}}{2} x^2 \tag{8.18}$$

since the angle must be 60° in an equilateral triangle.

8.1.3.2 part ii

The area, B, of the grey triangle is now given by the area of the whole triangle, minus the area of the small white triangle on the right. Using the equation found in part i:

$$B = \frac{\sqrt{3}}{2} \times \left(\frac{a}{2}\right)^2 \times 2 - \frac{\sqrt{3}}{2}(a-x)^2 \tag{8.19}$$

$$= \frac{\sqrt{3}}{4} a^2 - \frac{\sqrt{3}}{2}(a-x)^2 \tag{8.20}$$

8.1.4 Question 4

The area A_R of a rhombus:

$$A_R = \frac{ab}{2} \tag{8.21}$$

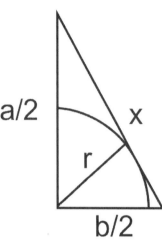

$$x = \sqrt{\frac{a^2}{4} + \frac{b^2}{4}} \tag{8.22}$$

By similar triangles:

$$\frac{a/2}{\sqrt{\frac{a^2}{4} + \frac{b^2}{4}}} = \frac{r}{b/2} \tag{8.23}$$

so

$$r = \frac{\frac{ab}{4}}{\sqrt{\frac{a^2}{4} + \frac{b^2}{4}}} \tag{8.24}$$

The area of the circle is now given by:

$$A_C = \pi r^2 \quad = \quad \pi \frac{a^2 b^2}{16} \frac{1}{\frac{a^2}{4} + \frac{b^2}{4}} \tag{8.25}$$

$$= \quad \frac{\pi a^2 b^2}{4(a^2 + b^2)} \tag{8.26}$$

so

$$\frac{A_C}{A_R} = \frac{\pi ab}{2(a^2 + b^2)} \tag{8.27}$$

8.1.5 Question 5

Given:

$$\log 5 \quad = \quad 0.7 \tag{8.28}$$

$$2^x \quad = \quad 10 \tag{8.29}$$

then

$$x \log 2 = \log 10 \tag{8.30}$$

$$x(\log 10 - \log 5) = \log 10 \tag{8.31}$$

$$x(1 - 0.7) = 1 \tag{8.32}$$

$$x = \frac{1}{0.3} \tag{8.33}$$

$$= 3.3 \tag{8.34}$$

8.1.6 Question 6

$$\sum_{r=1}^{6} 2^r + \frac{2r}{3} = \sum_{r=1}^{6} 2^r + \sum_{r=1}^{6} \frac{2r}{3} \tag{8.35}$$

$$\sum_{r=1}^{6} 2^r = 2 + 4 + 8 + 16 + 32 + 64 \tag{8.36}$$

$$= 126 \tag{8.37}$$

$$\sum_{r=1}^{6} \frac{2r}{3} = \frac{2}{3}(1 + 2 + 3 + 4 + 5 + 6) \tag{8.38}$$

$$= \frac{2 \times 21}{3} = \frac{42}{3} = 14 \tag{8.39}$$

$$\sum_{r=1}^{6} 2^r + \frac{2r}{3} = 126 + 14 \tag{8.40}$$

$$= 140 \tag{8.41}$$

Note we can't use

$$\sum^{\infty} = \frac{a}{1 - r} \tag{8.42}$$

since $|r| \geq 1$.

8.1.7 Question 7

The quickest way is to divide one polynomial by the other:

$$x^2 + 5x - \quad 6 \tag{8.43}$$

$$x^2 - x - 6 \overline{)x^4 + 4x^3 - \quad 17x^2 \quad -24x + 36} \tag{8.44}$$

$$-x^4 + x^3 + \quad 6x^2 \tag{8.45}$$

$$\overline{5x^3 - \quad 11x^2 \quad -24x + 36} \tag{8.46}$$

$$-5x^3 + \quad 5x^2 \quad +30x \tag{8.47}$$

$$\overline{ \quad 6x^2 \quad +6x + 36} \tag{8.48}$$

$$6x^2 \quad -6x - 36 \tag{8.49}$$

$$\overline{0} \tag{8.50}$$

Therefore $x^2 - x - 6$ and $x^2 + 5x - 6$ are factors. We now factorise these into brackets:

$$x^2 - x - 6 = 0 \tag{8.51}$$

$$(x-3)(x+2) = 0 \tag{8.52}$$

and

$$x^2 + 5x - 6 = 0 \tag{8.53}$$

$$(x-1)(x+6) = 0 \tag{8.54}$$

Therefore the roots are: $x = -6, -2, 1, 3$

8.1.8 Question 8

8.1.8.1 part i

Easiest to use method of partial fractions i.e. in the form:

$$\frac{x+2}{(x+1)(x-1)} = \frac{A}{x+1} + \frac{B}{x-1} \tag{8.55}$$

so multiplying both sides by $(x+1)(x-1)$:

$$A(x-1) + B(x+1) = x + 2 \tag{8.56}$$

Picking 'strategic' values so the terms vanish one at a time. If x=1:

$$A(1-1) + B(1+1) \quad = \quad 1+2 \tag{8.57}$$

$$2B \quad = \quad 3 \tag{8.58}$$

$$B \quad = \quad \frac{3}{2} \tag{8.59}$$

If x=-1:

$$A(-1-1) + B(-1+1) \quad = \quad -1+2 \tag{8.60}$$

$$-2A \quad = \quad 1 \tag{8.61}$$

$$A \quad = \quad -\frac{1}{2} \tag{8.62}$$

Therefore:

$$\int \frac{-\frac{1}{2}}{x+1} + \frac{\frac{3}{2}}{x-1} dx \quad = \quad -\frac{1}{2}\ln|x+1| + \frac{3}{2}\ln|x-1| + c \tag{8.63}$$

8.1.8.2   part ii

$$\int_0^1 \frac{1}{(x+1)^{\frac{1}{2}}} dx \quad = \quad \int_0^1 (x+1)^{-\frac{1}{2}} dx \tag{8.64}$$

$$= \quad \left[2(x+1)^{\frac{1}{2}}\right]_0^1 \tag{8.65}$$

$$= \quad 2\sqrt{2} - 2 \tag{8.66}$$

8.1.9   Question 9

$$y_1 - y_2 \quad = \quad x^2 - 3x^2 + 2x + 3 - x^2 + 3x + 4 \tag{8.67}$$

$$= \quad x^3 - 4x^2 + 5x + 7 \tag{8.68}$$

To find the maximum and minimum we must differentiate and then set the result to zero and solve:

$$\frac{d(y_1 - y_2)}{dx} \quad = \quad 3x^2 - 8x + 5 = 0 \tag{8.69}$$

$$\tag{8.70}$$

Using the quadratic equation:

$$x = \frac{8 \pm \sqrt{64 - 4 \times 3 \times 5}}{6} = \frac{8 \pm 2}{6} \tag{8.71}$$

$$x = = \frac{10}{6} \; and \; 1 \tag{8.72}$$

To find whether the points are a maximum or minimum find the second derivative and substitute in the above values of x. If the result is negative(positive) then the x value represents a maximum(minimum).

$$\frac{d^2(y_1 - y_2)}{dx^2} = 6x - 8 \tag{8.73}$$

$$\tag{8.74}$$

If $x = 10/6$:

$$\frac{6 \times 10}{6} - 8 = 2 \tag{8.75}$$

$$Minimum \tag{8.76}$$

If $x = 1$:

$$6 - 8 = -2 \tag{8.77}$$

$$Maximum \tag{8.78}$$

8.1.10   Question 10

Notice that

$$(x + y)^2 = x^2 + y^2 + 2xy \tag{8.79}$$

so

$$(x+y)^2 = s+t \tag{8.80}$$

$$\pm\sqrt{|s+t|} = x+y \tag{8.81}$$

$$\pm\sqrt{|s+t|} = x+\frac{t}{2x} \tag{8.82}$$

$$\pm\sqrt{|s+t|}x = x^2 + \frac{t}{2} \tag{8.83}$$

$$x^2 \pm \sqrt{|s+t|}x + \frac{t}{2} = 0 \tag{8.84}$$

$$x = \pm\frac{\sqrt{|s+t|} \pm \sqrt{|s+t| - 4\times\frac{t}{2}}}{2} \tag{8.85}$$

$$x = \pm\frac{\sqrt{|s+t|} \pm \sqrt{|s-t|}}{2} \tag{8.86}$$

Therefore:

$$y = \frac{t}{2x} = \pm\frac{t}{\sqrt{|s+t|} \pm \sqrt{|s-t|}} \tag{8.87}$$

8.1.11   Question 11

There are 36 possibilities from the two dice. The order matters since one score is labeled d_1 and the other d_2 and if $A \neq B$. This also means the probability of each score is equal. We also need to assume A and B are positive otherwise there will be negative solutions. Therefore a score of $d_1 = 6$ and $d_2 = 6$ must give 35 so:

$$6A + 6B + C = 35 \tag{8.88}$$

If $d_1 = 1$ and $d_2 = 1$ then we must get a score of zero:

$$A + B + C = 0 \tag{8.89}$$

$$-(A + B) = C \tag{8.90}$$

Substituting this into our first equation:

$$6A + 6B - A - B = 35 \tag{8.91}$$

$$5A + 5B = 35 \tag{8.92}$$

$$A + B = 7 \tag{8.93}$$

Therefore $C = -7$. The possibilities for A and B are 1 and 6, 2 and 5, 3 and 4. The simplest way to get each score between 0 and 35 is to have a resolution of 1 therefore we pick A=1 and B=6 (equivalently we could pick B=6 and A=1).

8.2 Part B - Physics

8.2.1 Question 12

The velocity is found from (d is distance and t is time):

$$v = \frac{d}{t} \tag{8.94}$$

But (f is frequency and λ is wavelength):

$$v = f\lambda \tag{8.95}$$

and (T is the period of the wave)

$$f = \frac{1}{T} \tag{8.96}$$

so

$$\lambda = \frac{dT}{t} = \frac{45 \times 2}{25} = \frac{90}{25} \tag{8.97}$$

Therefore the answer is C.

8.2.2 Question 13

$\alpha = 15$ and the temperature difference $T_S - T = 26 - 6 = 20$ so the power required is $15 \times 20 = 300W$. But since the efficiency is 30% the total power is 1000W. Therefore the answer is A.

8.2.3 Question 14

A lunar eclipse occurs when the moon passes behind the Earth, so that the Sun's rays are blocked from reaching the moon by the Earth. This can only occur when the moon is in the full moon phase. A full moon occurs when the Moon is on the far side of the Earth (but positioned out of the Earth's shadow) and reflects the Sun's rays from its surface. Therefore the answer is B.

8.2.4 Question 15

This is an application of the inverse square law. So if the star is twice as far away it must be $2^2 = 4$ times as bright. Therefore the answer is D.

8.2.5 Question 16

Remember that T^2 is proportional to R^3 according to Kepler's Third Law. So if T increases by a factor of 64. The cube root of 64 is 4 therefore R increases by a factor of 4. Therefore the answer is $0.4 \times 4 = 1.6AU$, so A.

8.2.6 Question 17

Repeatedly apply the standard series and parallel resistor formula. For 2 resistors in series:

$$R_T = R_1 + R_2 \tag{8.98}$$

and for 2 resistors in parallel:

$$\frac{1}{R_T} = \frac{1}{R_1} + \frac{1}{R_2} \tag{8.99}$$

Starting with the two resistors parallel and labeling this resistance Q:

$$\frac{1}{Q} = \frac{1}{R} + \frac{1}{R} \tag{8.100}$$

$$= \frac{2}{R} \tag{8.101}$$

$$Q = \frac{R}{2} \tag{8.102}$$

Moving on to consider the bottom line as two resistors in series and labeling this P:

$$P = Q + R \tag{8.103}$$

$$= \frac{R}{2} + R \tag{8.104}$$

$$= \frac{3R}{2} \tag{8.105}$$

Finally considering the two largest branches as a parallel circuit and labeling the total resistance N:

$$\frac{1}{N} = \frac{1}{R} + \frac{1}{P} \tag{8.106}$$

$$= \frac{1}{R} + \frac{2}{3R} \tag{8.107}$$

$$= \frac{5}{3R} \tag{8.108}$$

$$N = \frac{3R}{5} \tag{8.109}$$

Therefore the answer is D.

8.2.7 Question 18

We can consider this as a step down transformer. The turns follow the same ratio as the voltages. The voltage halves, so the number of turns do too. Therefore there are 25 and the answer is C. Alternatively we can apply the transformer equation:

$$\frac{V_p}{V_s} = \frac{N_p}{N_s} \tag{8.110}$$

where V is voltage, N is number of turns, p means the primary coil and s means the secondary coil.

8.2.8 Question 19

$$
\begin{align}
P &= VI \tag{8.111} \\
&= 6 \times 1 \tag{8.112} \\
&= 6J/s \tag{8.113} \\
\Delta E &= mgh \tag{8.114} \\
\frac{\Delta E}{t} &= mg\frac{h}{t} \tag{8.115} \\
\Delta P &= mgv \tag{8.116} \\
v &= \frac{\Delta P}{mg} \tag{8.117} \\
&= \frac{6}{0.1 \times 10} \tag{8.118} \\
&= 6m/s \tag{8.119}
\end{align}
$$

Therefore the answer is B.

8.2.9 Question 20

$$
\begin{align}
F &= mg\sin\theta \tag{8.120} \\
a &= g\sin\theta \tag{8.121} \\
&= 10\sin 30 \tag{8.122} \\
&= 5m/s^2 \tag{8.123}
\end{align}
$$

Therefore the answer is D.

8.2.10 Question 21

Draw a simple sketch:

$$\sin\theta = \frac{5}{10} \tag{8.124}$$

$$= \frac{1}{2} \tag{8.125}$$

$$\theta = 30° \tag{8.126}$$

Therefore the answer is C.

8.2.11   Question 22

8.2.11.1   part i

Equate the energy stored in the spring with the kinetic energy gained by the mass.

$$\frac{1}{2}k(x-l)^2 = \frac{1}{2}mv^2 \tag{8.127}$$

$$v = \sqrt{\frac{k}{m}}(x-l) \tag{8.128}$$

8.2.11.2   part ii

This time, the spring will require less force to extend to the same length as gravity will supply an additional force. Remember that the energy stored in a spring can be given by $1/2Fx$.

$$\frac{1}{2}mv^2 = \frac{1}{2}(k(x-l)-mg)(x-l) \tag{8.129}$$

$$mv^2 = k(x-l)^2 - mg(x-l) \tag{8.130}$$

$$v = \sqrt{\frac{k}{m}(x-l)^2 - g(x-l)} \tag{8.131}$$

8.2.11.3 part iii

Apply suvat:

$$s = ? \tag{8.132}$$

$$u = \sqrt{\frac{k}{m}(x-l)^2 - g(x-l)} \tag{8.133}$$

$$v = 0 \tag{8.134}$$

$$a = g \tag{8.135}$$

$$t = t \tag{8.136}$$

$$v^2 = u^2 + 2as \tag{8.137}$$

$$s = \frac{u^2}{2g} \tag{8.138}$$

$$= \frac{k}{2gm}(x-l)^2 - \frac{(x-l)}{2} \tag{8.139}$$

8.2.12   Question 23

Equate the electric and magnetic forces:

$$eE = evB \tag{8.140}$$

$$E = vB \tag{8.141}$$

$$v = \frac{E}{B} = \frac{1 \times 10^3}{1 \times 10^{-5}} \tag{8.142}$$

$$= 1 \times 10^8 m/s \tag{8.143}$$

We now know the velocity the electron needs to be accelerated to. By equating energies (we can find the accelerating potential, V:

$$qV = \frac{1}{2}mv^2 \tag{8.144}$$

$$V = \frac{mv^2}{2q} \tag{8.145}$$

$$= \frac{10^{-30} \times 10^{16}}{3.2 \times 10^{-19}} \tag{8.146}$$

$$= \frac{1 \times 10^{-14}}{3.2 \times 10^{-19}} \tag{8.147}$$

$$= 0.31 \times 10^5 \tag{8.148}$$

$$= 3.1 \times 10^4 Volts \tag{8.149}$$

8.2.13 Question 24

We can find the background count is 10 counts/sec. This needs to be subtracted from all the readings. After 10cm of air there are 90 counts/sec - this must be due to beta and gamma (10cm of air blocks alpha). After 1cm of aluminium there are 40 counts/sec so this must only be gamma (as the aluminium blocks alpha and beta). At a distance of 1cm there are 390 counts/sec - this will be alpha beta and gamma. Therefore we know gamma is 40 counts/sec. Beta must be 90-40 = 50 counts/sec. Finally alpha must be 390-50-40 = 300 counts/sec. Therefore the ratio $\alpha : \beta : \gamma$ is 30:5:4.

8.2.14 Question 25

Write some equations from the text. Use l, w, h to denote length, width and height and the subscripts s, m, l to denote small, medium, large boxes.

$$8l_s w_s h_s = l_m w_m h_m \tag{8.150}$$

$$l_s = h_m \tag{8.151}$$

$$w_l l_l = 9 w_s l_s \tag{8.152}$$

$$l_s + l_m + l_l = 2.4 \tag{8.153}$$

$$w_m = 2h_s \tag{8.154}$$

$$\frac{w_s}{l_s} = \frac{w_m}{l_m} = \frac{w_l}{l_l} \tag{8.155}$$

$$\frac{h_s}{l_s} = \frac{h_m}{l_m} = \frac{h_l}{l_l} \tag{8.156}$$

Statement A implies that the volume of one medium box is the same as the volume of eight small boxes. Since the boxes are similar it suggests that

$$l_m = \sqrt[3]{8} l_s \tag{8.157}$$

$$= 2 l_s \tag{8.158}$$

and from statement C (note the misprint in the paper)

$$l_l = \sqrt{9} l_s \tag{8.159}$$

$$= 3 l_s \tag{8.160}$$

Therefore:

$$l_s + l_m + l_l = 2.4 \tag{8.161}$$

$$l_s + 2l_s + 3l_s = 2.4 \tag{8.162}$$

$$6l_s = 2.4 \tag{8.163}$$

$$l_s = 0.4 \tag{8.164}$$

$$l_m = 0.8 \tag{8.165}$$

$$l_l = 1.2 \tag{8.166}$$

Returning to the equations from the question: simplify a few of these. Combine the first two:

$$8w_s h_s = l_m w_m \tag{8.167}$$

combining this with the fifth one:

$$8w_s = 2l_m \tag{8.168}$$

$$4w_s = l_m \tag{8.169}$$

Now:

$$l_m = 4w_s \tag{8.170}$$

$$w_s = 0.2 \tag{8.171}$$

Now:

$$\frac{w_s}{l_s} = \frac{w_m}{l_m} = \frac{w_l}{l_l} \tag{8.172}$$

$$\frac{0.2}{0.4} = \frac{w_m}{0.8} = \frac{w_l}{1.2} \tag{8.173}$$

Therefore:

$$w_m = 0.4 \tag{8.174}$$

$$w_l = 0.6 \tag{8.175}$$

Finally

$$w_m = 2h_s \tag{8.176}$$

$$h_s = 0.2 \tag{8.177}$$

$$\frac{h_s}{l_s} = \frac{h_m}{l_m} = \frac{h_l}{l_l} \tag{8.178}$$

$$\frac{0.2}{0.4} = \frac{h_m}{0.8} = \frac{h_l}{1.2} \tag{8.179}$$

$$h_m = 0.4 \tag{8.180}$$

$$h_l = 0.6 \tag{8.181}$$

So the ratio of width and height is 1 and the ratio of width and length is 0.5.

8.2.15   Question 26

Energy stored in the string is equivalent to kinetic energy:

$$\frac{1}{2}Fx = \frac{1}{2}mv^2 \tag{8.182}$$

$$v = \sqrt{\frac{Fx}{m}} \tag{8.183}$$

$$= \sqrt{\frac{120 \times 0.6}{0.02}} \tag{8.184}$$

$$= \sqrt{120 \times 30} \tag{8.185}$$

$$= \sqrt{3600} = 60m/s \tag{8.186}$$

Velocity is proportional to $\sqrt{energy}$ or $\sqrt{h}$ therefore:

$$\frac{5}{6} \times 60 = 50m/s \tag{8.187}$$

$$t = \frac{d}{v} = \frac{50}{50} \tag{8.188}$$

$$= 1s \tag{8.189}$$

Now use suvat:

$$s = \frac{1}{2}at^2 \tag{8.190}$$

$$= \frac{1}{2} \times 10 \times 1 \tag{8.191}$$

$$= 5m \tag{8.192}$$

To find the force of the arrow strike:

$$F = \frac{W}{d} \tag{8.193}$$

$$= \frac{0.5 \times mv^2}{d} \tag{8.194}$$

$$= \frac{0.5 \times 0.02 \times 2500}{0.005} \tag{8.195}$$

$$= 5000N \tag{8.196}$$

Finally, to find the velocity of the target apply the conservation of momentum:

$$m_1 v_1 = m_2 v_2 \tag{8.197}$$

$$v_2 = \frac{m_1 v_1}{m_2} \tag{8.198}$$

$$= \frac{0.02 \times 50}{5.02} \tag{8.199}$$

$$= \frac{1}{5.02} \approx 0.2 m/s \tag{8.200}$$

Chapter 9

Oxford Physics Aptitude Test 2012 Answers

9.1   Part A - Maths

9.1.1   Question 1

If we assume the area between means the area enclosed we need to consider x between -1 and 1. Let's integrate remembering that $|x|$ will be greater than x:

$$2 \times \left[\int_0^1 x - \int_0^1 x^2 \right] = \left[\frac{x^2}{2} - \frac{x^3}{3} \right]_0^1 \tag{9.1}$$

$$= 2 \times \left[\frac{1}{2} - \frac{1}{3} \right] \tag{9.2}$$

$$= \frac{1}{3} \tag{9.3}$$

9.1.2   Question 2

$$(4 + x)^4 = 4^4 \left(1 + \frac{x}{4} \right)^2 \tag{9.4}$$

$$= (2^2)4 \left[1 + 4\frac{x}{4} + \frac{4 \times 3}{2} \left(\frac{x}{4} \right)^2 + \frac{4 \times 3 \times 2}{6} \left(\frac{x}{4} \right)^3 \right] \tag{9.5}$$

$$= 256 \left[1 + \frac{1}{5} + \frac{3}{8}\frac{1}{25} + \frac{1}{16}\frac{1}{125} \right] \tag{9.6}$$

$$= 256 \left[1 + \frac{1}{5} + \frac{3}{200} + \frac{1}{2000} \right] \tag{9.7}$$

$$= 256 \left[\frac{2000 + 400 + 30 + 1}{2000} \right] \tag{9.8}$$

$$= 256 \left[\frac{2431}{2000} \right] \tag{9.9}$$

$$= 256 \times 1.2155 \tag{9.10}$$

$$= 311.17 \tag{9.11}$$

9.1.3 Question 3

$$\sum_{r=1}^{8}(2+4^r) = \sum_{r=1}^{8}2+\sum_{r=1}^{8}4^r \tag{9.12}$$

$$= 16+(4+16+64+256+1024+4096 \tag{9.13}$$

$$+16384+65536) \tag{9.14}$$

$$= 87396 \tag{9.15}$$

9.1.4 Question 4

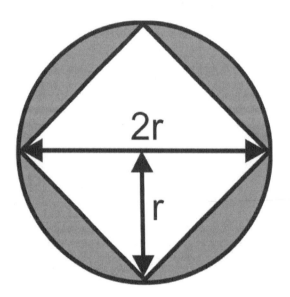

The area of the circle is

$$\pi r^2 \tag{9.16}$$

The area of the square is twice the area of the triangle

$$2 \times \frac{1}{2} \times 2r \times r \tag{9.17}$$

$$2r^2 \tag{9.18}$$

The shaded area is

$$\pi r^2 - 2r^2 \tag{9.19}$$

$$r^2(\pi - 2) \tag{9.20}$$

9.1.5   Question 5

Dividing the polynomial by (x-1) gives

$$x^2 \quad -5x \quad -14 \tag{9.21}$$

$$x-1\overline{|x^3 \quad -6x^2 \quad -9x+14} \tag{9.22}$$

$$\underline{-x^3 \quad +x^2} \tag{9.23}$$

$$-5x^2 \quad -9x+14 \tag{9.24}$$

$$\underline{5x^2 \quad -5x} \tag{9.25}$$

$$-14x+14 \tag{9.26}$$

$$\underline{14x-14} \tag{9.27}$$

$$0 \tag{9.28}$$

Factorising the resulting polynomial $x^2 - 5x - 14$ gives

$$x^2 - 5x - 14 = (x-7)(x+2) \tag{9.29}$$

and the other solutions as x=7 and x=-2.

9.1.6   Question 6

Draw a sketch of the graph $y = (x-2)^2$ and roughly what the line will look like given that it goes through the point (0,2) and must just touch the polynomial curve.

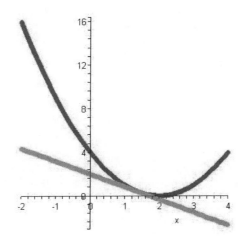

151

At the point of intersection the gradients must be the same:

$$y = (x-2)^2 \tag{9.30}$$

$$\frac{dy}{dx} = 2x-4 \tag{9.31}$$

So the equation of the line must be:

$$y = mx + c \tag{9.32}$$

$$y = (2x-4)x + c \tag{9.33}$$

The y co-ordinates must also be equal:

$$(x-2)^2 = (2x-4)x + 2 \tag{9.34}$$

$$x^2 - 4x + 4 = 2x^2 - 4x + 2 \tag{9.35}$$

$$0 = x^2 - 2 \tag{9.36}$$

$$x = \pm\sqrt{2} \tag{9.37}$$

The question asks for the touching point to be greater than zero, so we ignore the negative solution. Therefore the equation of the line is:

$$y = (2\sqrt{2}-4)x + c \tag{9.38}$$

The line also goes through the point (0,2) so

$$2 = (2\sqrt{2}-4) \times 0 + c \tag{9.39}$$

$$c = 2 \tag{9.40}$$

$$y = (2\sqrt{2}-4)x + 2 \tag{9.41}$$

9.1.7 Question 7

$$5 = \log_2 16 + \log_{10}\sqrt{0.01} + \log_3 x \tag{9.42}$$

$$5 = 4 + \log_{10} 0.1 + \log_3 x \tag{9.43}$$

$$5 = 4 - 1 + \log_3 x \tag{9.44}$$

$$2 = \log_3 x \tag{9.45}$$

$$x = 9 \tag{9.46}$$

9.1.8   Question 8

First, consider the ways in which 7 can be obtained:

Dice 1	Dice 1 Probability	Dice 2	Dice 2 Probability	Total Probability
6	$\frac{1}{6}$	1	$\frac{2}{6}$	$\frac{2}{36}$
5	$\frac{1}{6}$	2	$\frac{2}{6}$	$\frac{2}{36}$
4	$\frac{1}{6}$	3	$\frac{2}{6}$	$\frac{2}{36}$
				$\frac{6}{36}$

Therefore the answer is $\frac{1}{6}$.

9.1.9   Question 9

Using

$$\sin^2 \theta + \cos^2 \theta = 1 \tag{9.47}$$

Then

$$\cos^2 \theta + \sin \theta = 0 \tag{9.48}$$

$$1 - \sin^2 \theta + \sin \theta = 0 \tag{9.49}$$

$$\tag{9.50}$$

Making the substitution $x = \sin \theta$ gives:

$$1 - x^2 + x = 0 \tag{9.51}$$

$$x^2 - x - 1 = 0 \tag{9.52}$$

$$x = \frac{1 \pm \sqrt{1 - (4 \times -1)}}{2} \tag{9.53}$$

$$x = \frac{1 \pm \sqrt{5}}{2} \tag{9.54}$$

$$\sin \theta = \frac{1 - \sqrt{5}}{2} \tag{9.55}$$

9.1.10   Question 10

Points a and b tell us straightforward facts about our sketch. Point c tells us that there must be only one stationary point at $x = 4$. Point d tells us there must be two points of inflection at $x = 2$ and $x = 6$. Therefore the sketch should look like:

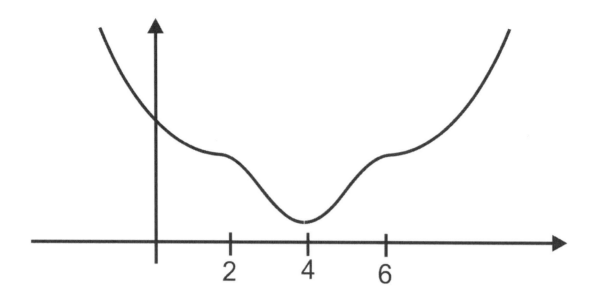

9.1.11 Question 11

$$-1 = -\frac{1}{x} + 2x \tag{9.56}$$

$$-x = -1 + 2x^2 \tag{9.57}$$

$$0 = 2x^2 + x - 1 \tag{9.58}$$

$$0 = (x+1)(x - \frac{1}{2}) \tag{9.59}$$

$$x = -1 \tag{9.60}$$

$$x = \frac{1}{2} \tag{9.61}$$

and

$$-\frac{1}{x} + 2x = 1 \tag{9.62}$$

$$-1 + 2x^2 = x \tag{9.63}$$

$$2x^2 - x - 1 = 0 \tag{9.64}$$

$$(x-1)(x + \frac{1}{2}) = 0 \tag{9.65}$$

$$x = 1 \tag{9.66}$$

$$x = -\frac{1}{2} \tag{9.67}$$

You now have four points which can be arranged on a number line. Substitute in points such as $x = 2$, $x = -2$, $x = 0.25$, $x = -0.25$, $x = 0.75$, $x = -0.75$ to test the inequalities. This gives:

$$-1 < x < -\frac{1}{2} \tag{9.68}$$

$$\frac{1}{2} < x < 1 \tag{9.69}$$

9.1.12 Question 12

Writing the equation as:

$$y = x^{-2} - x^{-1} - 1 \tag{9.70}$$

Finding the turning points:

$$\frac{dy}{dx} = -2x^{-3} + x^{-2} = 0 \tag{9.71}$$

$$= \frac{-2}{x^3} + \frac{1}{x^2} = 0 \tag{9.72}$$

$$\frac{-2}{x} + 1 = 0 \tag{9.73}$$

$$1 = \frac{2}{x} \tag{9.74}$$

$$x = 2 \tag{9.75}$$

At the point $x = 2$:

$$\frac{1 - 2 - 4}{4} = \frac{-5}{4} \tag{9.76}$$

The degree of the top is 2 and the degree of the bottom is 2. Therefore the limit as $x \to \infty$ is the leading coefficient of the top divided by the leading coefficient of the bottom which is $-1/1 = -1$. As $x \to 0$ the graph diverges in the positive direction and the function is even so this is true for positive and negative x. Therefore:

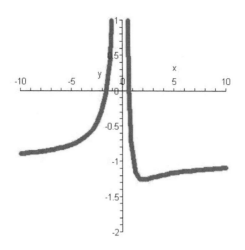

9.2   Part B - Physics

9.2.1   Question 13

Since

$$m \quad \propto \quad l^3 \tag{9.77}$$

$$m \quad = \quad kl^3 \tag{9.78}$$

$$6.5 \times 10^4 \quad = \quad k \times 1000 \tag{9.79}$$

$$65 \quad = \quad k \tag{9.80}$$

Therefore

$$1 \quad = \quad 65 \times l^3 \tag{9.81}$$

$$\frac{1}{65} \quad = \quad l^3 \tag{9.82}$$

$$\sqrt[3]{\frac{1}{65}} \quad = \quad l \tag{9.83}$$

$$\sqrt[3]{\frac{1}{65}} \quad \approx \quad \sqrt[3]{\frac{1}{64}} = \frac{1}{4} \tag{9.84}$$

$$l \quad = \quad 0.25m \tag{9.85}$$

Therefore the answer is C.

9.2.2   Question 14

$$P = \frac{nRT}{V} \tag{9.86}$$

$$= \frac{2 \times 8.3 \times (27 + 273)}{0.02} \tag{9.87}$$

$$= \frac{2 \times 8.3 \times 300}{0.02} \tag{9.88}$$

$$= 100 \times 8.3 \times 300 \tag{9.89}$$

$$= 100 \times 2490 \tag{9.90}$$

$$= 249,000 \tag{9.91}$$

Therefore the answer is D.

9.2.3   Question 15

Assuming electrical energy input in a second is equal to the work done in a second and the velocity of 36km/hr is 36,000 m/hr which is 36,000/3600 = 10 m/s then:

$$VI = Fv \tag{9.92}$$

$$160 \times 100 = F \times 10 \tag{9.93}$$

$$F = \frac{16000}{10} \tag{9.94}$$

$$= 1600N \tag{9.95}$$

Therefore the answer is B.

9.2.4   Question 16

The cube root of 125 is 5. Therefore the cube is $5 \times 5 \times 5$ blocks. There must be a $3 \times 3 \times 3$ cube in the middle with no paint which makes 27 cubes. Therefore the answer is C.

9.2.5   Question 17

Consider the forces acting radially on the object as it is going around the circle. There will be no normal reaction force (since the surface is frictionless $\mu = 0$).

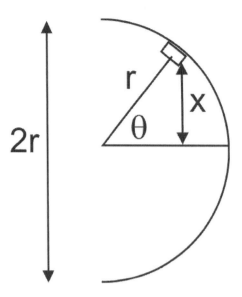

$$\frac{mv^2}{r} = mg\sin\theta \tag{9.96}$$

$$\frac{mv^2}{r} = mg\frac{x}{r} \tag{9.97}$$

$$v^2 = gx \tag{9.98}$$

Now lets consider conservation of energy. Initially the object will have GPE, when it falls from the circular track it will have GPE and KE:

$$mg2r = \frac{1}{2}mv^2 + mg(r + x) \tag{9.99}$$

$$mg2r = \frac{1}{2}mv^2 + mgr + mgx \tag{9.100}$$

Making a substitution for $v^2 = gx$:

$$mg2r = \frac{1}{2}mgx + mgr + mgx \tag{9.101}$$

$$mg2r = \frac{3}{2}mgx + mgr \tag{9.102}$$

$$2r = \frac{3}{2}x + r \tag{9.103}$$

$$r = \frac{3}{2}x \tag{9.104}$$

$$x = \frac{2r}{3} \tag{9.105}$$

Therefore the object does not reach the top and the answer is A.

9.2.6 Question 18

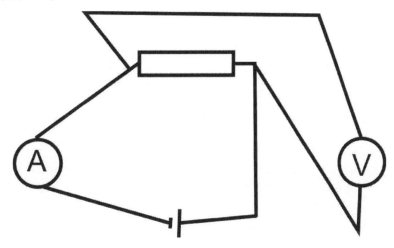

The current is:

$$I = \frac{V}{R} = \frac{12}{2000} = 0.006A \tag{9.106}$$

The time constant is

$$RC = 2000 \times 4 \times 10^{-6} = 8 \times 10^{-3}s \tag{9.107}$$

Therefore the current is not changing significantly after approximately 5RC which is $4 \times 10^{-2}s = 0.04s$. The current when the circuit is charging is:

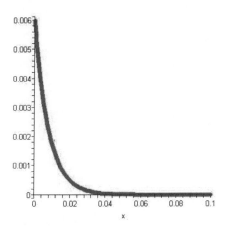

The current when the circuit is discharging is:

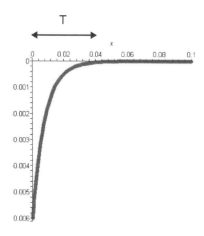

9.2.7   Question 19

The sound wave from the loud speaker and the sound wave reflected by the screen form a standing wave. Distance moved by the screen between maxima is $\lambda/2$ since we need a whole number of wavelengths difference in path length for constructive interference.

If the loudspeaker moves this would still create a standing wave and the maxima and minima would change position so would be recorded by the microphone.

If the microphone moves then it would record maxima and minima.

9.2.8   Question 20

Given that

$$\frac{N_{235}(t)}{N_{238}(t)} = 0.0072 \tag{9.108}$$

then

$$\frac{N_{235,0} \exp^{-\lambda_{235}t}}{N_{238,0} \exp^{-\lambda_{238}t}} = 0.0072 \tag{9.109}$$

$$\frac{N_{235,0} \exp^{-\lambda_{235} \times 10^9}}{N_{235,0} \exp^{-\lambda_{238} \times 10^9}} = 0.0072 \tag{9.110}$$

$$\frac{N_{235,0}}{N_{238,0}} = 0.0072 \times \frac{\exp^{-\lambda_{238} \times 10^9}}{\exp^{-\lambda_{235} \times 10^9}} \tag{9.111}$$

$$= 0.0072 \times \frac{\exp\left[-ln2 \times 10^9/4.5 \times 10^9\right]}{\exp\left[-ln2 \times 10^9/0.7 \times 10^9\right]} \tag{9.112}$$

$$= 0.0072 \times \frac{\exp\left[-ln2/4.5\right]}{\exp\left[-ln2/0.7\right]} \tag{9.113}$$

$$= 0.0072 \times \frac{\exp\left[-0.7/4.5\right]}{\exp\left[-0.7/0.7\right]} \tag{9.114}$$

$$= 0.0072 \times \exp\left[-0.7/4.5\right] \times 2.7 \tag{9.115}$$

$$= 0.0072 \times \left[1 - 0.7/4.5\right] \times 2.7 \tag{9.116}$$

$$= 0.0072 \times \frac{38}{45} \times 2.7 \tag{9.117}$$

$$= 0.016 \tag{9.118}$$

using the fact that $t_{1/2} = ln2/\lambda$

9.2.9 Question 21

Equate gravitational force and centripetal force:

$$\frac{Gm_1m_2}{r^2} = \frac{m_2v^2}{r} \tag{9.119}$$

$$v = \sqrt{\frac{GM}{R}} \tag{9.120}$$

G is the gravitational constant, M is the mass of the Earth and R is radius of the orbit.

Since the meteoroids have the same mass and opposite velocity, when they collide conservation of momentum says that the combined meteoroid will have zero velocity and will fall to Earth.

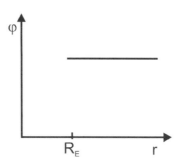

The kinetic energy is $0.5mv^2$ but $v^2 = \sqrt{(2gr)}$ so the kinetic energy is proportional to the distance fallen, but as it enters the Earths atmosphere at a distance of less than $2R_E$ it will begin to slow down and reach terminal velocity. Once it hits the Earth's surface the velocity will be zero.

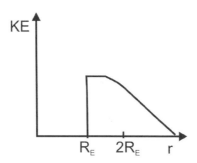

Above $2R_E$ there will be no heating as the effects of the atmosphere can be ignored, however below this height the temperature will increase as KE and GPE are converted to heat. As the meteoroid descends it will begin to cool as the atmosphere begins to conduct heat away from it:

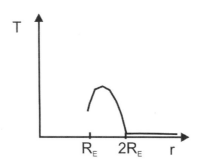

9.2.10   Question 22

9.2.10.1   part a1

Assume all the work is converted to kinetic energy. The work done is found from the area under the graph:

$$Fd = \frac{1}{2}mv^2 \tag{9.121}$$

$$10 \times 10 = \frac{1}{2} \times 1 \times v^2 \tag{9.122}$$

$$200 = v^2 \tag{9.123}$$

$$\sqrt{200} = v \tag{9.124}$$

$$14.1 = v \tag{9.125}$$

9.2.10.2   part a2

Firstly, find the distance at which the speed (and so the KE) will be zero. This happens when the area below the axis is the same as the area above since the same amount of work is done. The area under the F-x graph is 150. The area above the F-x graph is given by:

$$150 = \frac{1}{2} \times b^2 \tag{9.126}$$

$$b = \sqrt{300} \tag{9.127}$$

$$= 17.3 \tag{9.128}$$

Therefore the maximum distance is $-17.3 - 10 = -27.3m$. Since the rising force line has a gradient of 1 this gives the maximum force as $+17.3$N. Since the mass is 1kg, the maximum acceleration is also 17.3m/s^2.

The maximum velocity is found in the same way as part a1 but using the full area under the graph:

$$Fd = \frac{1}{2}mv^2 \tag{9.129}$$

$$10 \times 10 + \frac{1}{2} \times 10 \times = \frac{1}{2} \times 1 \times v^2 \tag{9.130}$$

$$150 = \frac{1}{2} \times 1 \times v^2 \tag{9.131}$$

$$300 = v^2 \tag{9.132}$$

$$\sqrt{300} = v \tag{9.133}$$

$$17.2 \approx v \tag{9.134}$$

The KE will follow the work done or area under the graph. It will have a constant gradient and increase from zero at $x = 10$ to $\frac{1}{2} \times 1 \times 200 = 100$ at $x = 0$ (check this at $x = 5$, the KE gained will be 50J). It will level off to a maximum of $\frac{1}{2} \times 1 \times 300 = 150$ by $x = -10$ and then decrease to zero by $x = -27.3$:

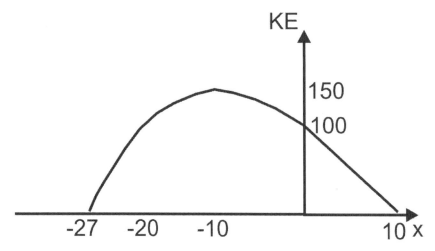

9.2.10.3   part a3

Since the acceleration is just $a = F/m$ and $m = 1$ then the acceleration is simply the force. You just need to turn it into a acceleration-time graph. Note also that the object behaves as SHM about the equilibrium point $x = -10$ for displacements less than zero, since the force is proportional to the displacement from $x = -10$

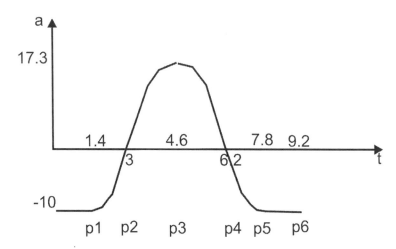

164

To find the time at point p1 apply suvat

$$s = 10 \tag{9.135}$$

$$u = 0 \tag{9.136}$$

$$v = 14.1 \tag{9.137}$$

$$a = -10 \tag{9.138}$$

$$t = ? \tag{9.139}$$

$$v = u + at \tag{9.140}$$

$$14.1 = -10t \tag{9.141}$$

$$t = 1.4 \tag{9.142}$$

To find the time between p2 and p4 consider the SHM. Recall

$$a = -\omega^2 s \tag{9.143}$$

where a is acceleration and s is displacement. Let's consider the point at x=0, the acceleration here is -10 and the displacement is 10 away from the equilibrium point. So:

$$\omega^2 = -\frac{a}{s} \tag{9.144}$$

$$= -\frac{-10}{10} \tag{9.145}$$

$$= 1 \tag{9.146}$$

$$\omega = 1 \tag{9.147}$$

Since

$$\omega = \frac{2\pi}{T} \tag{9.148}$$

$$T = 2\pi \tag{9.149}$$

Therefore the time between p2 and p4 is half a period or 3.14s. Since the period does not depend on amplitude the time between p1 and p2 will be 1.57s. To find the velocity graph remember that the acceleration is the gradient of this graph:

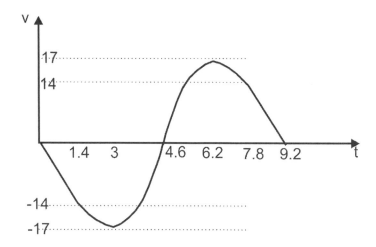

The velocity reached after 1.4s has been calculated in part a1. The maximum velocity reached in the negative direction will be given by the equating energies from the area under the graph between $x = -10$ and $x = 10$ and the kinetic energy:

$$10 \times 10 + \frac{1}{2} \times 10 \times 10 = \frac{1}{2} \times 1 \times v^2 \tag{9.150}$$

$$150 = \frac{1}{2} \times v^2 \tag{9.151}$$

$$\sqrt{300} = v \tag{9.152}$$

$$17.3 = v \tag{9.153}$$

9.2.10.4   part b1

When the object sets off it will have a resultant force of 9N, however when it returns it will have a resultant force of 11N. We therefore need to run through the same calculations above, but with these new forces:

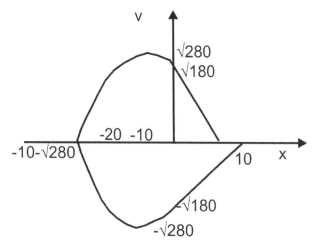

The velocity at x = 0 is given by assuming all the work is converted to kinetic energy. The work done is found from the area under the graph:

$$Fd = \frac{1}{2}mv^2 \tag{9.154}$$

$$9 \times 10 = \frac{1}{2} \times 1 \times v^2 \tag{9.155}$$

$$180 = v^2 \tag{9.156}$$

$$\sqrt{180} = v \tag{9.157}$$

$$13 \approx v \tag{9.158}$$

The maximum velocity is found in the same way as part a1 but using the full area under the graph:

$$Fd = \frac{1}{2}mv^2 \tag{9.159}$$

$$9 \times 10 + \frac{1}{2} \times 10 \times 10 = \frac{1}{2} \times 1 \times v^2 \tag{9.160}$$

$$140 = \frac{1}{2} \times 1 \times v^2 \tag{9.161}$$

$$280 = v^2 \tag{9.162}$$

$$\sqrt{280} = v \tag{9.163}$$

$$17 \approx v \tag{9.164}$$

9.2.10.5 part b2

Apply suvat:

$$s = \tag{9.165}$$

$$u = \sqrt{180} \tag{9.166}$$

$$v = 0 \tag{9.167}$$

$$a = -11 \tag{9.168}$$

$$t = \tag{9.169}$$

$$v^2 = u^2 + 2as \tag{9.170}$$

$$180 = 2 \times 11 \times s \tag{9.171}$$

$$\frac{180}{22} = s \tag{9.172}$$

$$8 \approx s \tag{9.173}$$

Therefore the total distance traveled is the original 10m plus 8m therefore 18m.

Chapter 10

Oxford Physics Aptitude Test 2013 Answers

10.1   Part A - Maths

Question 1

Here we have a sum of a geometric progression with first term $a = 2/3$ and common ratio $r = -1/3$ so:

$$
\begin{aligned}
S_\infty &= \frac{a}{1-r} & (10.1) \\
&= \frac{2/3}{1--1/3} & (10.2) \\
&= \frac{2/3}{4/3} & (10.3) \\
&= 0.5 & (10.4)
\end{aligned}
$$

Question 2

Use the first equation to substitute for y in the second equation.

$$
\begin{aligned}
\left(\sqrt{xv} - \sqrt{x}\right)\left(\sqrt{xv} - \sqrt{x}\right) &= u & (10.5) \\
xv - 2x\sqrt{v} + x &= u & (10.6) \\
x(v - 2\sqrt{v} + 1) &= u & (10.7) \\
x &= \frac{u}{v - 2\sqrt{v} + 1} & (10.8) \\
&= \frac{u}{(\sqrt{v} - 1)^2} & (10.9)
\end{aligned}
$$

Question 3

Write down some probabilities:

$$p(male) = \frac{20}{50} \tag{10.10}$$

$$p(female) = \frac{30}{50} \tag{10.11}$$

$$p(redhair) = \frac{8}{50} \tag{10.12}$$

$$p(blackhair) = \frac{3}{50} \tag{10.13}$$

$$p(otherhair) = \frac{39}{50} \tag{10.14}$$

$$\tag{10.15}$$

a

$$\frac{30}{50} \times \frac{8}{50} = \frac{240}{2500} \tag{10.16}$$

$$= \frac{24}{250} \tag{10.17}$$

$$= \frac{12}{125} \tag{10.18}$$

b

$$\frac{20}{50} \times \frac{39}{50} = \frac{780}{2500} \tag{10.19}$$

$$= \frac{78}{250} \tag{10.20}$$

$$= \frac{39}{125} \tag{10.21}$$

Question 4

a

To show that x=1 is a root, simply substitute this into the equation:

$$1^3 - 1^2 - 4 \times 1 + 4 = 0 \tag{10.22}$$

$$1 - 1 - 4 + 4 = 0 \tag{10.23}$$

To find the remaining roots, divide the polynomial by (x-1):

$$x^2 - \qquad 4 \tag{10.24}$$

$$x - 1 \overline{)x^3 - x^2 \quad -4x + 4} \tag{10.25}$$

$$-x^3 - x^2 \tag{10.26}$$

$$\overline{0 \quad -4x + 4} \tag{10.27}$$

$$-4x + 4 \tag{10.28}$$

$$\overline{0} \tag{10.29}$$

$$\tag{10.30}$$

Therefore the answer is:

$$(x - 1)(x^2 - 4) = (x - 1)(x - 2)(x + 2) \tag{10.31}$$

and the roots are x=1, x=2 and x=-2.

b

Smallest roots are -2 and 1. So to find the area, integrate:

$$\int_{-2}^{1} x^3 - x^2 - 4x + 4 = \left[\frac{x^4}{4} - \frac{x^3}{3} - \frac{4x^2}{2} + 4x \right]_{-2}^{1} \tag{10.32}$$

$$= \left(\frac{1}{4} - \frac{1}{3} - \frac{4}{2} + 4 \right) - \left(\frac{16}{4} + \frac{8}{3} - \frac{16}{2} - 8 \right) \tag{10.33}$$

$$= 1\frac{11}{12} + 9\frac{1}{3} \tag{10.34}$$

$$= 11\frac{1}{4} \tag{10.35}$$

Question 5

Take the equations one at a time and simplify, remembering that if $a^x = b$

$$\log_a b = x \tag{10.36}$$

So:

$$x = \log_{10} 100 + \log_5 25^{1/2} - \log_3 y^2 \tag{10.37}$$

$$= 2 + \frac{1}{2}\log_5 25 - 2\log_3 y \tag{10.38}$$

$$= 2 + \frac{1}{2} \times 2 - 2\log_3 y \tag{10.39}$$

$$x = 3 - 2\log_3 y \tag{10.40}$$

Turning to the other equation:

$$\frac{x}{2} = \log_2 8 - 9\log_{10} 10^{1/2} + 2\log_3 y \tag{10.41}$$

$$= 3 - 9 \times \frac{1}{2} + 2\log_3 y \tag{10.42}$$

$$= 3 - 4.5 + 2\log_3 y \tag{10.43}$$

$$x = -3 + 4\log_3 y \tag{10.44}$$

Equating the two equations we have for x:

$$3 - 2\log_3 y = -3 + 4\log_3 y \tag{10.45}$$

$$6 = 6\log_3 y \tag{10.46}$$

$$1 = \log_3 y \tag{10.47}$$

$$y = 3 \tag{10.48}$$

Substituting back:

$$x = 3 - 2\log_3 y \tag{10.49}$$

$$= 3 - 2 \times 1 \tag{10.50}$$

$$x = 1 \tag{10.51}$$

Question 6

The general equation of a circle is given by:

$$(x - a)^2 + (y - b)^2 = r^2 \tag{10.52}$$

where the centre is at (a, b). So lets rewrite the given equations in this form:

$$x^2 + 4x + y^2 - 2y = -1 \tag{10.53}$$

$$(x + 2)^2 + (y - 1)^2 = 4 \tag{10.54}$$

so the centre is at $(-2, 1)$, and

$$x^2 - 4x + y^2 - 6y = 3 \tag{10.55}$$

$$(x - 2)^2 + (y - 3)^2 = 16 \tag{10.56}$$

so the centre is at $(2, 3)$. The gradient is found using:

$$m = \frac{y_2 - y_1}{x_2 - x_1} = \frac{3 - 1}{2 - -2} \tag{10.57}$$

$$= \frac{1}{2} \tag{10.58}$$

Substituting into the equation of a straight line for the point $(2, 3)$ which is on the straight line:

$$y = \frac{1}{2}x + c \tag{10.59}$$

$$3 = \frac{1}{2} \times 2 + c \tag{10.60}$$

$$c = 2 \tag{10.61}$$

Therefore:

$$y = \frac{x}{2} + 2 \tag{10.62}$$

Question 7

Let's consider the Binomial expansion formula:

$$(1 + x)^n = 1 + nx + \frac{n(n - 1)}{2!}x^2 + \frac{n(n - 1)(n - 2)}{3!}x^3 + \ldots \tag{10.63}$$

Now let's rewrite $(3.12)^5$ in the format $(1 + x)n$ where $|x| < 1$:

$$3^5(1.04)^5 = 243(1 + 0.04)^5 \tag{10.64}$$

Now let's consider the largest size of the Binomial expansion term allowed, so that when it's multiplied by 243 is remains less than 0.05. This must be:

$$\frac{0.05}{243} \approx \frac{0.05}{250} = 0.0002 \tag{10.65}$$

Now let's look at powers of 0.04:

$$0.04^2 = 0.0016 \tag{10.66}$$

$$0.04^3 = 0.000064 \tag{10.67}$$

$$0.04^4 = 0.00000128 \tag{10.68}$$

Therefore we have to have terms as far as x^3, but lets just check that the coefficient of the x^4 term to see if this allows this term to be less than 0.0002:

$$\frac{n(n-1)(n-2)(n-3)}{4!}x^4 = \frac{5 \times 4 \times 3 \times 2}{24}0.00000128 \tag{10.69}$$

$$= 5 \times 0.00000128 \tag{10.70}$$

$$= 0.0000064 \tag{10.71}$$

Yes that's fine, so we need to include the x^3 term, but no further: which means there are 4 terms in total.

Question 8

Break up the inequalities and rearrange them:

$$1 = xy \tag{10.72}$$

$$y = \frac{1}{x} \tag{10.73}$$

and

$$2 = xy \tag{10.74}$$

$$y = \frac{2}{x} \tag{10.75}$$

and

$$\frac{1}{2} = \frac{y}{x} \tag{10.76}$$

$$y = \frac{x}{2} \tag{10.77}$$

and

$$y = \frac{x}{2} \tag{10.78}$$

$$y = 2x \tag{10.79}$$

Plot these lines:

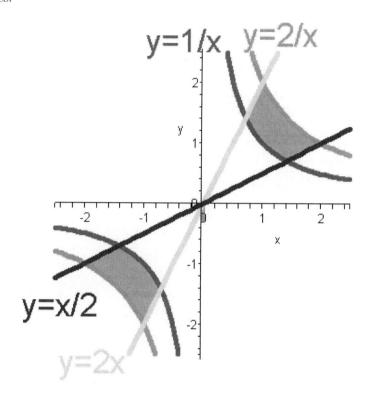

and then go through each inequality and work out the region in which it is true. The regions are shaded grey on the image.

Question 9

a

This is simply e^x reflected in the y axis:

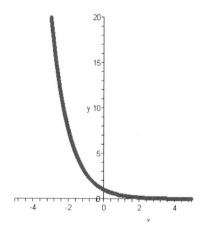

b

This is more difficult. Try to find out what sort of shaped graph it is, its limiting values and some points it goes through. Firstly lets spot that we can make both powers zero by taking $x = 1$. So:

$$y = 3(1 - 2) = -3 \tag{10.80}$$

So a point is (1,-3). Next let's consider when $x = 0$:

$$
\begin{aligned}
y &= 3\left[e^2 - 2e\right] && \text{(10.81)} \\
&= 3e(e - 2) && \text{(10.82)} \\
&\approx 3 \times 2.7 \times 0.7 && \text{(10.83)} \\
&\approx 6 && \text{(10.84)}
\end{aligned}
$$

since $e^1 \approx 2.7$, so another point is (0,6).

For large x the second term wins since the power of x is the same but the factor in front is -6 not 3. Therefore at large positive x:

$$y = -6e^{-(x-1)} \tag{10.85}$$

this will be negative, but approaching zero (compare with the graph you drew for part a).

Finally differentiate to find any turning points:

$$
\begin{aligned}
\frac{dy}{dx} &= 3\left[-2e^{-2(x-1)} + 2e^{-(x-1)}\right] && \text{(10.86)} \\
0 &= 6e^{-(x-1)} - 6e^{-2(x-1)} && \text{(10.87)} \\
6e^{-2(x-1)} &= 6e^{-(x-1)} && \text{(10.88)} \\
-2(x - 1) &= -(x - 1) && \text{(10.89)} \\
2(x - 1) &= x - 1 && \text{(10.90)} \\
2x - 2 &= x - 1 && \text{(10.91)} \\
x &= 1 && \text{(10.92)}
\end{aligned}
$$

We have already found the corresponding y value so the only turning point is (1,-3). So let's try a sketch:

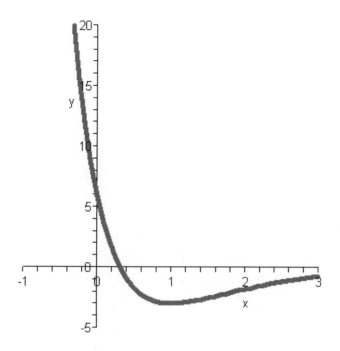

Question 10

Firstly, find the area of the small circle:

$$A_{sc} = \pi r^2 \tag{10.93}$$

Now consider the small circle and part of the small triangle. Since this is equilateral, all the angles are 60° and we can draw the following:

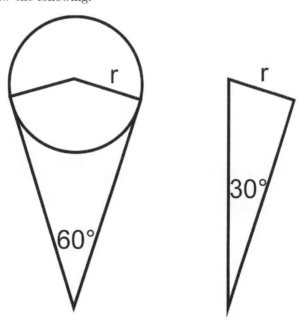

Looking at the right angle triangle we can find the hypotenuse:

$$\sin 30 = \frac{r}{h} \tag{10.94}$$

$$\frac{1}{2} = \frac{r}{h} \tag{10.95}$$

$$h = 2r \tag{10.96}$$

Using this, plus the radius of the small circle gives us the full height of the small triangle: this must be 3r. Next we need to find the length of the base of half the small equilateral triangle:

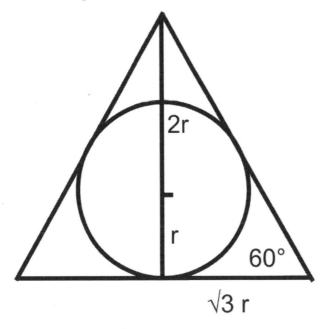

Applying trigonometry again:

$$\tan 60 = \frac{3r}{x} \tag{10.97}$$

$$\sqrt{3} = \frac{3r}{x} \tag{10.98}$$

$$x = \frac{3r}{\sqrt{3}} \tag{10.99}$$

$$= \sqrt{3}r \tag{10.100}$$

Now we can find the area of the small triangle:

$$A_{st} = \frac{1}{2} \times 2 \times \sqrt{3}r \times 3r \tag{10.101}$$

$$= 3\sqrt{3}r^2 \tag{10.102}$$

The radius of the large circle is given by the height of the first triangle which is 2r, so the area of the large circle is:

$$A_{lc} = \pi \times (2r)^2 \tag{10.103}$$

$$= 4\pi r^2 \tag{10.104}$$

Finally the area of the large triangle. The base is the given by twice the side length of the small equilateral triangle, this is $4\sqrt{3}r$. The height is given by twice the height of the small equilateral triangle: twice $3r$:

$$A_{lt} = \frac{1}{2} \times 4\sqrt{3}r \times 6r \tag{10.105}$$

$$= 12\sqrt{3}r^2 \tag{10.106}$$

So the areas of the shaded region is:

$$A = A_{lt} - A_{lc} + A_{st} - A_{sc} \tag{10.107}$$

$$= 12\sqrt{3}r^2 - 4\pi r^2 + 3\sqrt{3}r^2 - \pi r^2 \tag{10.108}$$

$$= 5\left(3\sqrt{3} - \pi\right)r^2 \tag{10.109}$$

10.2   Part B - Physics

Question 11

Consider the conservation of power (we usually assume transformers are 100% efficient.

$$V_p I_p = V_s I_s \tag{10.110}$$

$$100 \times 2.4 = V_s \times 4.8 \tag{10.111}$$

$$V_s = 50 \tag{10.112}$$

Now use the standard transformer equation:

$$\frac{N_s}{N_p} = \frac{V_s}{V_p} \tag{10.113}$$

$$\frac{N_s}{100} = \frac{50}{100} \tag{10.114}$$

$$N_s = 50 \tag{10.115}$$

Therefore the answer is B.

Question 12

Set x to be the number at atoms of B initially and draw a table:

days	A	B
0	2x	x
3	x	
6	x/2	x/2
9	x/4	
12	x/8	x/4
15		

Therefore the answer is C.

Question 13

Draw the equivalent circuits:

For the first diagram, the two resistors in series sum to $2R$. The two resistors in parallel are identical so their equivalent resistor must be $R/2$, so we can use the usual equation:

$$\frac{1}{R_t} = \frac{1}{R_1} + \frac{1}{R_2} \tag{10.116}$$

$$= \frac{1}{R} + \frac{1}{R} \tag{10.117}$$

$$= \frac{2}{R} \tag{10.118}$$

$$R_T = \frac{R}{2} \tag{10.119}$$

To find the second diagram, apply the parallel resistor formula again:

$$\frac{1}{R_T} = \frac{1}{2r} + \frac{2}{2R} \tag{10.120}$$

$$\frac{1}{R_T} = \frac{3}{2R} \tag{10.121}$$

$$R_T = \frac{2R}{3} \tag{10.122}$$

Finally to find the answer apply the equation again to the second diagram:

$$\frac{1}{R_T} = \frac{4}{2R} + \frac{3}{2R} \tag{10.123}$$

$$= \frac{7}{2R} \tag{10.124}$$

$$R_T = \frac{2R}{7} \tag{10.125}$$

Therefore the answer is A. As an alternative, consider this as 4 branches in parallel and use:

$$\frac{1}{R_T} = \frac{1}{R_1} + \frac{1}{R_2} + \frac{1}{R_3} + \frac{1}{R_4} \tag{10.126}$$

$$= \frac{1}{R} + \frac{1}{R} + \frac{1}{2R} + \frac{1}{R} \tag{10.127}$$

$$= \frac{7}{2R} \tag{10.128}$$

$$R_T = \frac{2R}{7} \tag{10.129}$$

Question 14

Remember the Kepler's Third Law gives us that the period squared is proportional to the radius cubed:

$$T^2 \propto R^3 \tag{10.130}$$

If the radius is halved, then the the net effect on radius cubed is to decrease by a factor of 8. Therefore the period must go down by a factor of $\sqrt{8}$ which is about 2.7. A geostationary satellite has a period of 24 hours so we need 24/2.7 which is about 8.5 hours. So the answer is B.

Question 15

Power follows the inverse square law so:

$$P \propto \frac{1}{r^2} \tag{10.131}$$

which means that

$$Pr^2 = k \tag{10.132}$$

where k is a constant. So:

$$P_1 r_1^2 = P_2 r_2^2 \tag{10.133}$$

$$20 \times 100^2 = 0.001 \times r^2 \tag{10.134}$$

$$\frac{200,000}{0.001} = r^2 \tag{10.135}$$

$$200,000,000 = r^2 \tag{10.136}$$

$$1000\sqrt{200} = r \tag{10.137}$$

$$10,000\sqrt{2} = r \tag{10.138}$$

$$10\sqrt{2}km = r \tag{10.139}$$

Therefore the answer is C.

Question 16

$$P = \frac{F}{A} \tag{10.140}$$

$$A = \frac{F}{A} \tag{10.141}$$

$$= \frac{1000 \times 10}{200,000} \tag{10.142}$$

$$= 0.05m^2 \tag{10.143}$$

but this if for 4 tyres, so the area is 0.0125m² per tyre.

Question 17

Consider the forces on M:

$$Mg - T = Ma \tag{10.144}$$

and the forces on m:

$$T - mg\sin\alpha = ma \tag{10.145}$$

The acceleration of mass m can be found be rearranging:

$$\frac{T - mg\sin\alpha}{m} = a \tag{10.146}$$

Assuming the acceleration of both masses to be the same (since they are connected by the string) we can equate the accelerations:

$$\frac{Mg - T}{M} = \frac{T - mg\sin\alpha}{m} \tag{10.147}$$

$$m(Mg - T) = M(T - mg\sin\alpha) \tag{10.148}$$

$$mMg - mT = MT - mMg\sin\alpha \tag{10.149}$$

$$mMg + mMh\sin\alpha = (M + m)T \tag{10.150}$$

$$\frac{mMg(1 + \sin\alpha)}{M + m} = T \tag{10.151}$$

For an acceleration of zero, study the first two equations given, $T = mg\sin\alpha$ or $T = Mg$ so:

$$Mg = mg\sin\alpha \tag{10.152}$$

$$M = m\sin\alpha \tag{10.153}$$

Question 18

Consider conservation of momentum:

$$p_{before} = p_{after} \tag{10.154}$$

$$0.2 \times 122 + 12 \times 0 = 12.2 \times v \tag{10.155}$$

$$\frac{0.2 \times 122}{12.2} = v \tag{10.156}$$

$$2 = v \tag{10.157}$$

Now the conservation of energy so that KE of ball and bullet is converted into GPE of the ball and bullet:

$$\frac{1}{2}mv^2 = mgh \tag{10.158}$$

$$\frac{1}{2} \times 12.2 \times 2^2 = 12.2 \times 10 \times h \tag{10.159}$$

$$24.4 = 12.2h \tag{10.160}$$

$$h = 0.2m \tag{10.161}$$

Question 19

Minima occur where there has been a $(n + \frac{1}{2})\lambda$ path difference between light arriving from each slit. This leads to destructive interference.

Maxima occur where there has been a $n\lambda$ (or whole number of wavelengths) path difference between light arriving from each slit. This leads to constructive interference.

For green light which has a shorter wavelength than red light and since $\lambda = dx/D$, x (the distance between the maxima) will be less and the peaks are closer together.

Question 20

part a

The mass of water in the pot is:

$$m = d \times v \tag{10.162}$$
$$= = 1 \times 10 \times 10 \times 15 \tag{10.163}$$
$$= 1500g \tag{10.164}$$

The energy need is found using:

$$E = mc\theta \tag{10.165}$$
$$= 1.5 \times 4200 \times 80 \tag{10.166}$$
$$= 120 \times 4200 \tag{10.167}$$
$$= 504,000J \tag{10.168}$$

part b

The reduction in air pressure

part c

The drop in boiling point of water at 6000m is:

$$\frac{6000}{300} = 20°C \tag{10.169}$$

so she needs to heat water from $10°$ to $80°C$.

$$
\begin{aligned}
E &= mc\theta & (10.170) \\
&= 0.1 \times 4200 \times 70 & (10.171) \\
&= 420 \times 7 & (10.172) \\
&= 29,400J & (10.173)
\end{aligned}
$$

part d

Neglect the heat capacity for the time being to simplify the maths. Initially the stove would output an energy of $1.5 \times 80 = 120$kgK in 15 minutes. So at 50% power this would be 60kgK in 15 minutes, which is 4kgK in 1 minute. She needs $0.1 \times 70 = 7$kgK to heat the water for her cup of tea. So it will take 7/4 minutes which is 1 minute 45 seconds.

Question 21

part a

Apply SUVAT:

$$
\begin{aligned}
s &= d & (10.174) \\
u &= v_0 & (10.175) \\
v &= ? & (10.176) \\
a &= \frac{f}{m} & (10.177) \\
v^2 &= u^2 + 2as & (10.178) \\
v^2 &= v_0^2 + \frac{2fd}{m} & (10.179) \\
v &= \sqrt{v_0^2 + \frac{2fd}{m}} & (10.180)
\end{aligned}
$$

part b

We assume the particle does not slow down over the distance D. Because the acceleration is always perpendicular to the velocity, this gives circular motion. So we use:

$$F = \frac{mv^2}{r} \tag{10.181}$$

$$\alpha v = \frac{mv^2}{r} \tag{10.182}$$

$$r = \frac{mv}{\alpha} \tag{10.183}$$

$$= \frac{m}{\alpha}\sqrt{v_0^2 + \frac{2fd}{m}} \tag{10.184}$$

so the y coordinate will be twice the radius:

$$y = \frac{2mv}{\alpha} = \frac{2m}{\alpha}\sqrt{v_0^2 + \frac{2fd}{m}} \tag{10.185}$$

part c

Just rearrange the equation from the previous question:

$$\Delta v = \frac{\alpha \Delta y}{2m} \tag{10.186}$$

part d

There are two ways to tackle this problem. Either remember that work is only done if the object moves in the direction of the force. So no work is done by force F. The particle moves through distance d and is affected by force f so the work done is $f \times d$.

Alternatively, the work done is equal to the energy gain (in this case kinetic energy):

$$W = \frac{1}{2}mv^2 \tag{10.187}$$

$$= \frac{1}{2}m\left(v_0^2 + \frac{2fd}{m}\right) \tag{10.188}$$

$$= \frac{1}{2}mv_0^2 + fd \tag{10.189}$$

But it already had kinetic energy of $1/2mv_0^2$ so the kinetic energy gained (and therefore the work done) is $f \times d$.

Chapter 11

Oxford Physics Aptitude Test 2014 Answers

11.1 Part A - Maths

Question 1

Let y=number of yellow, g=number of green, r=number of red and b=number of blue. The statements given suggest:

$$y = 2g \tag{11.1}$$

$$r = 2y = 4g \tag{11.2}$$

$$b = 2r = 8g \tag{11.3}$$

Including g green, you know there are 15g buttons in total. Therefore the probabilities are:

$$g = \frac{1}{15} \tag{11.4}$$

$$y = \frac{2}{15} \tag{11.5}$$

$$r = \frac{4}{15} \tag{11.6}$$

$$b = \frac{8}{15} \tag{11.7}$$

Question 2

This is a geometric progression with first term 1 and common ration e^{-x}. So:

$$\sum_{\infty} = \frac{a}{1-r} \tag{11.8}$$

$$= \frac{1}{1-e^{-x}} \tag{11.9}$$

This equation is valid for $|r| < 1$ therefore $e^{-x} < 1$ which is true when $x > 0$.

Question 3

part a

This is integration by substitution. We notice that the top is the differential of the bottom. So we make the substitution

$$u = 1 + \sin x \tag{11.10}$$

So:

$$du = \cos x\, dx \tag{11.11}$$

and

$$\int_0^{\pi/2} \frac{\cos x}{1 + \sin x} dx = \int_1^2 \frac{1}{u} du \tag{11.12}$$

$$= \left[\ln u\right]_1^2 \tag{11.13}$$

$$= \ln 2 - \ln 1 \tag{11.14}$$

$$= \ln 2 \tag{11.15}$$

Where we have calculated the new limits from:

$$u = 1 + \sin x \tag{11.16}$$

$$= 1 + \sin 0 \tag{11.17}$$

$$= 1 \tag{11.18}$$

and

$$u = 1 + \sin x \tag{11.19}$$

$$= 1 + \sin\left(\frac{\pi}{2}\right) \tag{11.20}$$

$$= 2 \tag{11.21}$$

part b

Here we need to adopt the partial fractions technique. We seek to express the expression as the sum of two fractions:

$$\frac{x}{(x+4)(x+2)} = \frac{A}{x+4} + \frac{B}{x+2} \tag{11.22}$$

Expressing this over a common denominator means:

$$\frac{x}{(x+4)(x+2)} = \frac{A(x+2) + B(x+4)}{(x+4)(x+2)} \tag{11.23}$$

Since the denominators are equal, so too must the numerators:

$$x = A(x+2) + B(x+4) \tag{11.24}$$

Letting $x = -2$, the first bracket cancels:

$$-2 = B(-2+4) \tag{11.25}$$

$$-2 = 2B \tag{11.26}$$

$$B = -1 \tag{11.27}$$

and letting $x = -4$, the second bracket cancels:

$$-4 = A(-4+2) \tag{11.28}$$

$$-4 = -2A \tag{11.29}$$

$$A = 2 \tag{11.30}$$

Therefore we need to integrate:

$$\int_0^2 \frac{2}{x+4} - \frac{1}{x+2} dx = [2\ln(x+4) - \ln(x+2)]_0^2 \tag{11.31}$$

$$= [2\ln(6) - \ln 4] - [2\ln 4 - \ln 2] \tag{11.32}$$

$$= 2\ln 6 - 3\ln 4 + \ln 2 \tag{11.33}$$

$$= 2(\ln 3 + \ln 2) - 3(2\ln 2) + \ln 2 \tag{11.34}$$

$$= 2\ln 3 - 3\ln 2 \tag{11.35}$$

$$= \ln \frac{9}{8} \tag{11.36}$$

Question 4

Consider where the x^7 terms come from. We need x^1 from the first bracket and x^6 from the second, x^2 and x^5, x^3 and x^4 and finally x^4 and x^3. Using Pascal's triangle for the coefficients and expressing:

$$(1+2x)^4(1-2x)^6 = (a+b)^4(c+d)^6 \tag{11.37}$$

For x^1 from the first bracket and x^6 from the second:

$$4a^3b^1 \times 1c^0d^6 \quad = \quad 4.1^3.2x \times 1. - 2^6.x^6 \tag{11.38}$$

$$= \quad 512x^7 \tag{11.39}$$

For x^2 from the first bracket and x^5 from the second:

$$6a^2b^2 \times 6c^1d^5 \quad = \quad 6.1^2.2^2x^2 \times 6.1^1. - 2^5.x^5 \tag{11.40}$$

$$= \quad -4608x^7 \tag{11.41}$$

For x^3 from the first bracket and x^4 from the second:

$$4a^1b^3 \times 15c^2d^4 \quad = \quad 4.1.2^3.x^3 \times 15.1^2. - 2^4.x^4 \tag{11.42}$$

$$= \quad 7608x^7 \tag{11.43}$$

For x^4 from the first bracket and x^3 from the second:

$$1a^1b^4 \times 20c^3d^3 \quad = \quad 1.1.2^4.x^4 \times 20.1^3. - 2^3.x^3 \tag{11.44}$$

$$= \quad -2560x^7 \tag{11.45}$$

This gives a total of:

$$(512 - 4608 + 7680 - 2560)x^7 = 1024x^7 \tag{11.46}$$

Question 5

Consider the sector in one of the circles. Assume an area A where:

$$A = \pi r^2 = \frac{60\pi r^2}{360} = \frac{\pi r^2}{360} \tag{11.47}$$

Now if we spot that the triangle must be an equilateral triangle, with area B:

$$B \quad = \quad \frac{1}{2} \times 2r \times 2r \times \sin 60 \tag{11.48}$$

$$= \quad \sqrt{3}r^2 \tag{11.49}$$

Therefore the shaded area is:

$$B - 3A \quad = \quad \sqrt{3}r^2 - \frac{3 \times \pi r^2}{6} \tag{11.50}$$

$$= \quad \left(\sqrt{3} - \frac{\pi}{2}\right)r^2 \tag{11.51}$$

Question 6

You need to equate volumes of clay. The small sphere has volume:

$$\frac{4}{3}\pi r^3 \tag{11.52}$$

the large sphere has volume:

$$\frac{4}{3}\pi 8r^3 \tag{11.53}$$

and the cylinder has volume:

$$\pi \left(\frac{r}{2}\right)^2 \times l \tag{11.54}$$

so:

$$\frac{4}{3}\pi r^3 + \frac{4}{3}\pi 8r^3 = \pi \left(\frac{r}{2}\right)^2 \times l \tag{11.55}$$

$$9 \times \frac{4}{3}\pi r^3 = \frac{\pi r^2}{4} \times l \tag{11.56}$$

$$12\pi r^3 = \frac{\pi r^2}{4} \times l \tag{11.57}$$

$$\frac{48\pi r^3}{\pi r^2} = l \tag{11.58}$$

$$48r = l \tag{11.59}$$

Question 7

You need to plot the lines:

$$y = x^2 \tag{11.60}$$

$$y = 4 \tag{11.61}$$

$$y = 0 \tag{11.62}$$

$$y = 2x - 4 \tag{11.63}$$

and shade the incorrect side of each line by testing the inequality.

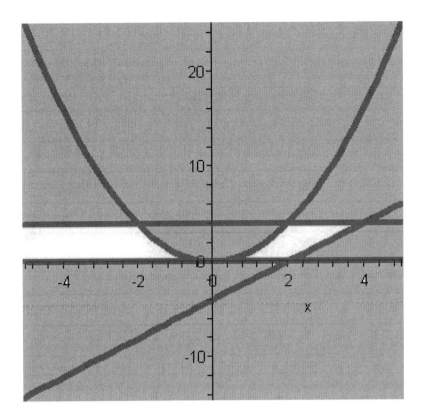

The area is found by noticing the region divides into an area under an x^2 graph and a triangle between x=2 and x=4. The area of the triangle is $\frac{1}{2} \times 4 \times 2 = 4$ and the area under the x^2 graph is $\int_0^2 x^2 = [x^3/3] = \frac{8}{3}$. Adding 4 and $\frac{8}{3}$ gives $6\frac{2}{3}$

Question 8

The graph of $f(x)$ is:

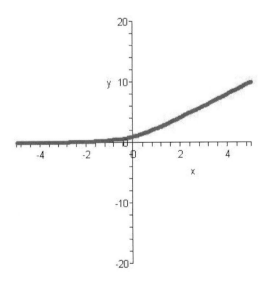

Since:

$$\frac{d}{dx}e^x = e^x \tag{11.64}$$

and since $f\prime(x) = 2 - e^{-x}$:

As $f\prime\prime(x) = e^{-x}$

and $f\prime\prime\prime(x) = -e^{-x}$

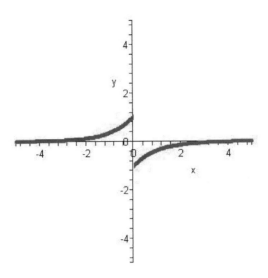

Question 9

The circle is centred on the origin and has a radius of $\sqrt{5}$. The radius is perpendicular to the tangent, be definition. We must consider another circle (not shown) centred on the point $(-4, 3)$. It will have radius $\sqrt{20}$ since:

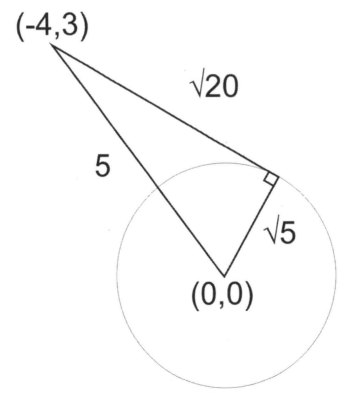

The equation of this new circle is:

$$(x+4)^2 + (y-3)^2 = 20 \tag{11.65}$$

We are looking for a point where these two circles intersect. Let us take the equation of the circle centred on the origin, rearrange and substitute into the equation of the circle centred on (-4,3) to eliminate x. Then solve for y.

$$(x+4)^2 + (y-3)^2 = 20 \tag{11.66}$$

$$x^2 + 8x + 16 + y^2 - 6y + 9 = 20 \tag{11.67}$$

$$x^2 + 8x + y^2 - 6y = -5 \tag{11.68}$$

$$\tag{11.69}$$

Now $x^2 = 5 - y^2$ so:

$$x^2 + 8x + y^2 - 6y = -5 \tag{11.70}$$

$$5 - y^2 + 8\sqrt{5 - y^2} + y^2 - 6y = -5 \tag{11.71}$$

$$8\sqrt{5 - y^2} - 6y = -10 \tag{11.72}$$

$$8\sqrt{5 - y^2} = 6y - 10 \tag{11.73}$$

$$64(5 - y^2) = (6y - 10)^2 \tag{11.74}$$

$$320 - 64y^2 = 36y^2 - 120y + 100 \tag{11.75}$$

$$0 = 100y^2 - 120y - 220 \tag{11.76}$$

$$0 = 10y^2 - 12y - 22 \tag{11.77}$$

$$0 = 5y^2 - 6y - 11 \tag{11.78}$$

$$0 = (5y - 11)(y + 1) \tag{11.79}$$

$$y = \frac{11}{5} \tag{11.80}$$

$$y = -1 \tag{11.81}$$

Now we use these two y coordinates to find the corresponding x coordinates and then find the equations of the lines joining the point (-4,3) each (x,y) point. For $y = 11/5$:

$$x^2 + y^2 = 5 \tag{11.82}$$

$$x^2 = \frac{125}{25} - \frac{121}{25} \tag{11.83}$$

$$x^2 = \frac{4}{25} \tag{11.84}$$

$$x = +\frac{2}{5} \tag{11.85}$$

(From looking at our diagram it is clear that we must consider the positive solution.) So the equation of the line joining (-4,3) and (2/5,11/5) is found:

$$m = \frac{3 - 11/5}{-4 - 2/5} = \frac{4/5}{-22/5} = -\frac{4}{22} = -\frac{2}{11} \tag{11.86}$$

$$y = -\frac{2}{11}x + c \tag{11.87}$$

$$3 = \frac{2}{11} \times 4 + c \tag{11.88}$$

$$c = \frac{25}{11} \tag{11.89}$$

$$y = -\frac{2}{11}x + \frac{25}{11} \tag{11.90}$$

$$11y = 25 - 2x \tag{11.91}$$

For $y = -1$:

$$x^2 + y^2 = 5 \tag{11.92}$$

$$x^2 = 5 - 1 \tag{11.93}$$

$$x^2 = 4 \tag{11.94}$$

$$x = -2 \tag{11.95}$$

Again considering out diagram we need to consider the negative solution only. So the equation of the line joining (-4,3) and (-2,-1) is found:

$$m = \frac{3 + 1}{-4 + 2} = -\frac{4}{2} \tag{11.96}$$

$$y = -2x + c \tag{11.97}$$

$$3 = 2 \times 4 + c \tag{11.98}$$

$$c = -5 \tag{11.99}$$

$$y = -2x - 5 \tag{11.100}$$

$$\tag{11.101}$$

11.2 Part B - Physics

Question 10

The duration of the day depends on its rotational speed. This is independent of distance from the Sun. The duration of the year depends on the time taken to complete one orbit of the Sun, this increases with greater distance from the Sun: this is correct. The size/volume is independent of distance from the Sun. The number of moons is independent of distance from the Sun. Ignoring Pluto, all the planets from Jupiter outwards are gas, so the planets do change from rocky to gas giants: this statement is correct. The answer is D.

Question 11

100GHz falls into the microwave part of the EM spectrum. So the answer is C. This is clearly above radio frequencies: think 99.1MHz for an FM station for example or the 800MHz/1600MHz used in mobile phones. You can also make a calculation of the lowest frequency which would be visible light:

$$f \quad = \quad \frac{v}{\lambda} \tag{11.102}$$

$$= \quad \frac{3 \times 10^8}{600 \times 10^{-9}} \tag{11.103}$$

$$= \quad 5 \times 10^{14} \tag{11.104}$$

$$= \quad 500,000 GHz \tag{11.105}$$

Question 12

If the velocity with respect to the ISS can be neglected, this means it is close to or exactly zero. This it will not move relative to ISS and so it will follow the ISS in its orbit. The answer is A.

Question 13

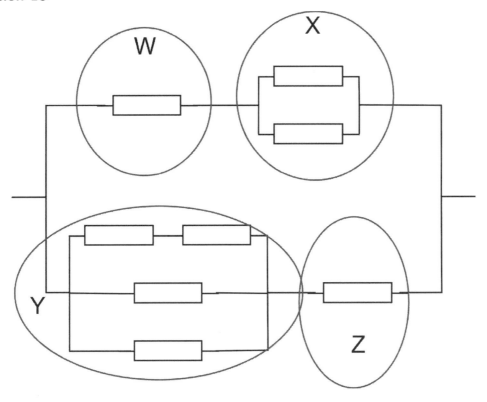

The total resistance of W is R. The total resistance of X is R/2. Therefore the total of the top branch is 3R/2. The total resistance of Y is:

$$\frac{1}{Y} = \frac{1}{2R} + \frac{1}{R} + \frac{1}{R} \tag{11.106}$$

$$= \frac{1}{2R} + \frac{2}{2R} + \frac{2}{2R} \tag{11.107}$$

$$= \frac{5}{2R} \tag{11.108}$$

$$Y = \frac{2R}{5} \tag{11.109}$$

The total resistance of the bottom branch is now:

$$\frac{2R}{5} + R = \frac{7R}{5} \tag{11.110}$$

Now adding the top and bottom branch in parallel:

$$\frac{1}{R} = \frac{2}{3R} + \frac{5}{7R} \tag{11.111}$$

$$= \frac{14 + 15}{21R} \tag{11.112}$$

$$= \frac{29}{21R} \tag{11.113}$$

$$R = \frac{21R}{29} \tag{11.114}$$

Question 14

The general equation for the period of mass spring system is:

$$T = 2\pi\sqrt{\frac{m}{k}} \tag{11.115}$$

If two springs are in series, consider how the k of the whole system will change. With two springs each experiencing force mg, the extension would double, so the k (i.e. the stiffness) of the whole system would half (since k=F/x). So:

$$T_s = \sqrt{2}T \tag{11.116}$$

If two springs are in parallel, consider how the k of the whole system will change. Each spring will now experience half the force, so the extension would half, so the k (i.e. the stiffness) of the whole system would double. So:

$$T_p = \frac{T}{\sqrt{2}} \tag{11.117}$$

Looking at the initial equation for the period, there is no dependence on g, therefore there is no effect on the period: it's T. (Further, if we consider this in the same way as we did above, both the force and the extension now double, leaving k for the whole system unchanged.)

Question 15

To find the current, consider conservation of energy. Electrical power input must equal the gravitational potential energy gained. (We assume that as the mass is moving at a constant speed, the kinetic energy is constant and the electric energy input only needs to be converted into GPE). The mass is raised by 0.5m every second:

$$\frac{E}{t} = \frac{mgh}{t} \tag{11.118}$$

$$= \frac{100 \times 10 \times 0.5}{1} \tag{11.119}$$

$$= 500W \tag{11.120}$$

$$I = \frac{P}{V} \tag{11.121}$$

$$= \frac{500}{230} = \frac{50}{23} = 2.2A \tag{11.122}$$

If we assume that the rope does not slip on the winding wheel, the speed of the rope will be the velocity of the edge of the wheel. But as the mass is attached to a pulley system, if the mass is moving upwards at 0.5m/s, the rope must be traveling at 1.5m/s. This can be easily understood by considering the length of rope between the two pulleys as x, the total length is therefore 3x. If the mass moves up 0.5m (in one second), then the total length of the string is no $3 \times (x - 0.5) = 3x - 1.5$. So the rope is 1.5m shorter. So the angular velocity is given by:

$$\omega = \frac{v}{r} \tag{11.123}$$

$$= \frac{1.5}{0.025} \tag{11.124}$$

$$= 60rad/s \tag{11.125}$$

Finally the force applied by the motor is:

$$F = \frac{P}{v} \tag{11.126}$$

$$= \frac{500}{1.5} \tag{11.127}$$

$$= 330N \tag{11.128}$$

Question 16

If C is positive with respect to D, the diode on the right will conduct as long as $V > 0.7V$. If D is positive with respect to C, the diode on the left will conduct as long as $V > 0.7V$. Thus the IV graph is:

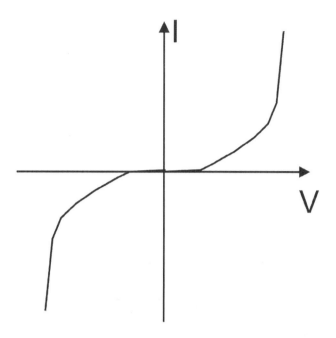

In normal operation up to 0.7V in forward bias a diode doesn't conduct. Therefore no matter which way round the pd is connected to A and B, no current will flow through CD. One diode will block it due to being in reverse, the other due to there being less than 0.7V. If a discharge occurs there will be a high pd between A and B or B and C. The large pd causes a large current to flow between C and D rather than through the sensitive ammeter. One diode is needed in each direction to short circuit the terminals due to a potential difference of either polarity between C and D.

Question 17

Label the particle with the lower mass, 1. Label the particle with the higher mass, 2. The potential energy is:

$$E_p = \frac{k \times Q \times 2Q}{d} = \frac{2kQ^2}{d} \tag{11.129}$$

The kinetic energy of the two particles is:

$$E_k = \frac{1}{2}m_1v_1^2 + \frac{1}{2}m_2v_2^2 \tag{11.130}$$

Since the particles exert the same force on each other:

$$F = m_1a_1 = m_2a_2 \tag{11.131}$$

Since $m_2 = 2m_1$, then $a_2 = a_1/2$. Since $v = at$, if a_2 has halved, then v_2 must be half of v_1. So the kinetic energy is

$$E_k = \frac{1}{2}m_1v_1^2 + \frac{1}{2}m_2v_2^2 \tag{11.132}$$

$$= \frac{1}{2}m(2v_2)^2 + \frac{1}{2} \times 2m \times v_2^2 \tag{11.133}$$

$$= 2mv_2^2 + mv_2^2 \tag{11.134}$$

$$= 3mv_2^2 \tag{11.135}$$

Since the kinetic energy comes from potential energy:

$$3mv_2^2 = \frac{2kQ^2}{d} \tag{11.136}$$

$$v_2 = \sqrt{\frac{2kQ^2}{3md}} \tag{11.137}$$

Question 18

part a

Total internal reflection is when a light ray from inside a fibre is incident on the wall of the fibre and reflects back into the fibre. This happens when the fibre is more dense than the material (air?) surrounding the fibre. The critical angle is the angle of incidence when the angle of refraction is $90°$. At angles of incidence greater than the critical angle, the light ray is reflected.

part b

Using Snell's Law:

$$n_1 \sin \theta_1 = n_2 \sin \theta_2 \tag{11.138}$$

$$n_1 \sin \theta_c = n_2 \sin 90 \tag{11.139}$$

$$\sin \theta_c = \frac{n_2}{n_1} \tag{11.140}$$

part c

At the entry point into the optical fibre apply Snell's law (assuming that the refractive index of air is 1:

$$1 \times \sin \theta_{max} = n_{core} \sin \theta_2 \tag{11.141}$$

$$\sin \theta_2 = \frac{\sin \theta_{max}}{n_{core}} \tag{11.142}$$

Then inside the fibre at the first point of incidence between the core and the cladding:

$$n_{core} \sin(90 - \theta_{max}) = n_{clad} \tag{11.143}$$

$$\cos \theta_2 = \frac{n_{clad}}{n_{core}} \tag{11.144}$$

Since $\sin^2 \theta + \cos^2 \theta = 1$:

$$\frac{\sin^2 \theta_{max}}{n_{core}^2} + \frac{n_{clad}^2}{n_{core}^2} = 1 \tag{11.145}$$

$$\sin^2 \theta_{max} = n_{core}^2 - n_{clad}^2 \tag{11.146}$$

part d

Consider a light ray exiting the fibre with $\theta_i > 0$. It will refract away from the normal, causing the beam to diverge as shown in the question. Now if the fibre ends in a tank of water (which has a lower refractive index than glass), the beam will not refract as much on exit into the air. This is because there is a smaller ratio of refractive indexes of water to air than glass to air.

part e

White light will split into component colours of the rainbow, since each colour refracts a different amount - this is called dispersion. So you would see concentric rings of different colours with red on the inside and blue on the outside.s

Question 19

part a

Assuming no friction, the resultant force acting is just the weight of m_2, therefore:

$$a = \frac{F}{m} = \frac{m_2 g}{m_1 + m_2} \tag{11.147}$$

Considering m_1 only, the tension must be given by:

$$T = m_1 a \tag{11.148}$$

$$= m_1 \frac{m_2 g}{m_1 + m_2} \tag{11.149}$$

or considering m_2 only,

$$m_2 g - T = m_2 \frac{m_2 g}{m_1 + m_2} \tag{11.150}$$

$$T = m_2 g - \frac{m_2^2 g}{m_1 + m_2} \tag{11.151}$$

$$= m_1 \frac{m_2 g}{m_1 + m_2} \tag{11.152}$$

part b

The resultant force now acting is:

$$F = m_2 g - \mu_d m_1 g \tag{11.153}$$

Therefore:

$$a = \frac{F}{m} = \frac{m_2 g - \mu_d m_1 g}{m_1 + m_2} \tag{11.154}$$

The tension must be given by

$$T - \mu_d m_1 g = m_1 a \tag{11.155}$$

$$T - \mu_d m_1 g = \frac{m_1 m_2 g - m_1^2 \mu_d g}{m_1 + m_2} \tag{11.156}$$

$$T = \frac{m_1 m_2 g - m_1^2 \mu_d g}{m_1 + m_2} + \mu_d m_1 g \tag{11.157}$$

For m_1 to accelerate:

$$m_2 > \mu_d m_1 \tag{11.158}$$

part c

In order for m_1 to continue moving in a circle it must be accelerating towards the centre of the circle. For it not to be moving radially, the resultant force acting on m_1 can only be the centripetal force (given by $m_1 \omega^2 r$):

$$m_2 g - m_1 \mu_s g = m_1 \omega^2 r \tag{11.159}$$

Therefore:

$$r = \frac{m_2 g - \mu_s m_1 g}{(m_1) \omega^2} \tag{11.160}$$

Now the frictional force can vary from zero up to a maximum of $\mu_s m_1 g$. Only once the force pulling on m_1 rises above $\mu_s m_1 g$ does it move in either direction (radially inwards or outwards). Therefore the minimum radius will be:

$$r_{min} = \frac{m_2 g - \mu_s m_1 g}{(m_1) \omega^2} \tag{11.161}$$

and the maximum radius will be:

$$r_{max} = \frac{m_2 g + \mu_s m_1 g}{m_1 \omega^2} \tag{11.162}$$

Chapter 12

Oxford Physics Aptitude Test Specimen Sept 2015 Answers

12.1 Part A - Maths

Question 1

Let y=number of yellow, g=number of green, r=number of red and b=number of blue. The statements given suggest:

$$y = 2g \tag{12.1}$$

$$r = 2y = 4g \tag{12.2}$$

$$b = 2r = 8g \tag{12.3}$$

Including g green, you know there are 15g buttons in total. Therefore the probabilities are:

$$g = \frac{1}{15} \tag{12.4}$$

$$y = \frac{2}{15} \tag{12.5}$$

$$r = \frac{4}{15} \tag{12.6}$$

$$b = \frac{8}{15} \tag{12.7}$$

Question 2

This is a geometric progression with first term 1 and common ration e^{-x}. So:

$$\sum_{\infty} = \frac{a}{1-r} \tag{12.8}$$

$$= \frac{1}{1-e^{-x}} \tag{12.9}$$

This equation is valid for $|r| < 1$ therefore $e^{-x} < 1$ which is true when $x > 0$.

Question 3

part a

This is integration by substitution. We notice that the top is the differential of the bottom. So we make the substitution

$$u = 1 + \sin x \tag{12.10}$$

So:

$$du = \cos x\, dx \tag{12.11}$$

and

$$\int_0^{\pi/2} \frac{\cos x}{1+\sin x} dx = \int_1^2 \frac{1}{u} du \tag{12.12}$$

$$= [\ln u]_1^2 \tag{12.13}$$

$$= \ln 2 - \ln 1 \tag{12.14}$$

$$= \ln 2 \tag{12.15}$$

Where we have calculated the new limits from:

$$u = 1 + \sin x \tag{12.16}$$

$$= 1 + \sin 0 \tag{12.17}$$

$$= 1 \tag{12.18}$$

and

$$u = 1 + \sin x \tag{12.19}$$

$$= 1 + \sin\left(\frac{\pi}{2}\right) \tag{12.20}$$

$$= 2 \tag{12.21}$$

Here we need to adopt the partial fractions technique. We seek to express the expression as the sum of two fractions:

$$\frac{x}{(x+4)(x+2)} = \frac{A}{x+4} + \frac{B}{x+2} \tag{12.22}$$

Expressing this over a common denominator means:

$$\frac{x}{(x+4)(x+2)} = \frac{A(x+2) + B(x+4)}{(x+4)(x+2)} \tag{12.23}$$

Since the denominators are equal, so too must the numerators:

$$x = A(x+2) + B(x+4) \tag{12.24}$$

Letting $x = -2$, the first bracket cancels:

$$-2 = B(-2+4) \tag{12.25}$$
$$-2 = 2B \tag{12.26}$$
$$B = -1 \tag{12.27}$$

and letting $x = -4$, the second bracket cancels:

$$-4 = A(-4+2) \tag{12.28}$$
$$-4 = -2A \tag{12.29}$$
$$A = 2 \tag{12.30}$$

Therefore we need to integrate:

$$\int_0^2 \frac{2}{x+4} - \frac{1}{x+2} dx = [2\ln(x+4) - \ln(x+2)]_0^2 \tag{12.31}$$
$$= [2\ln(6) - \ln 4] - [2\ln 4 - \ln 2] \tag{12.32}$$
$$= 2\ln 6 - 3\ln 4 + \ln 2 \tag{12.33}$$
$$= 2(\ln 3 + \ln 2) - 3(2\ln 2) + \ln 2 \tag{12.34}$$
$$= 2\ln 3 - 3\ln 2 \tag{12.35}$$

Question 4

Consider where the x^7 terms come from. We need x^1 from the first bracket and x^6 from the second, x^2 and x^5, x^3 and x^4 and finally x^4 and x^3. Using Pascal's triangle for the coefficients and expressing:

$$(1+2x)^4(1-2x)^6 = (a+b)^4(c+d)^6 \tag{12.36}$$

For x^1 from the first bracket and x^6 from the second:

$$4a^3b^1 \times 1c^0d^6 = 4.1^3.2x \times 1. - 2^6.x^6 \tag{12.37}$$

$$= 512x^7 \tag{12.38}$$

For x^2 from the first bracket and x^5 from the second:

$$6a^2b^2 \times 6c^1d^5 = 6.1^2.2^2x^2 \times 6.1^1. - 2^5.x^5 \tag{12.39}$$

$$= -4608x^7 \tag{12.40}$$

For x^3 from the first bracket and x^4 from the second:

$$4a^1b^3 \times 15c^2d^4 = 4.1.2^3.x^3 \times 15.1^2. \quad 2^4.x^4 \tag{12.41}$$

$$= 7608x^7 \tag{12.42}$$

For x^4 from the first bracket and x^3 from the second:

$$1a^1b^4 \times 20c^3d^3 = 1.1.2^4.x^4 \times 20.1^3. - 2^3.x^3 \tag{12.43}$$

$$= -2560x^7 \tag{12.44}$$

This gives a total of:
$$(512 - 4608 + 7680 - 2560)x^7 = 1024x^7 \tag{12.45}$$

Question 5

Consider the sector in one of the circles. Assume an area A where:

$$A = \pi r^2 = \frac{60\pi r^2}{360} = \frac{\pi r^2}{360} \tag{12.46}$$

Now if we spot that the triangle must be an equilateral triangle, with area B:

$$B = \frac{1}{2} \times 2r \times 2r \times \sin 60 \tag{12.47}$$

$$= \sqrt{3}r^2 \tag{12.48}$$

Therefore the shaded area is:

$$B - 3A = \sqrt{3}r^2 - \frac{3 \times \pi r^2}{6} \tag{12.49}$$

$$= \left(\sqrt{3} - \frac{\pi}{2}\right)r^2 \tag{12.50}$$

Question 6

You need to equate volumes of clay. The small sphere has volume:

$$\frac{4}{3}\pi r^3 \tag{12.51}$$

the large sphere has volume:

$$\frac{4}{3}\pi 8r^3 \tag{12.52}$$

and the cylinder has volume:

$$\pi \left(\frac{r}{2}\right)^2 \times l \tag{12.53}$$

so:

$$\frac{4}{3}\pi r^3 + \frac{4}{3}\pi 8r^3 = \pi \left(\frac{r}{2}\right)^2 \times l \tag{12.54}$$

$$9 \times \frac{4}{3}\pi r^3 = \frac{\pi r^2}{4} \times l \tag{12.55}$$

$$12\pi r^3 = \frac{\pi r^2}{4} \times l \tag{12.56}$$

$$\frac{48\pi r^3}{\pi r^2} = l \tag{12.57}$$

$$48r = l \tag{12.58}$$

Question 7

You need to plot the lines:

$$y = x^2 \tag{12.59}$$

$$y = 4 \tag{12.60}$$

$$y = 0 \tag{12.61}$$

$$y = 2x - 4 \tag{12.62}$$

$$x = 0 \tag{12.63}$$

and shade the incorrect side of each line by testing the inequality.

The area is found by noticing the region divides into an area under an x^2 graph and a triangle between x=2 and x=4. The area of the triangle is $\frac{1}{2} \times 4 \times 2 = 4$ and the area under the x^2 graph is $\int_0^2 x^2 = [x^3/3] = \frac{8}{3}$. Adding 4 and $\frac{8}{3}$ gives $6\frac{1}{3}$

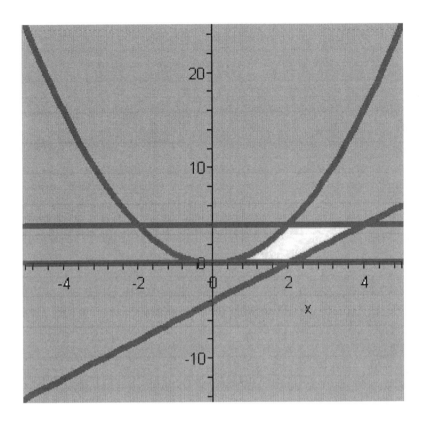

Question 8

The graph of $f(x)$ is:

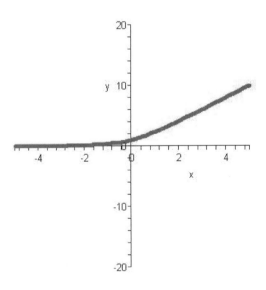

Since:

$$\frac{d}{dx}e^x = e^x \tag{12.64}$$

ad since $f\prime(x) = 2 - e^{-x}$:

As $f''(x) = e^{-x}$

and $f'''(x) = -e^{-x}$

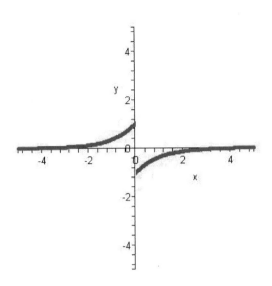

Question 9

The circle is centred on the origin and has a radius of $\sqrt{5}$. The radius is perpendicular to the tangent, be definition. We must consider another circle (not shown) centred on the point $(-4, 3)$. It will have radius $\sqrt{20}$ since:

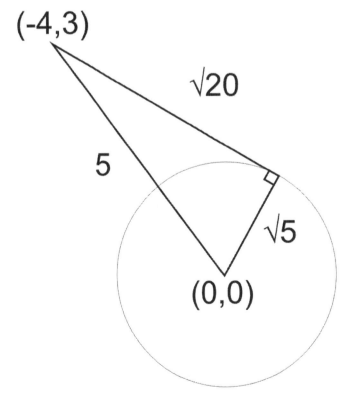

The equation of this new circle is:

$$(x+4)^2 + (y-3)^2 = 20 \tag{12.65}$$

We are looking for a point where these two circles intersect. Let us take the equation of the circle centred on the origin, rearrange and substitute into the equation of the circle centred on (-4,3) to eliminate x. Then solve for y.

$$
\begin{align}
(x+4)^2 + (y-3)^2 &= 20 \tag{12.66} \\
x^2 + 8x + 16 + y^2 - 6y + 9 &= 20 \tag{12.67} \\
x^2 + 8x + y^2 - 6y &= -5 \tag{12.68} \\
&\tag{12.69}
\end{align}
$$

Now $x^2 = 5 - y^2$ so:

$$
\begin{align}
x^2 + 8x + y^2 - 6y &= -5 \tag{12.70} \\
5 - y^2 + 8\sqrt{5 - y^2} + y^2 - 6y &= -5 \tag{12.71} \\
8\sqrt{5 - y^2} - 6y &= -10 \tag{12.72} \\
8\sqrt{5 - y^2} &= 6y - 10 \tag{12.73} \\
64(5 - y^2) &= (6y - 10)^2 \tag{12.74} \\
320 - 64y^2 &= 36y^2 - 120y + 100 \tag{12.75} \\
0 &= 100y^2 - 120y - 220 \tag{12.76} \\
0 &= 10y^2 - 12y - 22 \tag{12.77} \\
0 &= 5y^2 - 6y - 11 \tag{12.78} \\
0 &= (5y - 11)(y + 1) \tag{12.79} \\
y &= \frac{11}{5} \tag{12.80} \\
y &= -1 \tag{12.81}
\end{align}
$$

Now we use these two y coordinates to find the corresponding x coordinates and then find the equations of the lines joining the point (-4,3) each (x,y) point. For $y = 11/5$:

$$x^2 + y^2 = 5 \tag{12.82}$$

$$x^2 = \frac{125}{25} - \frac{121}{25} \tag{12.83}$$

$$x^2 = \frac{4}{25} \tag{12.84}$$

$$x = +\frac{2}{5} \tag{12.85}$$

(From looking at our diagram it is clear that we must consider the positive solution.) So the equation of the line joining (-4,3) and (2/5,11/5) is found:

$$m = \frac{3 - 11/5}{-4 - 2/5} = \frac{4/5}{-22/5} = -\frac{4}{22} = -\frac{2}{11} \tag{12.86}$$

$$y = -\frac{2}{11}x + c \tag{12.87}$$

$$3 = \frac{2}{11} \times 4 + c \tag{12.88}$$

$$c = \frac{25}{11} \tag{12.89}$$

$$y = -\frac{2}{11}x + \frac{25}{11} \tag{12.90}$$

$$11y = 25 - 2x \tag{12.91}$$

For $y = -1$:

$$x^2 + y^2 = 5 \tag{12.92}$$

$$x^2 = 5 - 1 \tag{12.93}$$

$$x^2 = 4 \tag{12.94}$$

$$x = -2 \tag{12.95}$$

Again considering out diagram we need to consider the negative solution only. So the equation of the line joining (-4,3) and (-2,-1) is found:

$$m = \frac{3 + 1}{-4 + 2} = -\frac{4}{2} \tag{12.96}$$

$$y = -2x + c \tag{12.97}$$

$$3 = 2 \times 4 + c \tag{12.98}$$

$$c = -5 \tag{12.99}$$

$$y = 2x - 5 \tag{12.100}$$

$$\tag{12.101}$$

12.2 Part B - Physics

Question 10

The horizontal and vertical components can be treated separately. If the projectile is fired at $200m/s$ and the rail car is traveling at $100m/s$ the horizontal component of the projectile's speed must be $100m/s$ so:

$$200\cos\theta = 100 \tag{12.102}$$

$$\cos\theta = \frac{1}{2} \tag{12.103}$$

$$\theta = 60° \tag{12.104}$$

Question 11

Firstly remember that perpendicular components of motion are independent and that a particle accelerated through a potential difference gains an energy of eV. So:

$$eV = \frac{1}{2}mv^2 \tag{12.105}$$

$$\frac{2eV}{m} = v^2 \tag{12.106}$$

$$\frac{2 \times 1.6 \times 10^{-19} \times 10^2}{10^{-30}} = v^2 \tag{12.107}$$

$$1.6 \times 10^{13} = v^2 \tag{12.108}$$

$$16 \times 10^{12} = v^2 \tag{12.109}$$

$$4 \times 10^6 = v \tag{12.110}$$

Using $v = d/t$

$$t = \frac{d}{v} = \frac{0.4}{4 \times 10^6} \tag{12.111}$$

$$= 0.1 \times 10^{-6}\text{s} \tag{12.112}$$

Now note down what you know for the vertical component of the motion:

$$u = 0 \tag{12.113}$$

$$a = 10 \tag{12.114}$$

$$t = 0.1 \times 10^{-6} \tag{12.115}$$

$$s = ? \tag{12.116}$$

Therefore:

$$s = ut + \frac{1}{2}at^2 \tag{12.117}$$

$$= \frac{1}{2} \times 10 \times (0.1 \times 10^{-6})^2 \tag{12.118}$$

$$= 5 \times 0.01 \times 10^{-12} \tag{12.119}$$

$$= 0.05 \times 10^{-12}\text{m} \tag{12.120}$$

$$= 5 \times 10^{-14}\text{m} \tag{12.121}$$

Question 12

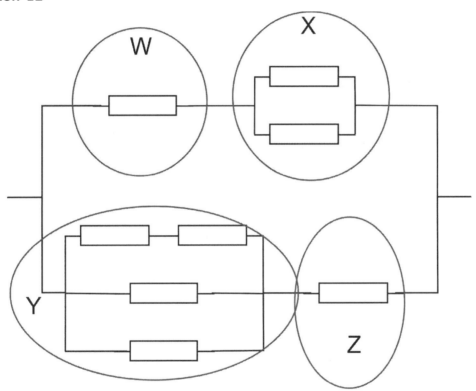

The total resistance of W is R. The total resistance of X is R/2. Therefore the total of the top branch is 3R/2. The total resistance of Y is:

$$\frac{1}{Y} = \frac{1}{2R} + \frac{1}{R} + \frac{1}{R} \tag{12.122}$$

$$= \frac{1}{2R} + \frac{2}{2R} + \frac{2}{2R} \tag{12.123}$$

$$= \frac{5}{2R} \tag{12.124}$$

$$Y = \frac{2R}{5} \tag{12.125}$$

The total resistance of the bottom branch is now:

$$\frac{2R}{5} + R = \frac{7R}{5} \tag{12.126}$$

Now adding the top and bottom branch in parallel:

$$\frac{1}{R} = \frac{2}{3R} + \frac{5}{7R} \tag{12.127}$$

$$= \frac{14 + 15}{21R} \tag{12.128}$$

$$= \frac{29}{21R} \tag{12.129}$$

$$R = \frac{21R}{29} \tag{12.130}$$

Question 13

The general equation for the period of mass spring system is:

$$T = 2\pi\sqrt{\frac{m}{k}} \tag{12.131}$$

If two springs are in series, consider how the k of the whole system will change. With two springs each experiencing force mg, the extension would double, so the k (i.e. the stiffness) of the whole system would half (since k=F/x). So:

$$T_s = \sqrt{2}T \tag{12.132}$$

If two springs are in parallel, consider how the k of the whole system will change. Each spring will now experience half the force, so the extension would half, so the k (i.e. the stiffness) of the whole system would double. So:

$$T_p = \frac{T}{\sqrt{2}} \tag{12.133}$$

Looking at the initial equation for the period, there is no dependence on g, therefore there is no effect on the period: it's T. (Further, if we consider this in the same way as we did above, both the force and the extension now double, leaving k for the whole system unchanged.)

Question 14

To find the current, consider conservation of energy. Electrical power input must equal the gravitational potential energy gained. (We assume that as the mass is moving at a constant speed, the kinetic energy is constant and the electric energy input only needs to be converted into GPE). The mass is raised by 0.5m every second:

$$\frac{E}{t} = \frac{mgh}{t} \tag{12.134}$$

$$= \frac{100 \times 10 \times 0.5}{1} \tag{12.135}$$

$$= 500W \tag{12.136}$$

$$I = \frac{P}{V} \tag{12.137}$$

$$= \frac{500}{230} = \frac{50}{23} = 2.2A \tag{12.138}$$

If we assume that the rope does not slip on the winding wheel, the speed of the rope will be the velocity of the edge of the wheel. But as the mass is attached to a pulley system, if the mass is moving upwards at 0.5m/s, the rope must be traveling at 1.5m/s. This can be easily understood by considering the length of rope between the two pulleys as x, the total length is therefore 3x. If the mass moves up 0.5m (in one second), then the total length of the string is no $3 \times (x - 0.5) = 3x - 1.5$. So the rope is 1.5m shorter. So the angular velocity is given by:

$$\omega = \frac{v}{r} \tag{12.139}$$

$$= \frac{1.5}{0.025} \tag{12.140}$$

$$= 60rad/s \tag{12.141}$$

Finally the force applied by the motor is:

$$F = \frac{P}{v} \tag{12.142}$$

$$= \frac{500}{1.5} \tag{12.143}$$

$$= 330N \tag{12.144}$$

Question 15

If C is positive with respect to D, the diode on the right will conduct as long as $V > 0.7V$. If D is positive with respect to C, the diode on the left will conduct as long as $V > 0.7V$. Thus the IV graph is:

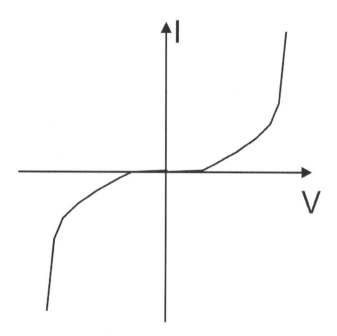

In normal operation up to 0.7V in forward bias a diode doesn't conduct. Therefore no matter which way round the pd is connected to A and B, no current will flow through CD. One diode will block it due to being in reverse, the other due to there being less than 0.7V. If a discharge occurs there will be a high pd between A and B or B and C. The large pd causes a large current to flow between C and D rather than through the sensitive ammeter. One diode is needed in each direction to short circuit the terminals due to a potential difference of either polarity between C and D.

Question 16

part a

Equate the energy stored in the spring with the kinetic energy gained by the mass.

$$\frac{1}{2}k(x-l)^2 \quad = \quad \frac{1}{2}mv^2 \tag{12.145}$$

$$v \quad = \quad \sqrt{\frac{k}{m}}(x-l) \tag{12.146}$$

part b

This time, the spring will require less force to extend to the same length as gravity will supply an additional force. Remember that the energy stored in a spring can be given by $1/2Fx$.

$$\frac{1}{2}mv^2 \quad = \quad \frac{1}{2}(k(x-l)-mg)(x-l) \tag{12.147}$$

$$mv^2 \quad = \quad k(x-l)^2 - mg(x-l) \tag{12.148}$$

$$v \quad = \quad \sqrt{\frac{k}{m}(x-l)^2 - g(x-l)} \tag{12.149}$$

Question 17

Label the particle with the lower mass, 1. Label the particle with the higher mass, 2. The potential energy is:

$$E_p = \frac{k \times Q \times 2Q}{d} = \frac{2kQ^2}{d} \tag{12.150}$$

The kinetic energy of the two particles is:

$$E_k = \frac{1}{2}m_1 v_1^2 + \frac{1}{2}m_2 v_2^2 \tag{12.151}$$

Since the particles exert the same force on each other:

$$F = m_1 a_1 = m_2 a_2 \tag{12.152}$$

Since $m_2 = 2m_1$, then $a_2 = a_1/2$. Since $v = at$, if a_2 has halved, then v_2 must be half of v_1. So the kinetic energy is

$$
\begin{aligned}
E_k &= \frac{1}{2}m_1 v_1^2 + \frac{1}{2}m_2 v_2^2 \tag{12.153} \\
&= \frac{1}{2}mv^2 + \frac{1}{2} \times 2m \times \left(\frac{v}{2}\right)^2 \tag{12.154} \\
&= \frac{1}{2}mv^2 + \frac{1}{4}mv^2 \tag{12.155} \\
&= \frac{3}{4}mv^2 \tag{12.156}
\end{aligned}
$$

Since the kinetic energy comes from potential energy:

$$
\begin{aligned}
\frac{3}{4}mv^2 &= \frac{2kQ^2}{d} \tag{12.157} \\
v &= \sqrt{\frac{8kQ^2}{3md}} \tag{12.158}
\end{aligned}
$$

Question 18

part a

Total internal reflection is when a light ray from inside a fibre is incident on the wall of the fibre and reflects back into the fibre. This happens when the fibre is more dense than the material (air?) surrounding the fibre. The critical angle is the angle of incidence when the angle of refraction is $90°$. At angles of incidence greater than the critical angle, the light ray is reflected.

part b

Using Snell's Law:

$$n_1 \sin \theta_1 = n_2 \sin \theta_2 \tag{12.159}$$

$$n_1 \sin \theta_c = n_2 \sin 90 \tag{12.160}$$

$$\sin \theta_c = \frac{n_2}{n_1} \tag{12.161}$$

part c

We notice that:

$$\theta_{max} + \theta_c = \frac{\pi}{2} \tag{12.162}$$

Therefore we can draw the following triangle:

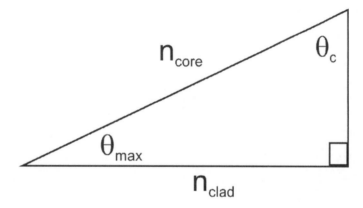

The lengths of the sides comes from reexpressing the answer to part b in term of n_{clad} and n_{core}:

$$\sin \theta_c = \frac{n_2}{n_1} = \frac{n_{clad}}{n_{core}} \tag{12.163}$$

Thus:

$$\cos \theta_{max} = \frac{n_{clad}}{n_{core}} \tag{12.164}$$

part d

Consider a light ray exiting the fibre with $\theta_i > 0$. It will refract away from the normal, causing the beam to diverge as shown in the question. Now if the fibre ends in a tank of water (which has a lower refractive index than glass), the beam will not refract as much on exit into the air. This is because there is a smaller ratio of refractive indexes of water to air than glass to air.

Question 19

part a

Assuming no friction, the resultant force acting is just the weight of m_2, therefore:

$$a = \frac{F}{m} = \frac{m_2 g}{m_1 + m_2} \tag{12.165}$$

Considering m_1 only, the tension must be given by:

$$T = m_1 a \tag{12.166}$$

$$= m_1 \frac{m_2 g}{m_1 + m_2} \tag{12.167}$$

or considering m_2 only,

$$m_2 g - T = m_2 \frac{m_2 g}{m_1 + m_2} \tag{12.168}$$

$$T = m_2 g - \frac{m_2^2 g}{m_1 + m_2} \tag{12.169}$$

$$= m_1 \frac{m_2 g}{m_1 + m_2} \tag{12.170}$$

part b

The resultant force now acting is:

$$F = m_2 g - \mu_s m_1 g \tag{12.171}$$

We must use the static coefficient of friction since the mass is not moving initially. Therefore:

$$a = \frac{F}{m} = \frac{m_2 g - \mu_s m_1 g}{m_1 + m_2} \tag{12.172}$$

The tension must be given by

$$T - \mu_s m_1 g = m_1 a \tag{12.173}$$

$$T - \mu_s m_1 g = \frac{m_1 m_2 g - m_1^2 \mu_s g}{m_1 + m_2} \tag{12.174}$$

$$T = \frac{m_1 m_2 g - m_1^2 \mu_s g}{m_1 + m_2} + \mu_s m_1 g \tag{12.175}$$

For m_1 to accelerate:

$$m_2 > \mu_s m_1 \tag{12.176}$$

Chapter 13

Oxford Physics Aptitude Test 2015 Answers

13.1 Part A - Maths

Question 1

Use the binomial expansion but use Pascal's triangle to get the coefficients:

$$(x+y)^n = \sum_{k=0}^{n} \binom{n}{k} x^{n-k} y^k \tag{13.1}$$

and

$n = 0$:　　　　　　　　1

$n = 1$:　　　　　　1　　　1

$n = 2$:　　　　1　　　2　　　1

$n = 3$:　　1　　3　　　3　　1

$n = 4$:　1　　4　　6　　4　　1

$n = 5$: 1　　5　　10　　10　　5　　1

So:

$$(a+b)^5 = a^5 + 5a^4b + 10a^3b^2 + 10a^2b^3 + 5ab^4 + b^5 \tag{13.2}$$

where $a = 2x$ and $b = x^2$ so

$$
\begin{aligned}
(2x + x^2)^5 &= 2^5x^5 + 5 \times 2^4x^4x^2 + 10 \times 2^3x^3(x^2)^2 + 10 \times 2^2x^2(x^2)^3 + 5 \times 2x(x^2)^4 + (x^2)^5 \\
&= 32x^5 + 80x^6 + 80x^7 + 40x^8 + 10x^9 + x^{10}
\end{aligned}
$$

Question 2

Since $\log_{10} 100 = 2$ and $10^2 = 100$ then we need to find to what power do we raise 4 to get 16: the answer is 2. So

$$\log_2 x + \log_4 16 \quad = \quad 2 \tag{13.3}$$

$$\log_2 x + 2 \quad = \quad 2 \tag{13.4}$$

So

$$\log_2 x \quad = \quad 0 \tag{13.5}$$

$$2^0 \quad = \quad x \tag{13.6}$$

$$x \quad - \quad 1 \tag{13.7}$$

Question 3

This is a geometric progression:

$$\sum_{n=1}^{5} \left(\frac{1}{3}\right)^n = \frac{1}{3} + \left(\frac{1}{3}\right)^2 + \left(\frac{1}{3}\right)^3 + \left(\frac{1}{3}\right)^4 + \left(\frac{1}{3}\right)^5 \tag{13.8}$$

where $a = 1/3$ and $r = 1/3$. It is simplest to calculate the sum to infinity first:

$$\sum_{\infty} = \frac{a}{1-r} = \frac{1/3}{2/3} = \frac{1}{2} \tag{13.9}$$

We can find the sum from term six to infinity and then subtract this from the sum from term 1 to infinity calculate above. In this case $a = 1/3^6$ and $r = 1/3$ and

$$\sum_{n=6}^{\infty} = \frac{1/3^6}{2/3} = \frac{1}{3^6} \times \frac{3}{2} = \frac{1}{2 \times 3^5} = \frac{1}{2 \times 243} = \frac{1}{486} \tag{13.10}$$

So the sum of the first 5 terms is

$$\sum_{n=1}^{5} \left(\frac{1}{3}\right)^n = \frac{1}{2} - \frac{1}{486} = \frac{243}{486} - \frac{1}{486} = \frac{242}{486} = \frac{121}{243} \tag{13.11}$$

Question 4

Note that

$$(x - 4)(x - 2) = x^2 - 6x + 8 \tag{13.12}$$

$$\frac{d}{dx}(x - 4)(x - 2) = 2x - 6 \tag{13.13}$$

Make the substitution:

$$u = (x - 4)(x - 2) \tag{13.14}$$

so

$$du = 2x - 6dx \tag{13.15}$$

To adjust the limits: If $x = 6$ then

$$u = (6 - 4)(6 - 2) \tag{13.16}$$

$$= 2 \times 4 \tag{13.17}$$

$$= 8 \tag{13.18}$$

and if $x = 4$ then

$$u = (4 - 4)(4 - 2) \tag{13.19}$$

$$= 0 \tag{13.20}$$

So:

$$\int_4^6 (2x - 6) \left[(x - 4)(x - 2) \right]^{1/2} dx = \int_0^8 u^{1/2} du \tag{13.21}$$

$$= \left[\frac{2u^{\frac{3}{2}}}{3} \right]_0^8 \tag{13.22}$$

$$= \frac{2 \times 8^{\frac{3}{2}}}{3} \tag{13.23}$$

$$= \frac{2 \times 2^{3 \times \frac{3}{2}}}{3} \tag{13.24}$$

$$= \frac{2^{\frac{11}{2}}}{3} \tag{13.25}$$

$$= \frac{2^5 \sqrt{2}}{3} \tag{13.26}$$

$$= \frac{32\sqrt{2}}{3} \tag{13.27}$$

Question 5

Simplify:

$$4x^2 + 8x - 8 = 4xm - 3m \tag{13.28}$$

$$4x^2 + (8 - 4m)x - (8 - 3m) = 0 \tag{13.29}$$

If the discriminant $(b^2 - 4ac) < 0$ then there are no real solutions so:

$$(8 - 4m)^2 + 4 \times 4 \times (8 - 3m) < 0 \tag{13.30}$$

$$64 - 64m + 16m^2 + 16(8 - 3m) < 0 \tag{13.31}$$

$$4 - 4m + m^2 + 8 - 3m < 0 \tag{13.32}$$

$$m^2 - 7m + 12 < 0 \tag{13.33}$$

$$(m - 4)(m - 3) < 0 \tag{13.34}$$

Therefore $m = 4$ and $m = 3$. Test values outside: if $m = 2$ then

$$(2 - 4)(2 - 3) = -2 \times -1 = 2 \tag{13.35}$$

$$2 > 0 \tag{13.36}$$

and if $m = 5$ then

$$(5 - 4)(5 - 3) = 1 \times 2 = 2 \tag{13.37}$$

$$2 > 0 \tag{13.38}$$

Therefore $3 < m < 4$.

Question 6

part a

The combinations are TTH, HTT and TTT each has probability of $(1/2)^3 = 1/8$. So the total of the three combinations is $3/8$.

part b

The combinations are HTT, TTH, THH and HHT each has probability of $(1/2)^3 = 1/8$. So the total of the four combinations is $4/8$.

part c

Any one result being a T, implies that none are H. Therefore the probability of this is $1 - P(HHH) = 1 - 1/8 = 7/8$. Only one combination has TTT so the probability of this is $1/8$. Therefore the answer is:

$$\frac{1/8}{7/8} = \frac{1}{7} \tag{13.39}$$

Question 7

Label the centre of the small circle O and the mid point of DC as F. Consider the triangle OCF. This angle FCO is 30°.

So:

$$\sin 30 = \frac{FO}{OC} \tag{13.40}$$

$$\frac{1}{2} = rOC \tag{13.41}$$

$$OC = 2r \tag{13.42}$$

Therefore $CE = 3r$.

Now consider the triangle DEC. The angle ECD is the same as angle FCO which is 30°.

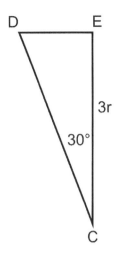

Therefore:

$$\tan 30 = \frac{DE}{3r} \tag{13.43}$$

$$\frac{1}{\sqrt{3}} = \frac{DE}{3r} \tag{13.44}$$

$$DE = \frac{3r}{\sqrt{3}} = \sqrt{3}r \tag{13.45}$$

$$DB = 2DE = 2\sqrt{3}r \tag{13.46}$$

The area of the large circle is:

$$\pi(3r)^2 = 9\pi r^2 \tag{13.47}$$

The area of the small circle is:

$$\pi r^2 \tag{13.48}$$

The area of triangle DBC is:

$$= \frac{1}{2} \times DB \times EC \tag{13.49}$$

$$= \frac{1}{2} \times 2\sqrt{3}r \times 3r \tag{13.50}$$

$$= 3\sqrt{3}r^2 \tag{13.51}$$

The area of triangle ABCD is twice that of triangle DBC:

$$= 6\sqrt{3}r^2 \tag{13.52}$$

Therefore the area of the shaded region is the area of the large circle, minus the area of triangle ABCD, plus the area of the small circle:

$$= \quad 9\pi r^2 - 6\sqrt{3}r^2 + \pi r^2 \tag{13.53}$$

$$= \quad 10\pi r^2 - 6\sqrt{3}r^2 \tag{13.54}$$

$$= \quad (10\pi - 6\sqrt{3})r^2 \tag{13.55}$$

Question 8

The normal line is a radius of the circle so it goes from the centre of the circle $(-3, 3)$ to the point $(1, 2)$. Its gradient must be:

$$m \quad = \quad \frac{y_2 - y_1}{x_2 - x_1} \tag{13.56}$$

$$= \quad \frac{2 - 3}{1 - -3} \tag{13.57}$$

$$= \quad \frac{-1}{4} \tag{13.58}$$

Therefore we have:

$$y = -\frac{1}{4}x + c \tag{13.59}$$

and so:

$$2 \quad = \quad -\frac{1}{4} \times 1 + c \tag{13.60}$$

$$c \quad = \quad 2\frac{1}{4} = \frac{9}{4} \tag{13.61}$$

So the equation of the line is:

$$y = -\frac{1}{4}x + \frac{9}{4} \tag{13.62}$$

Thus the slope is 1/4 and the y intercept is 9/4.

The tangent must be perpendicular to the normal line. The product of the gradients of perpendicular lines multiply to -1 therefore the gradient of the tangent must be 4. Therefore we have:

$$y = 4x + c \tag{13.63}$$

and so:

$$2 \quad = \quad 4 \times 1 + c \tag{13.64}$$

$$c \quad = \quad -2 \tag{13.65}$$

So the equation of the line is:

$$y = 4x - 2 \tag{13.66}$$

Thus the slope is 4 and the y intercept is -2.

Question 9

Try to step through sketching the graph in small steps from a graph you know of $y = 1/x^2$:

$y = 1/x^2$

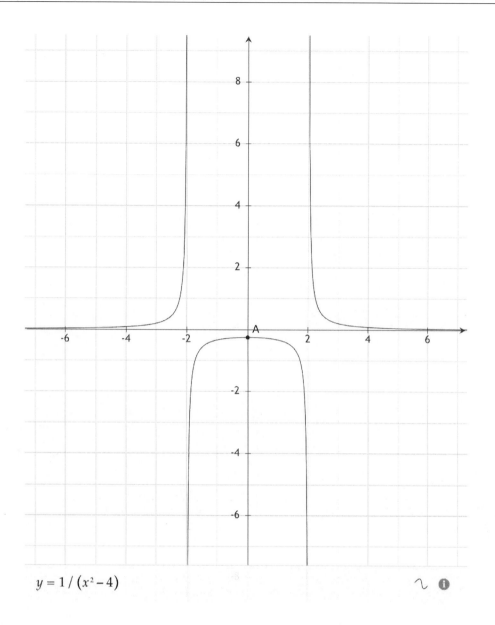

$y = 1 / \left(x^2 - 4 \right)$

$y = 8 / (x^2 - 4)$

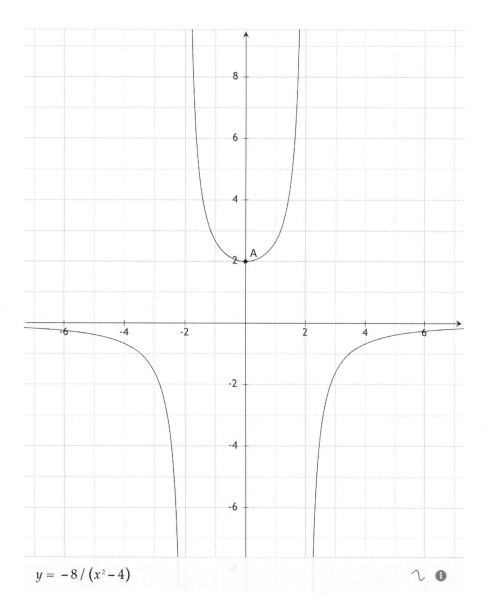

$$y = -8 / (x^2 - 4)$$

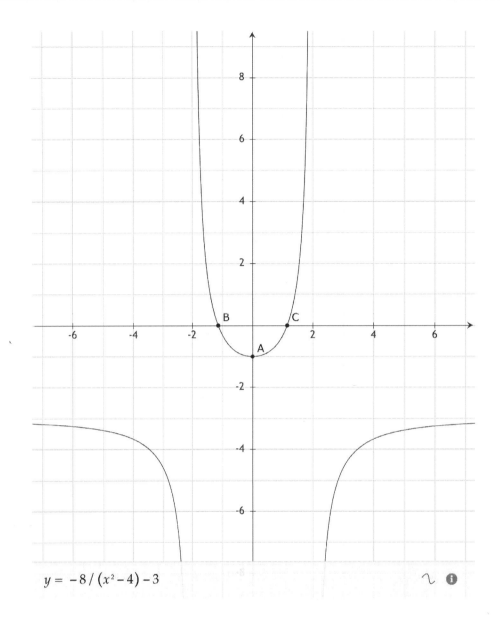

$$y = -8 / \left(x^2 - 4\right) - 3$$

Therefore when x has any real value y must be in the range $y < -3$ or $y \geq -1$.

Question 10

Break the inequality up and solve each part to find the key points.

$$-1 = \frac{3x + 4}{x - 6} \tag{13.67}$$

$$6 - x = 3x + 4 \tag{13.68}$$

$$2 = 4x \tag{13.69}$$

$$x = \frac{1}{2} \tag{13.70}$$

and

$$1 = \frac{3x + 4}{x - 6} \tag{13.71}$$

$$x - 6 = 3x + 4 \tag{13.72}$$

$$-10 = 2x \tag{13.73}$$

$$x = -5 \tag{13.74}$$

Now try substituting values either side of $x = 1/2$ and $x = 5$: For $x = 2$

$$\frac{3x + 4}{x - 6} = \frac{3 \times 2 + 4}{2 - 6} \tag{13.75}$$

$$= \frac{10}{-4} \tag{13.76}$$

$$= -2.5 \tag{13.77}$$

-2.5 does not lie between -1 and 1, so we can exclude the region $x > 1/2$.

For $x = 0$

$$\frac{3x + 4}{x - 6} = \frac{3 \times 0 + 4}{0 - 6} \tag{13.78}$$

$$= \frac{-4}{6} \tag{13.79}$$

$-4/6$ lies between -1 and 1, so we include the region $-5 < x < 1/2$.

For $x = -6$

$$\frac{3x + 4}{x - 6} = \frac{3 \times -6 + 4}{-6 - 6} \tag{13.80}$$

$$= \frac{-14}{-12} \tag{13.81}$$

$-14/12$ does not lie between -1 and 1, so we can exclude the region $x < -6$. Note there is also a singularity at $x = 6$, so we should check the other side of this too:

For $x = 7$

$$\frac{3x + 4}{x - 6} = \frac{3 \times 7 + 4}{7 - 6} \tag{13.82}$$

$$= \frac{25}{1} \tag{13.83}$$

25 does not lie between -1 and 1, so we can exclude the region $x > 6$.

Thus the inequality is satisfied for $-5 < x < 1/2$.

13.2 Part B - Physics

Question 11

You can either break this down into a number of parts or apply suvat (carefully) to the whole journey.

Firstly break it up: apply suvat from the launch point to the peak:

$$s = ? \tag{13.84}$$

$$u = 10\sin 30 \tag{13.85}$$

$$v = 0 \tag{13.86}$$

$$a = -10 \tag{13.87}$$

$$t = ? \tag{13.88}$$

$$v = u + at \tag{13.89}$$

$$0 = 10\sin 30 - 10t \tag{13.90}$$

$$t = \frac{1}{2} \tag{13.91}$$

Therefore the total time to get back to the cliff height will take 1 second and the ball will be traveling downwards at the same speed as the initial launch. Apply suvat from the cliff height down to the ground.

$$s = 10 \tag{13.92}$$

$$u = 10\sin 30 \tag{13.93}$$

$$v = 0 \tag{13.94}$$

$$a = 10 \tag{13.95}$$

$$t = ? \tag{13.96}$$

$$s = ut + \frac{1}{2}at^2 \tag{13.97}$$

$$10 = 10\sin 30 \times t + \frac{1}{2} \times 10 \times t^2 \tag{13.98}$$

$$10 = 5t + 5t^2 \tag{13.99}$$

$$2 = t + t^2 \tag{13.100}$$

$$0 = = t^2 + t - 2 \tag{13.101}$$

$$0 = (t+2)(t-1) \tag{13.102}$$

$$t = 1 \tag{13.103}$$

Adding this to the one second from earlier gives a total time of 2 seconds. Alternatively apply suvat to the whole journey:

$$s = -10 \tag{13.104}$$

$$u = 10\sin 30 \tag{13.105}$$

$$v = 0 \tag{13.106}$$

$$a = -10 \tag{13.107}$$

$$t = ? \tag{13.108}$$

$$s = ut + \frac{1}{2}at^2 \tag{13.109}$$

$$-10 = 10\sin 30 \times t - \frac{1}{2} \times 10 \times t^2 \tag{13.110}$$

$$-10 = 5t - 5t^2 \tag{13.111}$$

$$-2 = t - t^2 \tag{13.112}$$

$$0 = = t^2 - t - 2 \tag{13.113}$$

$$0 = (t-2)(t+1) \tag{13.114}$$

$$t = 2 \tag{13.115}$$

Questions 12

The height of the icecube is h from the floor and the height of the table is H from the floor. The ramp height must be $h - H$. If the ice cube is half way down the ramp then it must have fallen a height of $\frac{h-H}{2}$ so:

$$mgh = \frac{1}{2}mv^2 \tag{13.116}$$

$$g\left(\frac{h-H}{2}\right) = \frac{1}{2}v^2 \tag{13.117}$$

$$\sqrt{g(h-H)} = v \tag{13.118}$$

Question 13

At an solar eclipse the Sun and Moon seem to be the same angular size in the sky, where a is the distance from Earth to the object and o is the radius of the object. So:

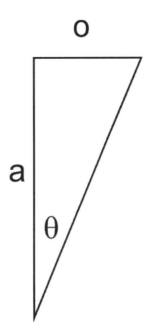

$\frac{o}{a}$ is constant for both the Sun and the moon. Thus:

$$\frac{700,000}{150,000,000} = \frac{r}{400,000} \tag{13.119}$$

$$\frac{7}{1500} = \frac{r}{400} \tag{13.120}$$

$$\frac{2800}{1500} = r \tag{13.121}$$

$$1.9 = r \tag{13.122}$$

Therefore the radius of the moon is around 1900km.

Question 14

$$n_1 \sin \theta_1 = n_2 \sin \theta_2 \tag{13.123}$$

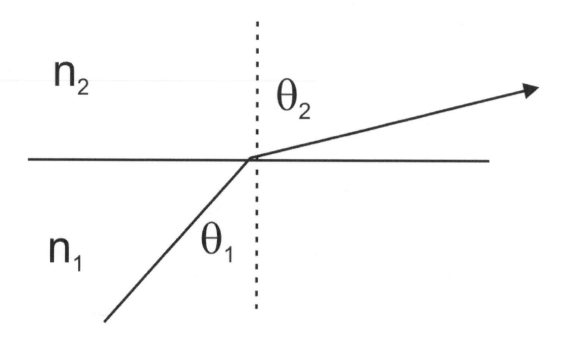

Total internal reflection will occur if $n_2 < n_1$ and $\theta_1 > \theta_c$ where θ_c is the critical angle.

Question 15

Resolve the forces horizontally:

$$A = C \cos 45 \tag{13.124}$$

$$A = \frac{C}{\sqrt{2}} \tag{13.125}$$

$$C = \sqrt{2}A \tag{13.126}$$

Resolve the forces vertically:

$$B = C \sin 45 \tag{13.127}$$

$$B = \frac{C}{\sqrt{2}} \tag{13.128}$$

$$C = \sqrt{2}B \tag{13.129}$$

Therefore A=B.

Question 16

If the collision is elastic this means that kinetic energy is conserved. Momentum must be conserved. Before the collision only the 2kg ball has velocity so:

$$p_{before} = 2 \times 1 = 2kgm/s \tag{13.130}$$

$$E_{before} = \frac{1}{2} \times 2 \times 1^2 = 1J \tag{13.131}$$

After the collision:

$$p_{after} = 2 = 1 \times v + 2 \times u \tag{13.132}$$

$$2 = v + 2u \tag{13.133}$$

$$E_{after} = 1 = \frac{1}{2} \times 1 \times v^2 + \frac{1}{2} \times 2 \times u^2 \tag{13.134}$$

$$1 = \frac{v^2}{2} + u^2 \tag{13.135}$$

$$2 = v^2 + 2u^2 \tag{13.136}$$

Therefore, rearranging the momentum equation for v and substituting into the energy equation:

$$v = 2 - 2u \tag{13.137}$$

$$2 = v^2 + 2u^2 \tag{13.138}$$

$$2 = (2 - 2u)^2 + 2u^2 \tag{13.139}$$

$$2 = 4 - 8u + 2u^2 + 2u^2 \tag{13.140}$$

$$0 = 6u^2 - 8u + 2 \tag{13.141}$$

$$0 = 3u^2 - 4u + 1 \tag{13.142}$$

$$0 = (3u - 1)(u - 1) \tag{13.143}$$

$$u = \frac{1}{3} \tag{13.144}$$

$$u = 1 \tag{13.145}$$

If $u = 1/3$ then:

$$v = 2 - \frac{2}{3} = \frac{4}{3}m/s \tag{13.146}$$

If $u = 1$ then:

$$v = 2 - 2 = 0m/s \tag{13.147}$$

Question 17

Since:

$$v = \frac{dy}{dt} = -A\omega \cos(kx - \omega t) \tag{13.148}$$

then

$$
\begin{aligned}
v_{max} &= -A\omega & \text{(13.149)} \\
&= 0.5 \times 0.4 \times \pi & \text{(13.150)} \\
&= 0.2\pi m/s & \text{(13.151)} \\
&= 0.2 \times 3.14 m/s & \text{(13.152)} \\
&= 0.628 = 0.63 m/s & \text{(13.153)}
\end{aligned}
$$

where

$$
\begin{aligned}
\omega &= 2\pi f & \text{(13.154)} \\
f &= \frac{v}{\lambda} = \frac{2}{10} = 0.2 Hz & \text{(13.155)} \\
\omega &= 2\pi \times 0.2 & \text{(13.156)} \\
\omega &= 0.4\pi & \text{(13.157)}
\end{aligned}
$$

Question 18

part a

If A is the cross sectional area and x is the volume per second then:

$$
\begin{aligned}
x &= Av & \text{(13.158)} \\
v &= \frac{x}{A} & \text{(13.159)}
\end{aligned}
$$

part bi

If the water falls down to the ground then the change in momentum will be given by the mass multiplied by the velocity, v. The mass, m, is given by density, ρ, multiplied by volume, V. x is the volume per second, so:

$$F = \frac{\Delta p}{\Delta t} = \frac{mv}{t} \tag{13.160}$$

$$= \frac{\rho V v}{t} \tag{13.161}$$

$$= \rho x v \tag{13.162}$$

part bii

If the water rebounds at the same speed then the momentum change will be from mv to $-mv$ so the total change is $2mv$ thus the force will be doubled: $F = 2\rho x v$.

Question 19

part a

Equate the gravitational force equation with the force in circular motion:

$$\frac{GMm}{r^2} = \frac{mv^2}{r} \tag{13.163}$$

$$v = \sqrt{\frac{GM}{r}} \tag{13.164}$$

note that the radius of the orbit must be measured from the centre of the Earth and we are taking r to mean a distance from the centre of the Earth and R to mean the radius of the Earth itself.

part b

We know that

$$g = \frac{GM}{R^2} \tag{13.165}$$

$$10 = \frac{GM}{R^2} \tag{13.166}$$

and from part a that:

$$v^2 = \frac{GM}{r} \tag{13.167}$$

so at sea level $r = R$, therefore:

$$v^2 = \frac{GM}{R} \tag{13.168}$$

$$= R\frac{GM}{R^2} \tag{13.169}$$

$$= R \times 10 \tag{13.170}$$

$$= 6400,000 \times 10 \tag{13.171}$$

$$v^2 = 64 \times 10^6 \tag{13.172}$$

$$v = 8 \times 10^3 m/s \tag{13.173}$$

$$\tag{13.174}$$

part c

Uneven height of land / obstacles.

Question 20

part a

Since $E = hc/\lambda$ the shortest wavelength implies the largest difference in energy:

$$E_1 - E_{10} = -\frac{R}{1^2} - -\frac{R}{10^2} \tag{13.175}$$

$$= -\frac{R}{1} + \frac{R}{100} \tag{13.176}$$

$$= -\frac{100R}{100} + \frac{R}{100} \tag{13.177}$$

$$= -\frac{99R}{100} \tag{13.178}$$

$$-\frac{hc}{\lambda} = -\frac{99R}{100} \tag{13.179}$$

$$\lambda = \frac{100hc}{99R} \tag{13.180}$$

part b

The longest wavelength corresponds to the smallest E thus this should be:

$$E_9 - E_{10} = -\frac{R}{9^2} - -\frac{R}{10^2} \tag{13.181}$$

$$= -\frac{R}{81} + \frac{R}{100} \tag{13.182}$$

$$= -\frac{100R}{8100} + \frac{81R}{8100} \tag{13.183}$$

$$= -\frac{19R}{8100} \tag{13.184}$$

$$-\frac{hc}{\lambda} = -\frac{19R}{8100} \tag{13.185}$$

$$\lambda = \frac{8100hc}{19R} \tag{13.186}$$

part c

Since the electron in energy level 10 can drop to either level 9,8,7,6,5,4,3,2,1 and the electron in energy level 9 can drop to 8 different levels, ending with the electron in energy level 2 which can only drop to level 1 the answer is simply the sum of the integer from 1 to 9. This is 45.

Question 21

part a

Apply the resistors in parallel formula to the three branches. Note that two identical resistors (both resistance R) in parallel have the total resistance $R/2$ - this is what we have on the bottom branch between A and D. This is useful fact to remember.

$$\frac{1}{R_{AB}} = \frac{1}{R} + \frac{1}{2R} + \frac{1}{\frac{3}{2}R} \tag{13.187}$$

$$= \frac{1}{R} + \frac{1}{2R} + \frac{2}{3R} \tag{13.188}$$

$$= \frac{6+3+4}{6R} \tag{13.189}$$

$$= \frac{13}{6R} \tag{13.190}$$

$$R_{AB} = \frac{6R}{13} \tag{13.191}$$

part b

The same pd, V, will be present across the bottom branch because all branches are in parallel. The pd is shared in proportion to the resistance for components in series. The resistance of the resistor between D and B has double the resistance of the pair between D and A and so the resistor between

D and B should have double the pd. That is we need three chunks of pd, 2 of which are across the resistor between D and B.

$$V_{acrossD} = \frac{2V}{3} \tag{13.192}$$

$$P = \frac{V^2}{R} \tag{13.193}$$

$$= \frac{(2/3V)^2}{R} \tag{13.194}$$

$$= \frac{4V^2}{9R} \tag{13.195}$$

part c

We can redraw the circuit with a quick sketch:

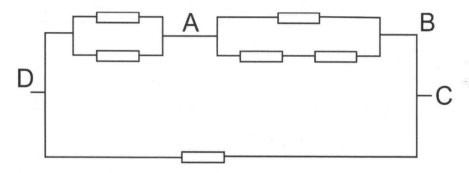

Now the resistance of AC is:

$$\frac{1}{R_{AC}} = \frac{1}{R} + \frac{1}{2R} \tag{13.196}$$

$$= \frac{2}{2R} + \frac{1}{2R} \tag{13.197}$$

$$= \frac{3}{2R} \tag{13.198}$$

$$R_{AC} = \frac{2R}{3} \tag{13.199}$$

The resistance of AD is $R/2$ so the total resistance of the top branch is:

$$R_{topbranch} = \frac{R}{2} + \frac{2R}{3} \tag{13.200}$$

$$= \frac{3R}{6} + \frac{4R}{6} \tag{13.201}$$

$$= \frac{7R}{6} \tag{13.202}$$

So the resistance DC is:

$$\frac{1}{R_{DC}} = \frac{1}{R} + \frac{6}{7R} \tag{13.203}$$

$$= \frac{7}{7R} + \frac{6}{7R} \tag{13.204}$$

$$= \frac{13}{7R} \tag{13.205}$$

$$R_{DC} = \frac{7R}{13} \tag{13.206}$$

Chapter 14

Oxford Physics Aptitude Test 2016 Answers

14.1   Part A - Maths

Question 1

Use the chain rule:

$$
\begin{aligned}
\frac{d}{dx}uv &= u\frac{dv}{dx} + v\frac{du}{dx} \tag{14.1}\\
&= x.2x\cos x^2 + \sin x^2 \tag{14.2}\\
&= 2x^2\cos x^2 + \sin x^2 \tag{14.3}
\end{aligned}
$$

Question 2

Make a substitution $x = \tan\theta$:

$$
\sqrt{3}x^2 - 2x - \sqrt{3} = 0 \tag{14.4}
$$

Then use the quadratic formula to solve:

$$
\begin{aligned}
x &= \frac{-b \pm \sqrt{b^2 - 4ac}}{2a} \tag{14.5}\\
&= \frac{2 \pm \sqrt{4 + 4.\sqrt{3}.\sqrt{3}}}{2\sqrt{3}} \tag{14.6}\\
&= \frac{2 \pm 4}{2\sqrt{3}} \tag{14.7}\\
&= \frac{6}{2\sqrt{3}} = \frac{3}{\sqrt{3}} = \sqrt{3} \tag{14.8}\\
&= \frac{-2}{2\sqrt{3}} = -\frac{1}{\sqrt{3}} \tag{14.9}
\end{aligned}
$$

From $x = \sqrt{3}$, $\theta = \tan^{-1}\sqrt{3} = 60°$ and from $x = -\frac{1}{\sqrt{3}}$, $\theta = \tan^{-1}\frac{1}{\sqrt{3}} = -30°$. Considering the shape of the $\tan\theta$ vs θ graph, this means theta must be 60° and (180+60)240° and (180-30)=150°

and 360-30=330°.

Question 3

Expand and simply the log in the given equations:

$$\log_4 \left(\frac{64^x}{16^y} \right) = 13 \tag{14.10}$$

$$\log_4 64^x - \log_4 16^y = 13 \tag{14.11}$$

$$x \log_4 64 - y \log_4 16 = 13 \tag{14.12}$$

$$3x - 2y = 13 \tag{14.13}$$

and

$$\log_{10} 10^x + \log_3 3^y = 1 \tag{14.14}$$

$$x \log_{10} 10 + y \log_3 3 = 1 \tag{14.15}$$

$$x + y = 1 \tag{14.16}$$

$$y = 1 - x \tag{14.17}$$

Substitute the second equation into the first:

$$3x - 2(1 - x) = 13 \tag{14.18}$$

$$3x - 2 + 2x = 13 \tag{14.19}$$

$$5x = 15 \tag{14.20}$$

$$x = 3 \tag{14.21}$$

Finally substitute $x = 3$ back into $y = 1 - x$ to find $y = -2$.

Question 4

Write out Pascal's triangle down to the row for $x^1 2$ which should look like this:

```
                          1
                      1       1
                   1      2      1
                1      3     3      1
             1     4      6     4      1
          1     5    10     10     5      1
       1     6    15     20     15     6      1
     1     7    21    35     35     21     7     1
   1     8    28    56    70     56     28     8     1
  1    9    36    84   126    126     84    36     9    1
 1   10   45  120   210   252    210   120    45    10   1
1  11   55  165  330   462    462   330   165    55    11  1
1 12  66  220  495  792   924   792   495   220    66   12   1
```

Remember that if the bracket is $(a+b)^n$ then the first coefficient is for $a^{12}b^0$ the second is for $a^{11}b^1$ etc. The term independent of x would be when we have x^8 and $\left(-\frac{1}{x^2}\right)^4$ or a^8b^4 which would have the coefficient 495.

Question 5

To pick a number in the 5 thousands you must pick 5 and then any 3 numbers from 4. Similarly for a number in the 6 and 7 thousands. $^4P_3 = \frac{n!}{n-r!} = \frac{4!}{1!} = 24$. But this can happen in three ways so: $24 \times 3 = 72$. You can also have a number in the thirty thousands - so pick a three and then any permutation of 4 numbers from four. Similarly for a number in the 40, 50, 60 and 70 thousands. So $^4P_4 = \frac{n!}{n-r!} = \frac{4!}{0!} = 24$ but this happens 5 ways so: $24 \times 5 = 120$. Finally $72 + 120 = 192$.

Question 6

After zero months you have a seed. After one month you have 1 twig and 2 leaves. After 2 months you still have the 1 twig and 2 leaves but you also have 2 new twigs and 4 new leaves. After three months you have the 3 old twigs and 6 old leaves but 4 new twigs and 8 new leaves. So really what you are doing is the sum of a geometric progression of leaves with first term 2 (after 1 month) and common ratio 2. After ten months:

$$\frac{a(1-r^n)}{1-r} = \frac{2(1-2^{10})}{(1-2)} \tag{14.22}$$

$$= \frac{2 \times -1023}{-1} \tag{14.23}$$

$$= 2046 \tag{14.24}$$

Question 7

part a

The sequence is is 10 throws long, therefore the player can't win from 8 throws.

part b

To get a specific number the probability is $\frac{1}{6}$ so to get ten throws as specified its $\frac{1}{6^{10}}$

part c

With twelve throws there are three ways to get a block of ten specified throws XXT, XTX and TXX where X is any number that we don't mind and T is the sequence of ten specified throws. So its $3 \times \frac{1}{6^{10}}$

Question 8

The area of the circle is πr^2. Let a be the side length of the octagon. The exterior angle of the octagon is $360/8 = 45°$ and $\cos 45 = \frac{1}{\sqrt{2}}$

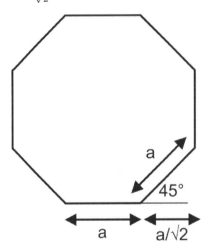

So the width of the octagon is given by:

$$x = a + 2 \times \frac{a}{\sqrt{2}} \tag{14.25}$$

$$= a + \sqrt{2}a \tag{14.26}$$

$$= a(1 + \sqrt{2}) \tag{14.27}$$

$$a = \frac{x}{1 + \sqrt{2}} \tag{14.28}$$

The area of the octagon is eight times the area of a triangle:

$$A = 8 \times \frac{1}{2} \times a \times \frac{x}{2} \tag{14.29}$$

$$= 8 \times \frac{1}{2} \times \frac{x}{1+\sqrt{2}} \times \frac{x}{2} \tag{14.30}$$

$$= \frac{2x^2}{1+\sqrt{2}} \tag{14.31}$$

Then, equating areas:

$$\frac{2x^2}{1+\sqrt{2}} = \pi r^2 \tag{14.32}$$

$$x^2 = \frac{\pi r^2(1+\sqrt{2})}{2} \tag{14.33}$$

$$x = \left(\frac{1}{2}\pi r^2(1+\sqrt{2})\right)^{\frac{1}{2}} \tag{14.34}$$

Question 9

Swap the inequality sign for an equals and solve:

$$5 - 3x = \frac{2}{x} \tag{14.35}$$

$$5x - 3x^2 = 2 \tag{14.36}$$

$$3x^2 - 5x + 2 = 0 \tag{14.37}$$

$$(3x - 2)(x - 1) = 0 \tag{14.38}$$

$$x = \frac{2}{3} \tag{14.39}$$

$$x = 1 \tag{14.40}$$

There is also a singularity at $x = 0$. Now try some values. Between $x = 0$ and $x = \frac{2}{3}$ lets try $x = \frac{1}{2}$. $5 - 3x = 3.5$ and $\frac{2}{x} = 4$. True. Now lets try a value between $x = \frac{2}{3}$ and $x = 1$, perhaps $x = \frac{3}{4}$. $5 - 3x = 2\frac{3}{4}$ and $\frac{2}{x} = 2\frac{2}{3}$. False. Finally try a value $x > 1$ for example $x = 2$. $5 - 3x = -1$ and $\frac{2}{x} = 1\frac{2}{3}$. False. So the inequality is valid for values of x: $0 < x < \frac{2}{3}$ and $x > 1$.

Question 10

Draw a quick sketch:

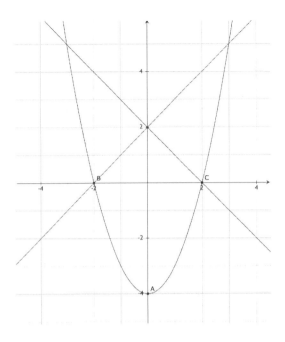

So the area above the x axis is just a triangle with area:

$$A = \frac{1}{2} \times 4 \times 2 \tag{14.41}$$

$$= 4 \tag{14.42}$$

The area below the axis is found by integrating:

$$A = \int_{-2}^{2} x^2 - 4\,dx \tag{14.43}$$

$$= \left[\frac{x^3}{3} - 4x\right]_{-2}^{2} \tag{14.44}$$

$$= \left(\frac{8}{3} - 8\right) - \left(\frac{-8}{3} + 8\right) \tag{14.45}$$

$$= \frac{8}{3} - 8 + \frac{8}{3} - 8 \tag{14.46}$$

$$= \frac{16}{3} - 16 \tag{14.47}$$

$$= \frac{-32}{3} \tag{14.48}$$

$$= -10\frac{2}{3} \tag{14.49}$$

Adding the areas and ignoring signs gives $14\frac{2}{3}$.

Question 11

Here we must find $\frac{dr}{dt}$. Begin by finding an equation for V and then making r the subject.

$$V \quad = \quad \pi r^2 h \tag{14.50}$$

$$r(t) \quad = \quad \left(\frac{V}{\pi h(t)}\right)^{\frac{1}{2}} \tag{14.51}$$

$$= \quad \left(\frac{V}{\pi(h_0 - \alpha t)}\right)^{\frac{1}{2}} \tag{14.52}$$

$$\tag{14.53}$$

Using the chain rule now differentiate this. In words this is the power, multiplied by the differential of the bracket, multiplied by the bracket with one subtracted from the power. First lets separately differentiate the contents of the bracket again using the chain rule:

$$\frac{d}{dt}\frac{V}{\pi(h_0 - \alpha t)} \quad = \quad \frac{d}{dt}V\pi^{-1}(h_0 - \alpha t)^{-1} \tag{14.54}$$

$$= \quad -V\pi^{-1} \times -\alpha \times (h_0 - \alpha t)^{-2} \tag{14.55}$$

$$= \quad \frac{\alpha V}{\pi(h_0 - \alpha t)^2} \tag{14.56}$$

Now lets do the main differentiation:

$$\frac{d}{dt}\left(\frac{V}{\pi(h_0 - \alpha t)}\right)^{\frac{1}{2}} \quad = \quad \frac{1}{2} \times \frac{\alpha V}{\pi(h_0 - \alpha t)^2} \times \left(\frac{V}{\pi(h_0 - \alpha t)}\right)^{-\frac{1}{2}} \tag{14.57}$$

$$= \quad \frac{1}{2} \times \frac{\alpha V}{\pi(h_0 - \alpha t)^2} \times \left(\frac{\pi(h_0 - \alpha t)}{V}\right)^{\frac{1}{2}} \tag{14.58}$$

$$= \quad \frac{\alpha}{2}\frac{V^{\frac{1}{2}}}{\pi^{\frac{1}{2}}}\left(\frac{1}{h_0 - \alpha t}\right)^{\frac{3}{2}} \tag{14.59}$$

As t increases, $h_0 - \alpha t$ decreases, $1/(h_0 - \alpha t)$ increases, so dr/dt increases.

14.2   Part B - Physics

Question 12

Since

$$mgh = \frac{1}{2}mv^2 \tag{14.60}$$

the kinetic energy is proportional to the height. So we want to solve the equation:

$$\left(\frac{3}{4}\right)^2 = 0.25 \tag{14.61}$$

This would be straightforward to solve with logs on a calculator, but without a calculator you just need to multiply 3/4 by itself and check the answer at each stage:

$$\frac{3}{4} \times \frac{3}{4} = \frac{9}{16} \tag{14.62}$$

$$\frac{9}{16} \times \frac{3}{4} = \frac{27}{64} \tag{14.63}$$

$$\frac{27}{64} \times \frac{3}{4} = \frac{81}{256} \tag{14.64}$$

$$\frac{81}{256} \times \frac{3}{4} = \frac{243}{1024} \tag{14.65}$$

$$\tag{14.66}$$

Thus, it's 5 times.

Question 13

An ideal wire has no resistance so the line should be along the x axis.

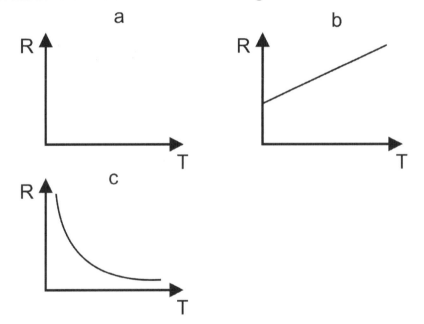

Question 14

Use Kepler's Law which tells us that:

$$T^2 \propto r^3 \tag{14.67}$$

So

$$\frac{T_e^2}{T_i^2} = \frac{r_e^3}{r_i^3} \tag{14.68}$$

$$\frac{T_e}{T_i} = \sqrt{\frac{r_e^3}{r_i^3}} \tag{14.69}$$

$$= \sqrt{1.6^3} \tag{14.70}$$

By long multiplication or recognising powers of 2, $1.6^3 = 4.096$ Then to 2sf $\sqrt{4.096} = 2.0$.

Question 15

Draw a triangle for the speeds (take care not to mix up values of distance here). If the river is 100, wide, to cross in 10 seconds her component of velocity across the river must be 10m/s. Down the river it is 7.5m/s.

7.5m/s

10m/s

Notice that this is effectively a 3-4-5 triangle with one 'unit' worth 2.m/s. So the speed must be 12.5m/s and the angle to the flow of the water is $\cos^{-1}\frac{3}{5}$.

Question 16

We need to assume the charge $-q$ is confined to the line joining the charges. If the charges are equal then there will be no net force at $x = a/2$. When the charges are not equal we need to consider the force from Q_1 and Q_2 separately.

$$F_1 = \frac{kQ_1q}{x^2} \tag{14.71}$$

$$F_2 = \frac{kQ_2q}{(a-x)^2} \tag{14.72}$$

$$\tag{14.73}$$

So equating F_1 and F_2:

$$\frac{Q_1}{x^2} = \frac{Q_2}{(a-x)^2} \tag{14.74}$$

$$Q_1(a-x)^2 = Q_2 x^2 \tag{14.75}$$

$$Q_1(a^2 - 2ax + x^2) = Q_2 x^2 \tag{14.76}$$

$$(Q_1 - Q_2)x^2 - 2aQ_1 x + Q_1 a^2 = 0 \tag{14.77}$$

Using the quadratic formula to solve this gives

$$x = \frac{aQ_1 \pm a\sqrt{Q_1 Q_2}}{(Q_1 - Q_2)} \tag{14.78}$$

Since both Q_1 and Q_2 are positive then we need the positive solution. The negative solution for x would correspond to the position of zero force if one of the charges was negative meaning there was attraction to one of the fixed point charges and repulsion from the other fixed point charge.

Question 17

part a

Find the area under the graph since work done = force x distance.

$$A = \frac{1}{2} \times 0.05 \times 10 = 0.25J \tag{14.79}$$

part b

$$0.25 = \frac{1}{2}mv^2 \tag{14.80}$$

$$0.5 = 0.02 \times v^2 \tag{14.81}$$

$$25 = v^2 \tag{14.82}$$

$$v = 5m/s \tag{14.83}$$

part c

Oscillate about displacement=0. This would be simple harmonic motion (SHM) as the force is directly proportional to the displacement.

Question 18

This is Stoke's Law - you may recognise it immediately and know the answer, but show your working. Recall that $F = ma$ so $N = kgms^{-2}$. So:

$$kgms^{-2} = m^x kg^y m^{-y} s^{-y} m^z s^{-z} \qquad (14.84)$$

$$= kg^y m^{x+z-y} s^{-(y+z)} \qquad (14.85)$$

By comparing powers $y = 1$, $x + z - y = 1$ and $y + z = 2$. Therefore $z = 1$ and then $y = 1$ and $x = 1$.

Question 19

part a

Use the equation:

$$\frac{hc}{\lambda} = \phi + KE_{max} \qquad (14.86)$$

Substitute in, but not that the suggestion they give for Planc's constant is not helpful. The Maths is significantly easier if you assume $h = 6.25 \times 10^{-34} Js$ rather than $h = 6.0 \times 10^{-34} Js$ - of course this is closer to the actual value of $h = 6.63 \times 10^{-34} Js$

$$\frac{6.25 \times 10^{-34} \times 3 \times 10^8}{6.25 \times 10^{-7}} = 1.6 \times 10^{-19} + \frac{1}{2} \times 1 \times 10^{-30} \times v^2 \qquad (14.87)$$

$$3 \times 10^{-19} = 1.6 \times 10^{-19} + \frac{1}{2} \times 1 \times 10^{-30} \times v^2 \qquad (14.88)$$

$$1.4 \times 10^{-19} = \frac{1}{2} \times 1 \times 10^{-30} \times v^2 \qquad (14.89)$$

$$\frac{2.8 \times 10^{-19}}{1 \times 10^{-30}} = v^2 \qquad (14.90)$$

$$2.8 \times 10^{11} = v^2 \qquad (14.91)$$

$$28 \times 10^{10} = v^2 \qquad (14.92)$$

$$5.3 \times 10^5 = v \qquad (14.93)$$

part b

5keV is significantly more energy that the maximum KE, so we can neglect this to 2sf, so:

$$5keV = \frac{1}{2} \times 1 \times 10^{-30} \times v^2 \tag{14.94}$$

$$5000 \times 1.6 \times 10^{-19} = \frac{1}{2} \times 1 \times 10^{-30} \times v^2 \tag{14.95}$$

$$\frac{8 \times 10^{-16} \times 2}{1 \times 10^{-30}} = v^2 \tag{14.96}$$

$$16 \times 10^{14} = v^2 \tag{14.97}$$

$$v = 4.0 \times 10^7 m/s \tag{14.98}$$

Question 20

Since all the resistors have equal resistance and all the heaters have equal resistance the potential at the junction above A is 42V and the junction below A is 42V. No current will flow through A (as there is no potential difference across it). There will be no energy dissipated in A so it will not heat the water. The pd across heater B is 42V, so the current will be $I = V/R = 42/6 = 7A$. The power dissipated in heater B will be $P = I^2R = 7^2 \times 6 = 294W$. The power dissipated in C will be the same. To find the time taken:

$$E = mc\Delta T \tag{14.99}$$

$$= 1 \times 4200 \times 7 \tag{14.100}$$

$$= 29,400 \tag{14.101}$$

and by long division

$$t = \frac{E}{P} \tag{14.102}$$

$$= \frac{29400}{294} \tag{14.103}$$

$$= 100s \tag{14.104}$$

Question 21

Add a tangent to the sphere at the point the ray meets the sphere. Then add the normal at 90°. Add some labels to the triangle formed within the sphere. Notice that θ_1 is the same as the angle at centre of the circle which can be found from the triangle labeled.

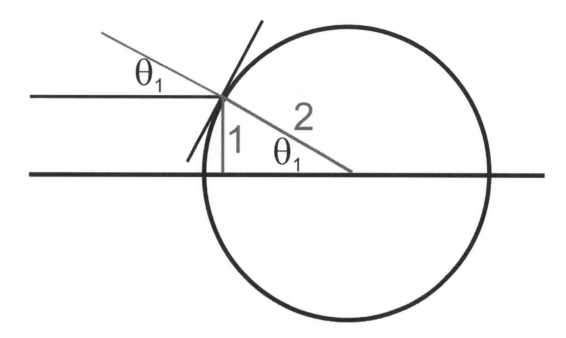

Recall the refractive index of vacuum is 1. Then apply Snell's Law:

$$n_1 \sin \theta_1 = n_2 \sin \theta_2 \tag{14.105}$$

$$n \times \frac{1}{2} = \sin 45 \tag{14.106}$$

$$n \times \frac{1}{2} = \frac{1}{\sqrt{2}} \tag{14.107}$$

$$n = 1.4 \tag{14.108}$$

For the second part we simply want total internal reflection at the surface of the sphere. This occurs where the angle of refraction (θ_2) is 90°. Again apply Snell's law:

$$n_1 \sin \theta_1 = n_2 \sin \theta_2 \tag{14.109}$$

$$\sqrt{2} \times \sin \theta_1 = \sin 90 \tag{14.110}$$

$$\sin \theta_1 = \frac{1}{\sqrt{2}} \tag{14.111}$$

$$\theta_1 = 45° \tag{14.112}$$

Chapter 15

Oxford Physics Aptitude Test Specimen Sept 2017 Answers

Question 1

Consider where the x^5 terms come from. We need x^0 from the first bracket and x^5 from the second, x^1 and x^4, x^2 and x^3, x^3 and x^2 and finally x^4 and x^1. Using Pascal's triangle for the coefficients and expressing:

$$(1+x)^4(1-x)^6 = (1+a)^4(1+b)^6 \tag{15.1}$$

For x^0 from the first bracket and x^5 from the second:

$$
\begin{aligned}
1a^0 \times 6b^5 &= 1.1 \times 6. - 1^5.x^5 \tag{15.2} \\
&= -6x^5 \tag{15.3}
\end{aligned}
$$

For x^1 from the first bracket and x^4 from the second:

$$
\begin{aligned}
4a^1 \times 15b^4 &= 4.x^1 \times 15. - 1^4.x^4 \tag{15.4} \\
&= 60x^5 \tag{15.5}
\end{aligned}
$$

For x^2 from the first bracket and x^3 from the second:

$$
\begin{aligned}
6a^2 \times 20b^3 &= 6.x^2 \times 20. - 1^3.x^3 \tag{15.6} \\
&= -120x^5 \tag{15.7}
\end{aligned}
$$

For x^3 from the first bracket and x^2 from the second:

$$4a^3 \times 15b^2 \quad = \quad 4.x^3 \times 15. - 1^2.x^2 \tag{15.8}$$

$$= \quad 60x^5 \tag{15.9}$$

For x^4 from the first bracket and x^1 from the second:

$$1a^4 \times 6b^1 \quad = \quad 1.x^4 \times 6. - 1^1.x^1 \tag{15.10}$$

$$= \quad -6x^5 \tag{15.11}$$

This gives a total of:

$$(-6 + 60 - 120 + 60 - 6)x^5 = -12x^5 \tag{15.12}$$

Answer is A.

Question 2

Since $\log_{10} 100 = 2$ and $10^2 = 100$ then we need to find to what power do we raise 4 to get 16: the answer is 2. So

$$\log_2 x + \log_4 16 \quad = \quad 2 \tag{15.13}$$

$$\log_2 x + 2 \quad = \quad 2 \tag{15.14}$$

So

$$\log_2 x \quad = \quad 0 \tag{15.15}$$

$$2^0 \quad = \quad x \tag{15.16}$$

$$x \quad = \quad 1 \tag{15.17}$$

Answer is B. (Also used as 2015 Q2)

Question 3

Use the chain rule:

$$\frac{d}{dx}uv \quad = \quad u\frac{dv}{dx} + v\frac{du}{dx} \tag{15.18}$$

$$= \quad x.2x\cos x^2 + \sin x^2 \tag{15.19}$$

$$= \quad 2x^2 \cos x^2 + \sin x^2 \tag{15.20}$$

Answer is E. (Also used as 2016 Q1)

Question 4

Simply use the gradient formula:

$$m = \frac{y_2 - y_1}{x_2 - x_1} \tag{15.21}$$

$$= \frac{-2 - 8}{5 - 4} \tag{15.22}$$

$$= \frac{-10}{1} \tag{15.23}$$

$$= -10 \tag{15.24}$$

Answer is A. (Also used as 2006 Q2).

Question 5

You can arrange the numbers in pairs:

$$(1 + 100) + (2 + 99) + ... + (50 + 51) \tag{15.25}$$

Each pair adds to 101 and there are 50 pairs so

$$101 \times 50 = 5050 \tag{15.26}$$

In the general case the sum of the integers from 1 to N is given by

$$\frac{N}{2}(N + 1) \tag{15.27}$$

Answer is C. (Also used as 2008 Q1).

Question 6

To pick a number in the 5 thousands you must pick 5 and then any 3 numbers from 4. Similarly for a number in the 6 and 7 thousands. $^4P_3 = \frac{n!}{n-r!} = \frac{4!}{1!} = 24$. But this can happen in three ways so: $24 \times 3 = 72$. You can also have a number in the thirty thousands - so pick a three and then any permutation of 4 numbers from four. Similarly for a number in the 40, 50, 60 and 70 thousands. So $^4P_4 = \frac{n!}{n-r!} = \frac{4!}{0!} = 24$ but this happens 5 ways so: $24 \times 5 = 120$. Finally $72 + 120 = 192$. Answer is C. (Also used as 2016 Q5).

Question 7

The duration of the day depends on its rotational speed. This is independent of distance from the Sun. The duration of the year depends on the time taken to complete one orbit of the Sun, this increases with greater distance from the Sun: this is correct. The size/volume is independent of distance from the Sun. The number of moons is independent of distance from the Sun. Ignoring Pluto, all the planets from Jupiter outwards are gas, so the planets do change from rocky to gas giants: this statement is correct. The answer is D. (Also used as 2014 Q10).

Question 8

100GHz falls into the microwave part of the EM spectrum. So the answer is C. This is clearly above radio frequencies: think 99.1MHz for an FM station for example or the 800MHz/1600MHz used in mobile phones. You can also make a calculation of the lowest frequency which would be visible light:

$$f \quad = \quad \frac{v}{\lambda} \tag{15.28}$$
$$= \quad \frac{3 \times 10^8}{600 \times 10^{-9}} \tag{15.29}$$
$$= \quad 5 \times 10^{14} \tag{15.30}$$
$$= \quad 500,000 GHz \tag{15.31}$$

Answer is C. Also used as 2014 Q11).

Question 9

If the velocity with respect to the ISS can be neglected, this means it is close to or exactly zero. This it will not move relative to ISS and so it will follow the ISS in its orbit. The answer is A. (Also used as 2014 Q12).

Question 10

Remember the Kepler's Third Law gives us that the period squared is proportional to the radius cubed:

$$T^2 \propto R^3 \tag{15.32}$$

If the radius is halved, then the the net effect on radius cubed is to decrease by a factor of 8. Therefore the period must go down by a factor of $\sqrt{8}$ which is about 2.7. A geostationary satellite has a period of 24 hours so we need 24/2.7 which is about 8.5 hours. So the answer is B. (Also used as 2013 Q14).

Question 11

Set x to be the number at atoms of B initially and draw a table:

days	A	B
0	2x	x
3	x	
6	x/2	x/2
9	x/4	
12	x/8	x/4
15		

Therefore the answer is C. (Also used as 2013 Q12)

Question 12

The cube root of 125 is 5. Therefore the cube is $5 \times 5 \times 5$ blocks. There must be a $3 \times 3 \times 3$ cube in the middle with no paint which makes 27 cubes. Therefore the answer is D. (Also used as 2012 Q16).

Question 13

Let y=number of yellow, g=number of green, r=number of red and b=number of blue. The statements given suggest:

$$y = 2g \tag{15.33}$$

$$r = 2y = 4g \tag{15.34}$$

$$b = 2r = 8g \tag{15.35}$$

Including g green, you know there are 15g buttons in total. Therefore the probabilities are:

$$g = \frac{1}{15} \tag{15.36}$$

$$y = \frac{2}{15} \tag{15.37}$$

$$r = \frac{4}{15} \tag{15.38}$$

$$b = \frac{8}{15} \tag{15.39}$$

Question 14

The horizontal and vertical components can be treated separately. If the projectile is fired at $200m/s$ and the rail car is traveling at $100m/s$ the horizontal component of the projectile's speed must be $100m/s$ so:

$$200\cos\theta = 100 \tag{15.40}$$

$$\cos\theta = \frac{1}{2} \tag{15.41}$$

$$\theta = 60° \tag{15.42}$$

(Also used as part of 2010 Q25).

Question 15

This is a geometric progression with first term 1 and common ration e^{-x}. So:

$$\sum_{\infty} = \frac{a}{1-r} \tag{15.43}$$

$$= \frac{1}{1-e^{-x}} \tag{15.44}$$

This equation is valid for $|r| < 1$ therefore $e^{-x} < 1$ which is true when $x > 0$. (Also used as 2014 Q2).

Question 16

Firstly remember that perpendicular components of motion are independent and that a particle accelerated through a potential difference gains an energy of eV. So:

$$eV = \frac{1}{2}mv^2 \tag{15.45}$$

$$\frac{2eV}{m} = v^2 \tag{15.46}$$

$$\frac{2 \times 1.6 \times 10^{-19} \times 50}{10^{-30}} = v^2 \tag{15.47}$$

$$1.6 \times 10^{13} = v^2 \tag{15.48}$$

$$16 \times 10^{12} = v^2 \tag{15.49}$$

$$4 \times 10^6 = v \tag{15.50}$$

This gives us the final velocity when the electron reaches the second plate, but the average velocity over its journey is half this. Using $v = d/t$

$$t = \frac{d}{v} = \frac{0.4}{2 \times 10^6} \tag{15.51}$$

$$= 0.2 \times 10^{-6}\text{s} \tag{15.52}$$

Now note down what you know for the vertical component of the motion:

$$u = 0 \tag{15.53}$$

$$a = 10 \tag{15.54}$$

$$t = 0.2 \times 10^{-6} \tag{15.55}$$

$$s = ? \tag{15.56}$$

Therefore:

$$s = ut + \frac{1}{2}at^2 \tag{15.57}$$

$$= \frac{1}{2} \times 10 \times (0.2 \times 10^{-6})^2 \tag{15.58}$$

$$= 5 \times 0.04 \times 10^{-12} \tag{15.59}$$

$$= 0.2 \times 10^{-12}\text{m} \tag{15.60}$$

$$= 2 \times 10^{-13}\text{m} \tag{15.61}$$

(Also used as 2009 Q26).

Question 17

part a

This is integration by substitution. We notice that the top is the differential of the bottom. So we make the substitution

$$u = 1 + \sin x \tag{15.62}$$

So:

$$du = \cos x\, dx \tag{15.63}$$

and

$$\int_0^{\pi/2} \frac{\cos x}{1 + \sin x} dx = \int_1^2 \frac{1}{u} du \tag{15.64}$$

$$= [\ln u]_1^2 \tag{15.65}$$

$$= \ln 2 - \ln 1 \tag{15.66}$$

$$= \ln 2 \tag{15.67}$$

Where we have calculated the new limits from:

$$u = 1 + \sin x \tag{15.68}$$

$$= 1 + \sin 0 \tag{15.69}$$

$$= 1 \tag{15.70}$$

and

$$u = 1 + \sin x \tag{15.71}$$

$$= 1 + \sin(\frac{\pi}{2}) \tag{15.72}$$

$$= 2 \tag{15.73}$$

part b

Here we need to adopt the partial fractions technique. We seek to express the expression as the sum of two fractions:

$$\frac{x}{(x+4)(x+2)} = \frac{A}{x+4} + \frac{B}{x+2} \tag{15.74}$$

Expressing this over a common denominator means:

$$\frac{x}{(x+4)(x+2)} = \frac{A(x+2) + B(x+4)}{(x+4)(x+2)} \tag{15.75}$$

Since the denominators are equal, so too must the numerators:

$$x = A(x+2) + B(x+4) \tag{15.76}$$

Letting $x = -2$, the first bracket cancels:

$$-2 = B(-2 + 4) \tag{15.77}$$

$$-2 = 2B \tag{15.78}$$

$$B = -1 \tag{15.79}$$

270

and letting $x = -4$, the second bracket cancels:

$$-4 \quad = \quad A(-4 + 2) \tag{15.80}$$

$$-4 \quad = \quad -2A \tag{15.81}$$

$$A \quad = \quad 2 \tag{15.82}$$

Therefore we need to integrate:

$$\int_0^2 \frac{2}{x+4} - \frac{1}{x+2} dx \quad = \quad [2\ln(x+4) - \ln(x+2)]_0^2 \tag{15.83}$$

$$= \quad [2\ln(6) - \ln 4] - [2\ln 4 - \ln 2] \tag{15.84}$$

$$= \quad 2\ln 6 - 3\ln 4 + \ln 2 \tag{15.85}$$

$$= \quad 2(\ln 3 + \ln 2) - 3(2\ln 2) + \ln 2 \tag{15.86}$$

$$= \quad 2\ln 3 - 3\ln 2 \tag{15.87}$$

$$= \quad \ln \frac{9}{8} \tag{15.88}$$

(Also used as 2014 Q3).

Question 18

The general equation for the period of mass spring system is:

$$T = 2\pi \sqrt{\frac{m}{k}} \tag{15.89}$$

If two springs are in series, consider how the k of the whole system will change. With two springs each experiencing force mg, the extension would double, so the k (i.e. the stiffness) of the whole system would half (since k=F/x). So:

$$T_s = \sqrt{2}T \tag{15.90}$$

If two springs are in parallel, consider how the k of the whole system will change. Each spring will now experience half the force, so the extension would half, so the k (i.e. the stiffness) of the whole system would double. So:

$$T_p = \frac{T}{\sqrt{2}} \tag{15.91}$$

Looking at the initial equation for the period, there is no dependence on g, therefore there is no effect on the period: it's T. (Further, if we consider this in the same way as we did above, both the force and the extension now double, leaving k for the whole system unchanged.) (Also used as 2014 Q14).

Question 19

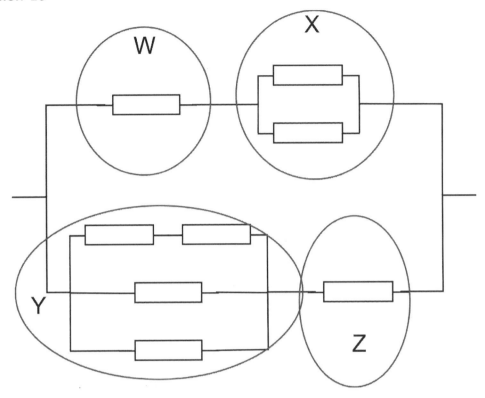

The total resistance of W is R. The total resistance of X is R/2. Therefore the total of the top branch is 3R/2. The total resistance of Y is:

$$\frac{1}{Y} = \frac{1}{2R} + \frac{1}{R} + \frac{1}{R} \tag{15.92}$$

$$= \frac{1}{2R} + \frac{2}{2R} + \frac{2}{2R} \tag{15.93}$$

$$= \frac{5}{2R} \tag{15.94}$$

$$Y = \frac{2R}{5} \tag{15.95}$$

The total resistance of the bottom branch is now:

$$\frac{2R}{5} + R = \frac{7R}{5} \tag{15.96}$$

Now adding the top and bottom branch in parallel:

$$\frac{1}{R} = \frac{2}{3R} + \frac{5}{7R} \tag{15.97}$$

$$= \frac{14 + 15}{21R} \tag{15.98}$$

$$= \frac{29}{21R} \tag{15.99}$$

$$R = \frac{21R}{29} \tag{15.100}$$

(Also used as 2014 Q13).

Question 20

Consider the sector in one of the circles. Assume an area A where:

$$A = \pi r^2 = \frac{60\pi r^2}{360} = \frac{\pi r^2}{360} \tag{15.101}$$

Now if we spot that the triangle must be an equilateral triangle, with area B:

$$B = \frac{1}{2} \times 2r \times 2r \times \sin 60 \tag{15.102}$$

$$= \sqrt{3}r^2 \tag{15.103}$$

Therefore the shaded area is:

$$B - 3A = \sqrt{3}r^2 - \frac{3 \times \pi r^2}{6} \tag{15.104}$$

$$= \left(\sqrt{3} - \frac{\pi}{2}\right)r^2 \tag{15.105}$$

(Also used as 2014 Q5).

Question 21

If C is positive with respect to D, the diode on the right will conduct as long as $V > 0.7V$. If D is positive with respect to C, the diode on the left will conduct as long as $V > 0.7V$. Thus the IV graph is:

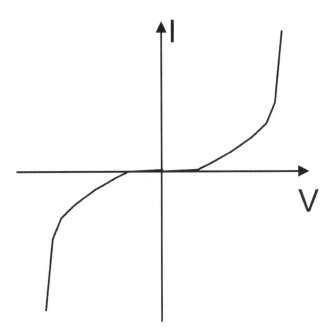

In normal operation up to 0.7V in forward bias a diode doesn't conduct. Therefore no matter which way round the pd is connected to A and B, no current will flow through CD. One diode will block it due to being in reverse, the other due to there being less than 0.7V. If a discharge occurs there will be a high pd between A and B or B and C. The large pd causes a large current to flow between C and D rather than through the sensitive ammeter. One diode is needed in each direction to short circuit the terminals due to a potential difference of either polarity between C and D. (Also used as 2014 Q16).

Question 22

You need to equate volumes of clay. The small sphere has volume:

$$\frac{4}{3}\pi r^3 \tag{15.106}$$

the large sphere has volume:

$$\frac{4}{3}\pi 8r^3 \tag{15.107}$$

and the cylinder has volume:

$$\pi \left(\frac{r}{2}\right)^2 \times l \tag{15.108}$$

so:

$$\frac{4}{3}\pi r^3 + \frac{4}{3}\pi 8r^3 = \pi \left(\frac{r}{2}\right)^2 \times l \tag{15.109}$$

$$9 \times \frac{4}{3}\pi r^3 = \frac{\pi r^2}{4} \times l \tag{15.110}$$

$$12\pi r^3 = \frac{\pi r^2}{4} \times l \tag{15.111}$$

$$\frac{48\pi r^3}{\pi r^2} = l \tag{15.112}$$

$$48r = l \tag{15.113}$$

(Also used as 2016 Q6).

Question 23

To find the current, consider conservation of energy. Electrical power input must equal the gravitational potential energy gained. (We assume that as the mass is moving at a constant speed, the kinetic energy is constant and the electric energy input only needs to be converted into GPE). The mass is raised by 0.5m every second:

$$\frac{E}{t} = \frac{mgh}{t} \tag{15.114}$$

$$= \frac{100 \times 10 \times 0.5}{1} \tag{15.115}$$

$$= 500W \tag{15.116}$$

$$I = \frac{P}{V} \tag{15.117}$$

$$= \frac{500}{230} = \frac{50}{23} = 2.2A \tag{15.118}$$

If we assume that the rope does not slip on the winding wheel, the speed of the rope will be the velocity of the edge of the wheel. But as the mass is attached to a pulley system, if the mass is moving upwards at 0.5m/s, the rope must be traveling at 1.5m/s. This can be easily understood by considering the length of rope between the two pulleys as x, the total length is therefore 3x. If the mass moves up 0.5m (in one second), then the total length of the string is no $3 \times (x - 0.5) = 3x - 1.5$. So the rope is 1.5m shorter. So the angular velocity is given by:

$$\omega = \frac{v}{r} \tag{15.119}$$

$$= \frac{1.5}{0.025} \tag{15.120}$$

$$= 60 rad/s \tag{15.121}$$

Finally the force applied by the motor is:

$$F = \frac{P}{v} \tag{15.122}$$

$$= \frac{500}{1.5} \tag{15.123}$$

$$= 330N \tag{15.124}$$

(Also used as 2014 Q15).

Question 24

You need to plot the lines:

$$y = x^2 \tag{15.125}$$

$$y = 4 \tag{15.126}$$

$$y = 0 \tag{15.127}$$

$$y = 2x - 4 \tag{15.128}$$

$$x = 0 \tag{15.129}$$

and shade the incorrect side of each line by testing the inequality.

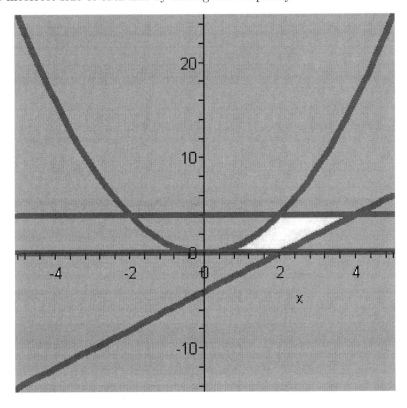

The area is found by noticing the region divides into an area under an x^2 graph and a triangle between x=2 and x=4. The area of the triangle is $\frac{1}{2} \times 4 \times 2 = 4$ and the area under the x^2 graph is $\int_0^2 x^2 = [x^3/3] = \frac{8}{3}$. Adding 4 and $\frac{8}{3}$ gives $6\frac{2}{3}$ (Also used as 2014 Q7).

Question 25

part a

Assuming no friction, the resultant force acting is just the weight of m_2, therefore:

$$a = \frac{F}{m} = \frac{m_2 g}{m_1 + m_2} \tag{15.130}$$

Considering m_1 only, the tension must be given by:

$$T = m_1 a \tag{15.131}$$
$$= m_1 \frac{m_2 g}{m_1 + m_2} \tag{15.132}$$

or considering m_2 only,

$$m_2 g - T = m_2 \frac{m_2 g}{m_1 + m_2} \tag{15.133}$$
$$T = m_2 g - \frac{m_2^2 g}{m_1 + m_2} \tag{15.134}$$
$$= m_1 \frac{m_2 g}{m_1 + m_2} \tag{15.135}$$

part b

The resultant force now acting is:

$$F = m_2 g - \mu_d m_1 g \tag{15.136}$$

Therefore:

$$a = \frac{F}{m} = \frac{m_2 g - \mu_d m_1 g}{m_1 + m_2} \tag{15.137}$$

The tension must be given by

$$T - \mu_d m_1 g = m_1 a \tag{15.138}$$
$$T - \mu_d m_1 g = \frac{m_1 m_2 g - m_1^2 \mu_d g}{m_1 + m_2} \tag{15.139}$$
$$T = \frac{m_1 m_2 g - m_1^2 \mu_d g}{m_1 + m_2} + \mu_d m_1 g \tag{15.140}$$

For m_1 to accelerate:

$$m_2 > \mu_d m_1 \tag{15.141}$$

(Also used as 2014 Q19)

Question 26

The circle is centred on the origin and has a radius of $\sqrt{5}$. The radius is perpendicular to the tangent, be definition. We must consider another circle (not shown) centred on the point $(-4, 3)$. It will have radius $\sqrt{20}$ since:

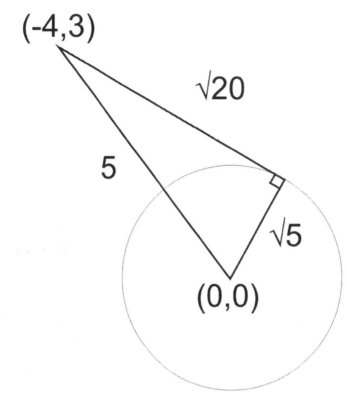

The equation of this new circle is:

$$(x + 4)^2 + (y - 3)^2 = 20 \tag{15.142}$$

We are looking for a point where these two circles intersect. Let us take the equation of the circle centred on the origin, rearrange and substitute into the equation of the circle centred on (-4,3) to eliminate x. Then solve for y.

$$(x + 4)^2 + (y - 3)^2 \quad = \quad 20 \tag{15.143}$$

$$x^2 + 8x + 16 + y^2 - 6y + 9 \quad = \quad 20 \tag{15.144}$$

$$x^2 + 8x + y^2 - 6y = -5 \tag{15.145}$$

$$\tag{15.146}$$

Now $x^2 = 5 - y^2$ so:

$$x^2 + 8x + y^2 - 6y = -5 \tag{15.147}$$

$$5 - y^2 + 8\sqrt{5 - y^2} + y^2 - 6y = -5 \tag{15.148}$$

$$8\sqrt{5 - y^2} - 6y = -10 \tag{15.149}$$

$$8\sqrt{5 - y^2} = 6y - 10 \tag{15.150}$$

$$64(5 - y^2) = (6y - 10)^2 \tag{15.151}$$

$$320 - 64y^2 = 36y^2 - 120y + 100 \tag{15.152}$$

$$0 = 100y^2 - 120y - 220 \tag{15.153}$$

$$0 = 10y^2 - 12y - 22 \tag{15.154}$$

$$0 = 5y^2 - 6y - 11 \tag{15.155}$$

$$0 = (5y - 11)(y + 1) \tag{15.156}$$

$$y = \frac{11}{5} \tag{15.157}$$

$$y = -1 \tag{15.158}$$

Now we use these two y coordinates to find the corresponding x coordinates and then find the equations of the lines joining the point (-4,3) each (x,y) point. For $y = 11/5$:

$$x^2 + y^2 = 5 \tag{15.159}$$

$$x^2 = \frac{125}{25} - \frac{121}{25} \tag{15.160}$$

$$x^2 = \frac{4}{25} \tag{15.161}$$

$$x = +\frac{2}{5} \tag{15.162}$$

(From looking at our diagram it is clear that we must consider the positive solution.) So the equation of the line joining (-4,3) and (2/5,11/5) is found:

$$m = \frac{3 - 11/5}{-4 - 2/5} = \frac{4/5}{-22/5} = -\frac{4}{22} = -\frac{2}{11} \tag{15.163}$$

$$y = -\frac{2}{11}x + c \tag{15.164}$$

$$3 = \frac{2}{11} \times 4 + c \tag{15.165}$$

$$c = \frac{25}{11} \tag{15.166}$$

$$y = -\frac{2}{11}x + \frac{25}{11} \tag{15.167}$$

$$11y = 25 - 2x \tag{15.168}$$

For $y = -1$:

$$x^2 + y^2 = 5 \tag{15.169}$$

$$x^2 = 5 - 1 \tag{15.170}$$

$$x^2 = 4 \tag{15.171}$$

$$x = -2 \tag{15.172}$$

Again considering out diagram we need to consider the negative solution only. So the equation of the line joining (-4,3) and (-2,-1) is found:

$$m = \frac{3+1}{-4+2} = -\frac{4}{2} \tag{15.173}$$

$$y = -2x + c \tag{15.174}$$

$$3 = 2 \times 4 + c \tag{15.175}$$

$$c = -5 \tag{15.176}$$

$$y = -2x - 5 \tag{15.177}$$

$$\tag{15.178}$$

(Also used as 2014 Q9).

Question 27

part a

Total internal reflection is when a light ray from inside a fibre is incident on the wall of the fibre and reflects back into the fibre. This happens when the fibre is more dense than the material (air?) surrounding the fibre. The critical angle is the angle of incidence when the angle of refraction is $90°$. At angles of incidence greater than the critical angle, the light ray is reflected.

part b

Using Snell's Law:

$$n_1 \sin \theta_1 = n_2 \sin \theta_2 \tag{15.179}$$

$$n_1 \sin \theta_c = n_2 \sin 90 \tag{15.180}$$

$$\sin \theta_c = \frac{n_2}{n_1} \tag{15.181}$$

part c

At the entry point into the optical fibre apply Snell's law (assuming that the refractive index of air is 1:

$$1 \times \sin \theta_{max} = n_{core} \sin \theta_2 \tag{15.182}$$

$$\sin \theta_2 = \frac{\sin \theta_{max}}{n_{core}} \tag{15.183}$$

Then inside the fibre at the first point of incidence between the core and the cladding:

$$n_{core} \sin(90 - \theta_{max}) = n_{clad} \tag{15.184}$$

$$\cos \theta_2 = \frac{n_{clad}}{n_{core}} \tag{15.185}$$

Since $\sin^2 \theta + \cos^2 \theta = 1$:

$$\frac{\sin^2 \theta_{max}}{n_{core}^2} + \frac{n_{clad}^2}{n_{core}^2} = 1 \tag{15.186}$$

$$\sin^2 \theta_{max} = n_{core}^2 - n_{clad}^2 \tag{15.187}$$

(Also used as 2014 Q18).

Chapter 16

Oxford Physics Aptitude Test 2017 Answers

Question 1

Use the chain rule. If $y = uv$ then $u = 2x$ and $v = \cos x$. So

$$
\begin{aligned}
\frac{dy}{dx} &= u\frac{dv}{dx} + v\frac{du}{dx} \tag{16.1}\\
&= -2x \sin x + 2 \cos x \tag{16.2}
\end{aligned}
$$

Therefore the answer is D.

Question 2

Divide by 2 and then factorise.

$$
\begin{aligned}
x^2 - x - 6 &= 0 \tag{16.3}\\
(x+2)(x-3) &= 0 \tag{16.4}
\end{aligned}
$$

Therefore the answer is A.

Question 3

This is geometric progression. To find the sum from terms 0 to 10, take the sum to infinity from term 0 and subtract the sum to infinity from term 11. So for the sum to infinity from term 0, the first term $a = 1$ and the common ratio is $r = -e^{-1}$.

$$
\begin{aligned}
\sum_{\infty} &= \frac{a}{1-r} \tag{16.5}\\
&= \frac{1}{1+e^{-1}} \tag{16.6}
\end{aligned}
$$

And for the sum to infinity from term 11, the first term $a = (-e^{-1})^{11} = -e^{-11}$ and the common ratio is $r = -e^{-1}$.

$$\sum_{\infty} = \frac{a}{1-r} \tag{16.7}$$

$$= \frac{-e^{-11}}{1+e^{-1}} \tag{16.8}$$

So:

$$\sum_{n=0}^{10}(-e^{-1})^n = \frac{1}{1+e^{-1}} + \frac{-e^{-11}}{1+e^{-1}} \tag{16.9}$$

$$= \frac{1+e^{-11}}{1+e^{-1}} \tag{16.10}$$

Therefore the answer is E.

Question 4

Glance at the given options and realise that you should use the laws of logs to remove the powers of a and b and then simplify. So:

$$(3-x)\log a + 5x \log b = (x+5)\log a + 3x \log b \tag{16.11}$$

$$3\log a - x\log a + 5x \log b = x\log a + 5\log a + 3x \log b \tag{16.12}$$

$$2x\log b = 2x\log a + 2\log a \tag{16.13}$$

$$x\log b = x\log a + \log a \tag{16.14}$$

$$x(\log b - \log a) = \log a \tag{16.15}$$

$$x = \frac{\log a}{\log b - \log a} \tag{16.16}$$

Therefore the answer is D.

Question 5

Definite integrals are zero if the function is odd and the limits are symmetric about the origin. Remember even times even and odd times odd make even function. Odd times even make odd functions. Integral 1 is an odd power of x only so must be an odd function, so has answer 0. Integral 2 and 3 and both even as they reflect in the y axis so are not 0. Integral 4 is odd and so has answer 0. Therefore it must be B.

Question 6

There are singularities at $x = -3$ and $x = 1$. Equation E has singularities when the denominator is zero so at $x = -3$ and $x = 3$, so it's not E. Equation A only has terms in $1/x$ and so gives a $1/x$ type graph, so it can't be A. Equation D has an additional singularity at $x = -1$, so it's not D. Equation B has a negative sign which would reflect the familiar shapes to the bottom right and bottom left quadrants. Therefore it must be equation C.

Question 7

The moon has no air resistance (which is something we usually assume in suvat calculations) and approximately one sixth the gravitational field strength as on Earth. So it would behave similarly to Earth - so the answer is C.

Question 8

Perhaps recall an pneumonic to help you remember the order of the electromagnetic spectrum. Consider Gay X-man Usually Live In Music Rooms: Gamma, X-ray, UV, Visible Light, Infrared, Microwaves, Radiowaves. Therefore the answer is E.

Question 9

First calculate the effective resistance of the pair of resistors in parallel.

$$\frac{1}{R_T} = \frac{1}{R} + \frac{1}{2R} \tag{16.17}$$

$$= \frac{3}{2R} \tag{16.18}$$

$$R_T = \frac{2R}{3} \tag{16.19}$$

Now add resistors in series to give:

$$\frac{2R}{3} + R = \frac{5R}{3} \tag{16.20}$$

$$V = IR \tag{16.21}$$

$$I = \frac{V}{R} = \frac{3V}{5R} \tag{16.22}$$

Therefore the answer is B.

Question 10

Recall the equation linking capacitance to area:

$$C = \frac{\epsilon_0 \epsilon_r A}{d} \tag{16.23}$$

So it area halves, capacitance halves. Therefore the answer is A.

Question 11

Consider forces acting on mass m. There is mg downwards due to weight. Therefore the total tension in the two ropes upwards must equal mg. Therefore the tension in one of the ropes is $mg/2$. So the answer is B.

Question 12

Begin by equating the electric potential energy gained to the kinetic energy lost:

$$qV = \frac{1}{2}mv^2 \tag{16.24}$$

$$\frac{2qV}{v} = mv \tag{16.25}$$

But the average velocity is given by both:

$$\frac{d}{t} = \frac{v}{2} \tag{16.26}$$

so

$$v = \frac{2d}{t} \tag{16.27}$$

Substituting this into the earlier equation for momentum:

$$mv = 2qV \times \frac{t}{2d} \tag{16.28}$$

$$= \frac{qVt}{d} \tag{16.29}$$

Therefore the answer is A.

Question 13

Use the binomial expansion:

$$(a+b)^n = \sum_{k=0}^{n} \binom{n}{k} a^{n-k} b^k \tag{16.30}$$

$$(3+2x)^5 = \binom{5}{0} 3^5 + \binom{5}{1} 3^4 2x + \binom{5}{2} 3^3 (2x)^2 + \binom{5}{3} 3^2 (2x)^3 \tag{16.31}$$

$$+ \binom{5}{4} 3(2x)^4 + \binom{5}{5} (2x)^5 \tag{16.32}$$

Using Pascal's triangle for the values of the combinations:

$$(3+2x)^5 = 3^5 + 5 \times 3^4 \times 2x + 10 \times 3^3 (2x)^2 + 10 \times 3^2 (2x)^3 \tag{16.33}$$

$$+ 5 \times 3(2x)^4 + (2x)^5 \tag{16.34}$$

$$= 243 + 810x + 1080x^2 + 720x^3 + 240x^4 + 32x^5 \tag{16.35}$$

Question 14

part a

Multiply the probability that each person is individually busy:

$$\frac{1}{2} \times \frac{3}{4} \times \frac{1}{5} = \frac{3}{40} \tag{16.36}$$

part b

Multiply the probability that each person is individually available:

$$\frac{1}{2} \times \frac{1}{4} \times \frac{4}{5} = \frac{4}{40} \tag{16.37}$$

Note that this is not one minus the answer to part a. This would include times when, for example, person A was available but person B was busy etc.

Question 15

The block m will just move when the restoring force of the spring is equal to the maximum frictional force. The maximum frictional force is $\mu_s mg$. The force given by the spring is kx. So the block M must be moved by:

$$x = \frac{\mu_s mg}{k} \tag{16.38}$$

Question 16

The volume of sphere is:

$$\frac{4}{3}\pi r^3 \tag{16.39}$$

The volume of cone is:

$$\frac{1}{3}\pi R^2 h \tag{16.40}$$

If the height of the cone is $2r$, then:

$$\frac{1}{3}\pi R^2 \times 2r \;=\; \frac{4}{3}\pi r^3 \tag{16.41}$$

$$2R^2 \;=\; 4r^2 \tag{16.42}$$

$$R^2 \;=\; 2r^2 \tag{16.43}$$

$$R \;=\; \sqrt{2}r \tag{16.44}$$

$$=\; 1.41r \tag{16.45}$$

Question 17

αv^2 must have units of force (kgms^{-2})to match all the other terms. Since v^2 has units of m^{2}s^{-2} then α must have units of kg/m.

Terminal velocity occurs when the acceleration (or dv/dt) is zero. So:

$$mg \;=\; \alpha v^2 \tag{16.46}$$

$$v^2 \;=\; \frac{mg}{\alpha} \tag{16.47}$$

$$v \;=\; \sqrt{\frac{mg}{\alpha}} \tag{16.48}$$

To find the work done take the average force multiplied by the distance traveled. The average force can be estimated as the final force over 2: so $\alpha v^2/2$ where v is the terminal velocity found earlier. So:

$$W \;=\; \frac{\alpha v^2}{2} \times h \tag{16.49}$$

$$=\; \frac{\alpha}{2} \times \frac{mg}{\alpha} \times h \tag{16.50}$$

$$=\; \frac{mgh}{2} \tag{16.51}$$

Question 18

Since

$$v = f\lambda \tag{16.52}$$

and

$$\omega = 2\pi f \tag{16.53}$$

Then:

$$v = \frac{\omega_1 \lambda_1}{2\pi} = \frac{\omega_2 \lambda_2}{2\pi} \tag{16.54}$$

Now use the trig identity given in the hint and make a substitution for $\frac{2\pi x}{\lambda_1} = \omega_1/v$

$$
\begin{aligned}
y_1 + y_2 &= A \cos \left[\frac{2\pi x}{\lambda_1} - \omega_1 t \right] + A \cos \left[\frac{2\pi x}{\lambda_2} - \omega_2 t \right] \tag{16.55} \\
&= 2A \cos \frac{1}{2} \left[\frac{2\pi x}{\lambda_1} - \omega_1 t + \frac{2\pi x}{\lambda_2} - \omega_2 t \right] \tag{16.56} \\
&\times \cos \frac{1}{2} \left[\frac{2\pi x}{\lambda_1} - \omega_1 t - \frac{2\pi x}{\lambda_2} + \omega_2 t \right] \tag{16.57} \\
&= 2A \cos \frac{1}{2} \left[\frac{\omega_1 x}{v} - \omega_1 t + \frac{\omega_2 x}{v} - \omega_2 t \right] \tag{16.58} \\
&\times \cos \frac{1}{2} \left[\frac{\omega_1 x}{v} - \omega_1 t - \frac{\omega_2 x}{v} + \omega_2 t \right] \tag{16.59}
\end{aligned}
$$

For a sketch as a function of x at some time t, it is best to pick a time $t = 0$ so then equation becomes:

$$
\begin{aligned}
y_1 + y_2 &= 2A \cos \frac{1}{2} \left[\frac{\omega_1 x}{v} + \frac{\omega_2 x}{v} \right] \cos \frac{1}{2} \left[\frac{\omega_1 x}{v} - \frac{\omega_2 x}{v} \right] \tag{16.60} \\
&= 2A \cos \frac{x}{2v} [\omega_1 + \omega_2] \cos \frac{x}{2v} [\omega_1 - \omega_2] \tag{16.61}
\end{aligned}
$$

The term with $\omega_1 - \omega_2$ gives the lower frequency and the term with $\omega_1 + \omega_2$ gives the higher frequency (since $\omega = 2\pi f$:

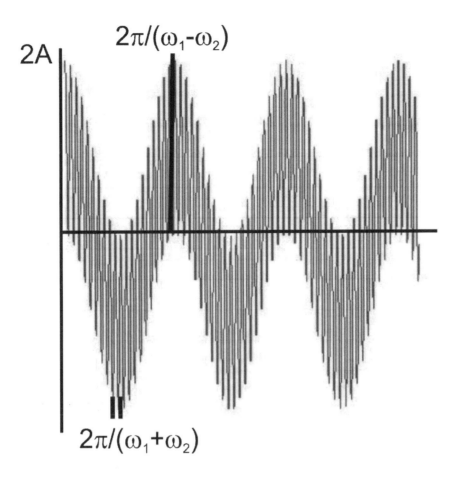

You would hear a frequency which corresponds to the difference in frequencies - i.e. a wave with frequency $2\pi/(\omega_1 - \omega_2)$. This is called the beat frequency.

To find the distance between the points where the sound disappears look at the previous equation. A point at which the amplitude is zero is found by setting the $\cos\frac{x}{2v}[\omega_1 - \omega_2]$ term equal to zero and solving.

$$\cos\frac{x}{2v}[\omega_1 - \omega_2] = 0 \tag{16.62}$$
$$\frac{x}{2v}[\omega_1 - \omega_2] = \frac{\pi}{2} \tag{16.63}$$
$$x = \frac{2v\pi}{2[\omega_1 - \omega_2]} \tag{16.64}$$
$$= \frac{v\pi}{[\omega_1 - \omega_2]} \tag{16.65}$$

the adjacent point is found by:

$$\cos \frac{x}{2v} \left[\omega_1 - \omega_2\right] = 0 \tag{16.66}$$

$$\frac{x}{2v} \left[\omega_1 - \omega_2\right] = \frac{3\pi}{2} \tag{16.67}$$

$$x = \frac{6v\pi}{2\left[\omega_1 - \omega_2\right]} \tag{16.68}$$

$$= \frac{3v\pi}{\left[\omega_1 - \omega_2\right]} \tag{16.69}$$

So the distance between the two points is:

$$\frac{3v\pi}{\left[\omega_1 - \omega_2\right]} - \frac{v\pi}{\left[\omega_1 - \omega_2\right]} = \frac{2v\pi}{\left[\omega_1 - \omega_2\right]} \tag{16.70}$$

Question 19

Set $y = 0$ and then solve the second equation for ωt.

$$\sqrt{3} = 2\cos \omega t \tag{16.71}$$

$$\frac{\sqrt{3}}{2} = \cos \omega t \tag{16.72}$$

$$\omega t = \frac{\pi}{6} \tag{16.73}$$

There is also a solution at:

$$\omega t = 2\pi - \frac{\pi}{6} = \frac{11\pi}{6} \tag{16.74}$$

Now substitute these values into the first equation:

$$x = a\left[\frac{\pi}{6} - \sin \frac{\pi}{6}\right] \tag{16.75}$$

$$= a\left[\frac{\pi}{6} - \frac{1}{2}\right] \tag{16.76}$$

$$= \frac{a}{6}(\pi - 3) \tag{16.77}$$

and

$$x = a\left[\frac{11\pi}{6} - \sin \frac{11\pi}{6}\right] \tag{16.78}$$

$$= a\left[\frac{11\pi}{6} + \frac{1}{2}\right] \tag{16.79}$$

$$= \frac{a}{6}(11\pi + 3) \tag{16.80}$$

Question 20

Consider the case of the two stars to begin.

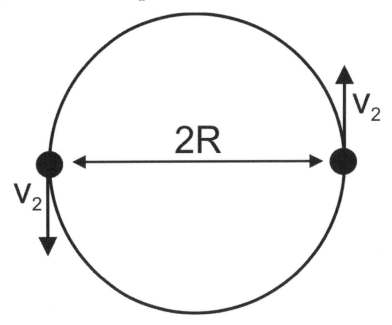

If the gravitational force and centripetal force are equated:

$$\frac{Gmm}{(2R)^2} = \frac{mv_2^2}{2R} \tag{16.81}$$

$$\frac{Gm}{2R} = v_2^2 \tag{16.82}$$

Now consider the case of the three stars.

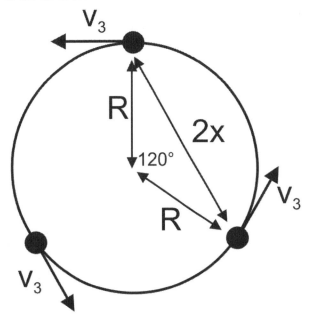

Applying trigonometry to the top half of the triangle formed inside the circle in the diagram:

$$\sin 60 = \frac{x}{R} \tag{16.83}$$

$$\frac{\sqrt{3}}{2} = \frac{x}{R} \tag{16.84}$$

$$x = \frac{\sqrt{3}}{2}R \tag{16.85}$$

$$2x = \sqrt{3}R \tag{16.86}$$

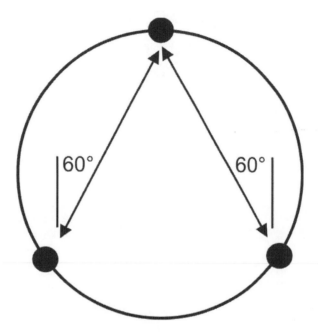

The vertical component of the force on the top star due to the bottom right star is given by:

$$F = \frac{Gmm}{(\sqrt{3}R)^2}\cos 60 \tag{16.87}$$

This is the same as from the bottom left star. The total vertical force on the top star is:

$$F = 2 \times \frac{Gmm}{(\sqrt{3}R)^2}\cos 60 \tag{16.88}$$

$$= \frac{2Gm^2}{3R^2} \times \frac{1}{2} \tag{16.89}$$

$$= \frac{Gm^2}{3R^2} \tag{16.90}$$

The horizontal components of the forces from the bottom stars on the top star cancel out. Setting the vertical force equal to the centripetal force with the radius from the common centre of mass as

R:

$$\frac{mv_3^2}{R} = \frac{Gm^2}{3R^2} \tag{16.91}$$

$$v_3^2 = \frac{Gm}{3R} \tag{16.92}$$

So calculating:

$$\frac{v_3^2}{v_2^2} = \frac{Gm}{3R} \times \frac{2R}{GM} \tag{16.93}$$

$$= \frac{2}{3} \tag{16.94}$$

$$v_3 = \sqrt{\frac{2}{3}}v_2 \tag{16.95}$$

Question 21

Start at the inside with the integration. Then substitute the limits. Finally complete the differentiation.

$$\frac{d}{dt}\int_0^{2t^2}(xt)^4 dx = \frac{d}{dt}\int_0^{2t^2}x^4t^4 dt \tag{16.96}$$

$$= \frac{d}{dt}t^4\int_0^{2t^2}x^4 dx \tag{16.97}$$

$$= \frac{d}{dt}t^4\left[\frac{x^5}{5}\right]_0^{2t^2} \tag{16.98}$$

$$= \frac{d}{dt}t^4\left[\frac{(2t^2)^5}{5}\right] \tag{16.99}$$

$$= \frac{d}{dt}t^4\frac{32t^{10}}{5} \tag{16.100}$$

$$= \frac{d}{dt}\frac{32}{5}t^{14} \tag{16.101}$$

$$= 14 \times \frac{32}{5}t^{13} \tag{16.102}$$

$$= 89.6t^{13} \tag{16.103}$$

Question 22

The general equation of a circle is given by:

$$(x-a)^2 + (y-b)^2 = r^2 \tag{16.104}$$

where the centre of the circle is at (a,b). For circle C_1 express the given equation in the form of the general equation:

$$4(x^2 + 6x + y^2 - 4y + \frac{43}{4}) = 0 \tag{16.105}$$

Complete the square on the x term and the y term separately:

$$x^2 + 6x = x^2 + 6x + 9 - 9 = (x+3)^2 - 9 \tag{16.106}$$
$$y^2 - 4y = y^2 - 4y + 4 - 4 = (y-2)^2 - 4 \tag{16.107}$$

Substituting this back in:

$$(x+3)^2 - 9 + (y-2)^2 - 4 + \frac{43}{4} = 0 \tag{16.108}$$
$$(x+3)^2 + (y-2)^2 = 9 + 4 + \frac{43}{4} \tag{16.109}$$
$$(x+3)^2 + (y-2)^2 = 2.25 \tag{16.110}$$
$$(x+3)^2 + (y-2)^2 = 1.5^2 \tag{16.111}$$

Do the same to the circle C_2:

$$4(x^2 - 10x + y^2 - 2y + \frac{79}{4}) = 0 \tag{16.112}$$
$$x^2 - 10x = x^2 - 10x + 25 - 25 \tag{16.113}$$
$$= (x-5)^2 - 25 \tag{16.114}$$
$$y^2 - 2y = y^2 - 2y + 1 - 1 \tag{16.115}$$
$$= (y-1)^2 - 1 \tag{16.116}$$
$$(x-5)^2 - 25 + (y-1)^2 - 1 + \frac{79}{4} = 0 \tag{16.117}$$
$$(x-5)^2 + (y-1)^2 = 25 + 1 - \frac{79}{4} \tag{16.118}$$
$$(x-5)^2 + (y-1)^2 = 6.25 \tag{16.119}$$
$$(x-5)^2 + (y-1)^2 = 2.5^2 \tag{16.120}$$

The plot looks like this:

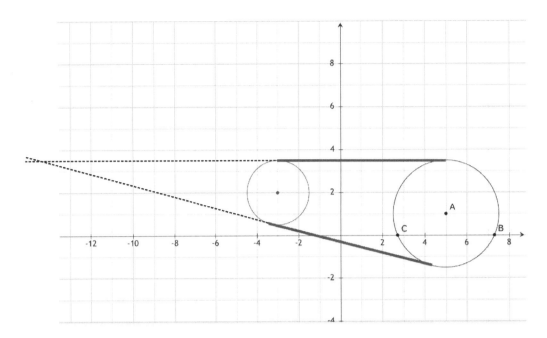

Remember that two tangents to a circle meet at a point. The lengths of the lines are equal. Since the tangents to the small circle will be the same length and the tangents to large circle will be the same length, the lengths of the segment lines joining the tangent points will have equal length. The top segment line starts at the point (-3,3.5) and ends at (5,3.5) so its length is 8 units. The other two tangents are show here:

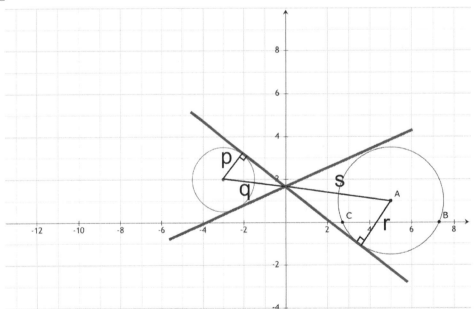

Since the circles have radi in the ratio $1.5/2.5 = 0.6$ then the crossing point of the two tangents will be between the circle centers in the same ratio. So vertically the centers are at 1 and 2, so the crossing point will be at $(0.6/1.6) \times 1 = 0.375$ from the center of the small circle. Horizontally the centers are at -3 and 5 so the crossing point will be $(0.6/1.6) \times 8 = 3$ from the small circle center. Thus the center will be at $(0, 1.625)$. To find the length look at the triangle containing p and q.

Length p is 1.5 and length q is $\sqrt{3^2 + 0.375^2}$. The length of the tangent in the second quadrant is then $\sqrt{3^2 + 0.375^2 - 1.5^2} = 2.625$. Similarly with the triangle containing r and s. The length s is $\sqrt{5^2 + 0.625^2}$ and the length of the tangent is the fourth quadrant is $\sqrt{5^2 + 0.625^2 - 2.5^2} = 4.375$. So the total length of the tangent is $2.625 + 4.375 = 7$.

Question 23

Draw a complete diagram which takes in account the light ray crossing the boundary from n_2 to n_1. Call the angle this ray makes with the normal θ_2.

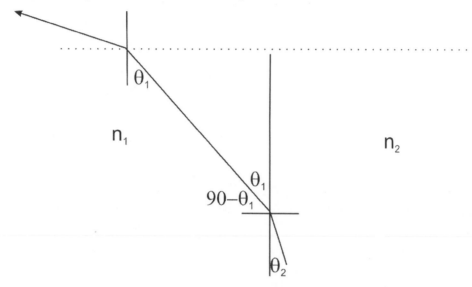

As the ring drops, the angle θ_2 must get larger. The maximum value it can take is $90°$ and so $\sin\theta_2 \rightarrow 1$. So applying Snell's Law at the boundary between n_2 and n_1:

$$n_2 = n_1 \sin(90 - \theta_1) \qquad (16.121)$$
$$= n_1 \cos\theta_1 \qquad (16.122)$$
$$\cos\theta_1 = \frac{n_2}{n_1} \qquad (16.123)$$

Now using a quick sketch we can find $\sin\theta_1$.

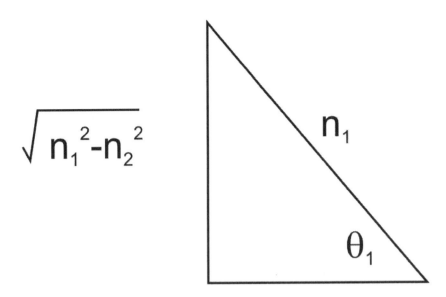

$$\sin \theta_1 = \frac{\sqrt{n_1^2 - n_2^2}}{n_1} \tag{16.124}$$

So applying Snell's Law at the boundary between n_1 and air:

$$\sin \theta_0 = n_1 \times \frac{\sqrt{n_1^2 - n_2^2}}{n_1} \tag{16.125}$$

$$= \sqrt{n_1^2 - n_2^2} \tag{16.126}$$

Using the following diagram we can find the apparent depth, x.

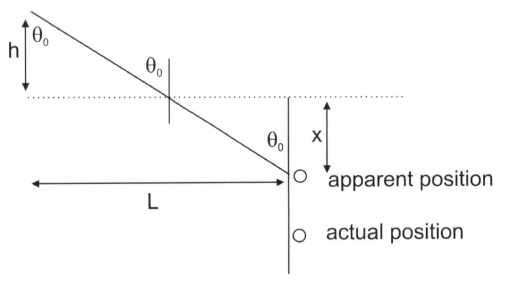

$$\sqrt{n_1^2 - n_2^2} = \frac{L}{\sqrt{(h+x)^2 + L^2}} \tag{16.127}$$

$$n_1^2 - n_2^2 = \frac{L^2}{(h+x)^2 + L^2} \tag{16.128}$$

$$(h+x)^2 = \frac{L^2}{n_1^2 - n_2^2} - L^2 \tag{16.129}$$

$$x = \sqrt{\frac{L^2}{n_1^2 - n_2^2} - L^2} - h \tag{16.130}$$

Chapter 17

Oxford Physics Aptitude Test 2018 Answers

Question 1

Find the differences between successive terms. This gives 1,4,5,9. Spot that the next difference is the sum of the previous two differences. This is a similar idea to the Fibonacci series. So the difference to the next term is 5+9=14. 23 + 14 gives 37. Therefore the answer is C.

Question 2

Motion in a straight line only occurs when the resultant force is zero. Since there is only a gravitational force acting, there can't be motion in a straight line. So orbit 5 is not possible. Therefore the answer is C.

Question 3

Option A: $CVm^{-1} = N$ since $F = qE$ and units for E can be Vm^{-1}. Option B: $ATm = N$ since $F = BIL$. Option C: $kgms^{-2} = N$ since $F = ma$. Option D: $Jm^{-1} = N$ since $W = Fd$. Finally option E does not equal Newtons, so must be the odd one out. Therefore the answer is E.

Question 4

You can either draw a tree diagram and multiply along each branch or consider all the possible permutations. Option A: RRR

$$\frac{2}{3} \times \frac{2}{3} \times \frac{2}{3} = \frac{8}{27} \qquad (17.1)$$

for option B: LLL

$$\frac{1}{3} \times \frac{1}{3} \times \frac{1}{3} = \frac{1}{27} \qquad (17.2)$$

for option C: LRR, RLR or RRL

$$\frac{1}{3} \times \frac{2}{3} \times \frac{2}{3} \times 3 = \frac{12}{27} \qquad (17.3)$$

301

for option D: RLL, LRL or LLR

$$\frac{2}{3} \times \frac{1}{3} \times \frac{1}{3} \times 3 = \frac{6}{27} \tag{17.4}$$

Therefore the answer is C, since this has the largest probability.

Question 5

Sketch a table with the cup number and the volume of tea:

cup	1	2	3	4
volume	V	α V	α^2 V	α^3 V

This is a geometric progression, so we use the equation for the sum to infinity and set this equal to $3V$. The first term is V and the common ratio is α:

$$\sum_{\infty} = \frac{a}{1-r} \tag{17.5}$$

$$3V = \frac{V}{1-\alpha} \tag{17.6}$$

$$3 = \frac{1}{1-\alpha} \tag{17.7}$$

$$1-\alpha = \frac{1}{3} \tag{17.8}$$

$$\alpha = \frac{2}{3} \tag{17.9}$$

Therefore the answer is C.

Question 6

If the centre of the string is held, there must be node at the centre. Therefore there must be the same number of loops each side of the centre and so the standing waves which can be set up must have an even number of loops so n=2,4,6 etc. The general equation of the wavelength is:

$$\lambda = \frac{2L}{n} \tag{17.10}$$

and here n=2,4,6 etc so:

$$\lambda = \frac{2L}{2} = L \tag{17.11}$$

$$\lambda = \frac{2L}{4} = \frac{L}{2} \tag{17.12}$$

$$\lambda = \frac{2L}{6} = \frac{L}{3} \tag{17.13}$$

so the answer is B.

Question 7

The work done by the brakes must transfer all the kinetic energy of the car away from kinetic energy and into thermal energy so we can equate work done with kinetic energy:

$$\frac{1}{2}mv^2 = Fd \tag{17.14}$$

$$F = \frac{1}{2}\frac{mv^2}{d} \tag{17.15}$$

Therefore the answer is A.

Question 8

If we a looking for a minimum, we should differentiate the function and set this equal to zero and solve for x:

$$y = x^2 + x - 3x - 3 \tag{17.16}$$

$$= x^2 - 2x - 3 \tag{17.17}$$

$$\frac{dy}{dx} = 2x - 2 \tag{17.18}$$

$$2x - 2 = 0 \tag{17.19}$$

$$2x = 2 \tag{17.20}$$

$$x = 1 \tag{17.21}$$

Therefore the answer is A.

Question 9

Lines which intersect at right angles have gradients which multiply to -1. As the gradient of the line $y = mx + c$ is m, the gradient of the line $y = 2x - 2$ is 2 so the gradient of the line we are looking for is $-\frac{1}{2}$. At $x = 1$ the line $y = 2x - 2$ goes through the point $(1, 0)$ so we know the line we require also goes through this point. Since we now have the gradient and a point, we can find the equation of the line by substitution into $y = mx + c$:

$$y = mx + c \tag{17.22}$$

$$0 = -\frac{1}{2} \times 1 + c \tag{17.23}$$

$$c = \frac{1}{2} \tag{17.24}$$

$$y = -\frac{1}{2}x + \frac{1}{2} \tag{17.25}$$

Therefore the answer is B.

Question 10

Replace the inequality sign with an equals and try to solve:

$$x^3 - x^2 - x + 1 = 0 \tag{17.26}$$

We can't solve a cubic (easily) but we notice that all our answer options are related to -1 and 1. So we test some values each side of -1 and 1: when $x = -2$ the function is equal to -9, when $x = 0$ the function is equal to 1 and when $x = 2$ the function is equal to 3. Therefore the answer is E.

Question 11

First calculate the area of the roof:

$$A = 100 \times 50 = 5000m^2 \tag{17.27}$$

Then calculate the mass of the roof:

$$
\begin{aligned}
m &= massperunitarea \times area \tag{17.28} \\
&= 100 \times 5000 \tag{17.29} \\
&= 500,000 kg \tag{17.30}
\end{aligned}
$$

Find the perimeter of the walls:

$$
\begin{aligned}
p &= 100 + 100 + 50 + 50 \tag{17.31} \\
&= 300m \tag{17.32}
\end{aligned}
$$

Then find the cross sectional area of the walls which have thickness 0.1m:

$$A = 300 \times 0.1 = 30m^2 \tag{17.33}$$

Finally find the stress:

$$\sigma \quad = \quad \frac{F}{A} \tag{17.34}$$

$$= \quad \frac{500,000 \times 10}{30} \tag{17.35}$$

$$= \quad 1.7 \times 10^5 N/m^2 \tag{17.36}$$

$$= \quad 0.17 N/mm^2 \tag{17.37}$$

We have used $1m^2 = 1 \times 10^6 mm^2$ and multiplied the mass by g to find the force. So the answer must be C.

Question 12

When a light ray travels into a material with a higher refractive index (a more dense medium) the wave slows down and refracts towards the normal. If it travelled through a large number of plates with increasing refractive index the wave will be travelling along the normal - making an angle of $0°$ to the normal. Therefore the answer is C. This is similar to the way waves on the shore approach parallel to the beach as the wave has slowed down and refracted towards the normal as the sea depth gradually reduces up to the beach.

Question 13

Consider one branch at a time. So the top branch simplifies to C/2 since they combine like resistors in parallel and the total resistance of two identical resistors in parallel is R/2. Now considering the middle branch: the two capacitors in parallel on the right simplify to 2C. Then following the formula to find the total capacitance of capacitors C and 2C in series:

$$\frac{1}{C_T} \quad = \quad \frac{1}{C} + \frac{1}{2C} \tag{17.38}$$

$$= \quad \frac{2}{2C} + \frac{1}{2C} \tag{17.39}$$

$$= \quad \frac{3}{2C} \tag{17.40}$$

$$C_T \quad = \quad \frac{2C}{3} \tag{17.41}$$

Finally the bottom branch gives a capacitance of 3C. Combining all the branches simply means adding the capacitances of each individual branch:

$$C_T \quad = \quad \frac{C}{2} + \frac{2C}{3} + 3C \tag{17.42}$$

$$= \quad \frac{25C}{6} \tag{17.43}$$

Question 14

Use the identity:

$$\log_a b = \frac{\log_c b}{\log_c a} \tag{17.44}$$

to rewrite $\log_x 25$ matching the base to the base used on the other side of the equation:

$$\log_x 25 = \frac{\log_5 25}{\log_5 x} \tag{17.45}$$

so:

$$\frac{\log_5 25}{\log_5 x} = \log_5 x \tag{17.46}$$

$$\frac{2}{\log_5 x} = \log_5 x \tag{17.47}$$

$$2 = (\log_5 x)^2 \tag{17.48}$$

$$\sqrt{2} = \log_5 x \tag{17.49}$$

$$5^{\sqrt{2}} = x \tag{17.50}$$

Question 15

part a

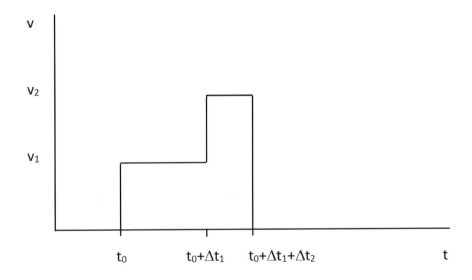

part b

$$\langle v \rangle_t = \frac{distance}{time} = \frac{area}{time} \tag{17.51}$$

$$= \frac{\Delta t_1 v_1 + \Delta t_2 v_2}{\Delta t_1 + \Delta t_2} \tag{17.52}$$

$$= \frac{2 \times 1 + 1 \times 2}{2 + 1} \tag{17.53}$$

$$= \frac{4}{3} m/s \tag{17.54}$$

part c

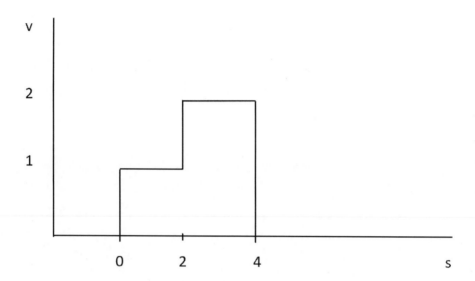

part d

$$\langle v \rangle_s = \frac{area}{displacement} \tag{17.55}$$

$$= \frac{\Delta s_1 v_1 + \Delta s_2 v_2}{\Delta s_1 + \Delta s_2} \tag{17.56}$$

$$= \frac{1 \times 2 + 2 \times 2}{2 + 2} \tag{17.57}$$

$$= \frac{6}{4} = 1.5 m/s \tag{17.58}$$

part e

$$\langle v \rangle_c = \langle v \rangle_t$$

part f

Integrate and divide by t.

Question 16

The area of the lead is given by πr^2. To find the area of the hexagon, consider of the triangles which make it up:

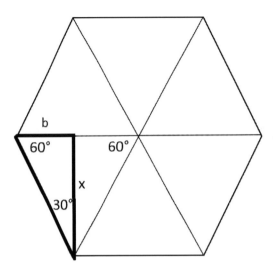

The side length b of the black triangle is given by $\tan 60 = x/b$, so $b = x \tan 60 = x/\sqrt{3}$. The area of the black triangle is:

$$
\begin{align}
A &= \frac{1}{2} \times b \times h \tag{17.59}\\
&= \frac{1}{2} \times x/\sqrt{3} \times x \tag{17.60}\\
&= \frac{x^2}{2\sqrt{3}} \tag{17.61}
\end{align}
$$

The area of the hexagon is 12 times this area:

$$
A = \frac{6x^2}{\sqrt{3}} \tag{17.62}
$$

So then equating the area of the hexagon with 4 times the area of the circle:

$$
\begin{align}
\frac{6x^2}{\sqrt{3}} &= 4\pi r^2 \tag{17.63}\\
x^2 &= \frac{4\pi\sqrt{3}r^2}{6} \tag{17.64}\\
x &= \sqrt{\frac{4\pi\sqrt{3}}{6}}r \tag{17.65}
\end{align}
$$

Question 17

Use the binomial expansion with the coefficients from Pascal's triangle:

$$\int_0^{0.1} (1+9)^9 dx = \int_0^{0.1} 1 + 9x + 35x^2 + 84x^3 + \tag{17.66}$$

$$126x^4 + 126x^5 + 84x^6 + 36x^7 + 9x^8 + x^9 dx \tag{17.67}$$

$$= x + \frac{9x^2}{2} + \frac{36x^3}{3} + \frac{84x^4}{4} + \frac{126x^5}{5} \tag{17.68}$$

$$+ \frac{126x^6}{6} + \frac{84x^7}{7} + \frac{36x^8}{8} + \frac{x^9}{9} + \frac{x^{10}}{10} \Big|_0^{0.1} \tag{17.69}$$

$$= 0.1 + \frac{9}{2} \times 0.01 + 12 \times 1 \times 10^{-3} + 21 \times 1 \times 10^{-4} \tag{17.70}$$

$$+ 25.2 \times 1 \times 10^{-5} + 21 \times 1 \times 10^{-6} \tag{17.71}$$

$$+ 12 \times 1 \times 10^{-7} + 4.5 \times 1 \times 10^{-8} + 1 \times 10^{-9} \tag{17.72}$$

$$+ 1 \times 10^{-11} \tag{17.73}$$

$$= 0.159374246 \tag{17.74}$$

90 percent of this value is 0.143436821, so we get to within 10 percent of the final value using just the first two terms, so we only need to expand as far as x^1.

Question 18

part a

Resolve forces acting on one of the balls vertically and horizontally. Note that the separation of masses is $(x - 2\delta x)$. So vertically:

$$T \cos\theta = mg \tag{17.75}$$

and horizontally:

$$T \sin\theta = \frac{Gmm}{(x - 2\delta x)^2} \tag{17.76}$$

Dividing these equations:

$$\frac{T \sin\theta}{T \cos\theta} = \frac{Gm}{g(x - 2\delta x)^2} \tag{17.77}$$

$$\tan\theta = \frac{Gm}{g(x^2 - 4x\delta x + 4\delta x^2)} \tag{17.78}$$

Since $\delta x << L$ then $\tan\theta \approx \delta x/L$ so

$$\frac{\delta x}{L} = \frac{Gm}{g(x^2 - 4x\delta x + 4\delta x^2)} \tag{17.79}$$

$$\delta x(x^2 - 4x\delta x + 4\delta x^2) = \frac{GmL}{g} \tag{17.80}$$

$$\delta x x^2 - 4x\delta x^2 + 4\delta x^3 = \frac{GmL}{g} \tag{17.81}$$

$$\tag{17.82}$$

Since δx is small we can ignore the term δx^3 since this will be almost zero.

$$\delta x x^2 - 4x\delta x^2 = \frac{GmL}{g} \tag{17.83}$$

$$\frac{\delta x x^2}{4} - x\delta x^2 = \frac{GmL}{4g} \tag{17.84}$$

$$x\delta x^2 - \frac{x^2}{4}\delta x + \frac{GmL}{4g} = 0 \tag{17.85}$$

$$\delta x^2 - \frac{x}{4}\delta x + \frac{GmL}{4xg} = 0 \tag{17.86}$$

Using the quadratic formula with $a = 1$, $b = -x/4$ and $c = GmL/4gx$ gives:

$$\frac{\frac{x}{4} \pm \sqrt{\frac{x^2}{16} - \frac{4GmL}{4gx}}}{2} = \delta x \tag{17.87}$$

$$\frac{x}{8} - \sqrt{\left(\frac{x}{8}\right)^2 - \frac{GmL}{4gx}} = \delta x \tag{17.88}$$

We are not using the positive answer as in the limit $m \to 0$ the deflection $\delta x \to 0$. This can only happen with the negative solution selected and the square root becoming equal to $x/8$.

part b

The wires would hang vertically when the electric force of repulsion is equal to the gravitational force of attraction:

$$\frac{Gmm}{r^2} = \frac{kQQ}{r^2} \tag{17.89}$$

$$Gm^2 = kQ^2 \tag{17.90}$$

$$Q = \sqrt{\frac{G}{k}}m \tag{17.91}$$

Question 19

part a

Calculate the resistance of each bulb when connected individually to the 100V supply. The question states we can assume the resistance of each bulb is then constant.

$$P = \frac{V^2}{R} \tag{17.92}$$

$$R = \frac{V^2}{P} \tag{17.93}$$

$$R_A = \frac{100^2}{100} \tag{17.94}$$

$$= 100\Omega \tag{17.95}$$

$$R_B = \frac{100^2}{20} \tag{17.96}$$

$$= 500\Omega \tag{17.97}$$

We can now say that since the current through the two bulbs in series is the same and $P = I^2 R$ the brightest bulb is the one with the highest resistance: bulb B. The ratio of the brightness is given by:

$$\frac{P_A}{P_B} = \frac{I^2 R_A}{I^2 R_B} \tag{17.98}$$

$$= \frac{R_A}{R_B} \tag{17.99}$$

$$= \frac{100}{500} = \frac{1}{5} \tag{17.100}$$

part b

If the bulbs were connected in parallel then the lower resistance bulb would draw more current. Since $P = I^2 R$ resistance would be lower once over, but current is higher twice over since it is squared, so bulb A will now be brighter.

Question 20

part a

Simple cubic. Since it can't be body centred cubic because $1 + 1 + 1 = 3$ which is not 2 times an integer. It can't be face centred cubic either because of the third word in the bullet point referring to all the planes being all even or odd.

part b

$$a = d\sqrt{h^2 + k^2 + l^2} \tag{17.101}$$

$$= 0.224\sqrt{3} = 0.38798 \tag{17.102}$$

$$= 0.195\sqrt{4} = 0.39 \tag{17.103}$$

$$= 0.137\sqrt{8} = 0.38749 \tag{17.104}$$

$$= 0.117\sqrt{11} = 0.38885 \tag{17.105}$$

Finding the average of these gives $a = 0.389$.

part c

Since volume is equal to length cubed and volume is constant:

$$V = L^3 = N^2 a^3 \tag{17.106}$$

$$N^2 a^3 = x^2 \times \frac{2}{3} N a \tag{17.107}$$

$$\frac{3N^2 a^2}{2} = x^2 \tag{17.108}$$

$$\sqrt{\frac{3}{2}} N a = x \tag{17.109}$$

Question 21

part a

$$F(r) = m\omega^2 r \tag{17.110}$$

part b

$$W = \int F(r)dr = \int_0^{r_0} m\omega^2 r\, dr \tag{17.111}$$

part c

Rotational kinetic energy, increase in angular velocity.

part d

$$J = I\omega \tag{17.112}$$

$$= (mr^2 + I_p)\omega \tag{17.113}$$

$$\omega = \frac{J}{mr^2 + I_p} \tag{17.114}$$

part e

$$W = \int_0^{r_0} m\frac{J^2 r}{(mr^2 + I_p)^2}\,dr \tag{17.115}$$

$$= J^2 \int_0^{r_0} \frac{r}{\left(r^2 + \frac{I_p}{m}\right)^2}\,dr \tag{17.116}$$

$$= J^2 \left[\frac{-1}{2\left(\frac{I_p}{m} + r^2\right)}\right]_0^{r_0} \tag{17.117}$$

$$= J^2 \left[\frac{1}{\frac{2I_p}{m}} - \frac{1}{\frac{2}{m}\left(I_p + mr_0^2\right)}\right] \tag{17.118}$$

$$= \frac{J^2 m}{2}\left[\frac{1}{I_p} - \frac{1}{I_p + mr_0^2}\right] \tag{17.119}$$

Question 22

The general equation of a circle is given by $(x-a)^2 + (y-b)^2 = r^2$. We need to try to write the equation given in this form since we then know the radius, r, and the centre (a, b).

$$(x-4)^2 + (y+2)^2 + c = x^2 + y^2 - 8x + 4y + 4 \tag{17.120}$$

$$x^2 - 8x + 16 + y^2 + 4y + 4 + c = x^2 + y^2 - 8x + 4y + 4 \tag{17.121}$$

$$x^2 + y^2 - 8x + 4y + 20 + c = x^2 + y^2 - 8x + 4y + 4 \tag{17.122}$$

$$20 + c = 4 \tag{17.123}$$

$$c = -16 \tag{17.124}$$

$$(x-4)^2 + (y+2)^2 - 16 = 0 \tag{17.125}$$

$$(x-4)^2 + (y+2)^2 = 4^2 \tag{17.126}$$

It is then useful to draw a sketch of the circle and the lines:

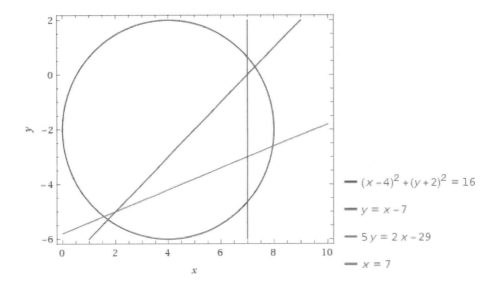

We now need to find the coordinates of the three vertices of the triangle. The top right is where lines $x = 7$ and $y = x - 7$ cross. This is at the point $(7, 0)$. The bottom right is where the lines $x = 7$ and $5y = 2x - 29$ cross. This is at $(7,-3)$. Finally the bottom left is where the lines $5y = 2x - 29$ and $y = x - 7$ meet which is at $(2, -5)$. We can find the area of the triangle using the base as the side of the triangle from $(7, 0)$ to $(7, -3)$ and the height as the distance from the point $(2, -5)$ to the line $x = 7$:

$$A = \frac{1}{2} \times 3 \times 5 \tag{17.127}$$

$$= 7.5 \tag{17.128}$$

So the area required is:

$$16\pi - 7.5 \tag{17.129}$$

Question 23

The natural log a number ≤ 0 is undefined. So:

$$3x + 10 > 0 \tag{17.130}$$

$$x > \frac{-10}{3} \tag{17.131}$$

The natural log of 1 is 0, and we can't have a divide by zero so we can't have:

$$3x + 10 = 1 \tag{17.132}$$

$$x = -3 \tag{17.133}$$

We can't take the square root of a negative number so:

$$x^2 - 2 \geq 0 \tag{17.134}$$

$$x^2 \geq 2 \tag{17.135}$$

$$|x| \geq \sqrt{2} \tag{17.136}$$

So the range is:

$$\frac{-10}{3} < \quad x \quad < -3 \tag{17.137}$$

$$-3 < \quad x \quad \leq -\sqrt{2} \tag{17.138}$$

$$x \quad \geq \sqrt{2} \tag{17.139}$$

Chapter 18

Oxford Physics Aptitude Test 2019 Answers

Question 1

There is a common ratio of -1/3 between each term. So the next term is $-12 \times -1/3 = 4$. So the answer is D.

Question 2

Noticing that the right hand side of the second equation is $\log 2$ and that $2^5 = 32$:

$$\log x + 2 \log y = 5 \log 2 \tag{18.1}$$

$$\log y - \log x = \log 2 \tag{18.2}$$

Substituting the second equation into the first:

$$\log x + 2 \log y = 5(\log y - \log x) \tag{18.3}$$

$$\log x + 2 \log y = 5 \log y - 5 \log x \tag{18.4}$$

$$6 \log x = 3 \log y \tag{18.5}$$

$$2 \log x = \log y \tag{18.6}$$

$$\log x^2 = \log y \tag{18.7}$$

$$x^2 = y \tag{18.8}$$

This is only true for answer A.

Question 3

$$\langle E_{tot} \rangle = \langle T_{tot} \rangle + \langle V_{tot} \rangle \tag{18.9}$$

$$= \frac{n}{2} \langle V_{tot} \rangle + \langle V_{tot} \rangle \tag{18.10}$$

$$\tag{18.11}$$

Since for gravity $V(r) = -GMm/r$ then $n = -1$:

$$\langle E_{tot} \rangle = -\frac{1}{2} \langle V_{tot} \rangle + \langle V_{tot} \rangle \tag{18.12}$$

$$= \frac{\langle V_{tot} \rangle}{2} \tag{18.13}$$

So the answer is C.

Question 4

$$g_{Earth} = \frac{GM}{R^2} \tag{18.14}$$

If the radius is half, the volume is an eighth since $V = 4\pi r^3/3$. This means the mass is an eighth (assuming constant density). Since density is double, the mass is a quarter, rather than an eighth. So:

$$g_{planet} = \frac{2G(M/4)}{(R/2)^2} \tag{18.15}$$

$$= \frac{2GM}{R^2} \tag{18.16}$$

$$\frac{g_{planet}}{g_{Earth}} = \frac{2GM}{R^2} \frac{R^2}{GM} = 2 \tag{18.17}$$

So the answer is A.

Question 5

Re-write as:

$$\frac{1}{\cos^2 \theta} + \alpha \frac{\sin \theta}{\cos \theta} = 0 \tag{18.18}$$

Then make a substitution $y = 1/\cos\theta$:

$$y^2 + \alpha y \sin \theta = 0 \tag{18.19}$$

To find real solutions the discriminant, $b^2 - 4ac$ must be greater than or equal to zero, so:

$$\alpha^2 \sin^2 \theta - 4 \times 1 \times 0 \geq 0 \tag{18.20}$$

$\sin^2 \theta$ is always greater than or equal to 1, so α must be greater than or equal to 0. So the answer is D.

Question 6

Find the probability but dividing the number of outcomes we want by the total number of outcomes and adding the possible combinations of achieving this. So we either want a red ball then a blue or a blue then a red:

$$\frac{r}{b+r} \times \frac{b}{b+r-1} + \frac{b}{b+r} \times \frac{r}{b+r-1} = \frac{2br}{(b+r)(b+r-1)} \tag{18.21}$$

So the answer is A.

Question 7

This is like binary counting. A finger can in two states either stretched out or curled up. So we just need to work out $2^{10} = 1024$.

Question 8

Odd functions with symmetric limits give an area under the graph (i.e. an integral) that is zero, since area below the x axis is negative and area above the x axis is positive. For I_1 this is an even function multiplied by an odd function. This gives an odd function so the area is zero. For I_2 this is an even function since be have x^2 so this gives a non-zero result. For I_3 this is an even function again giving a non-zero result. For I_4 this is an odd function multiplied by an even function giving an odd function which has a zero area. Thus the answer is A.

Question 9

For the magnetic field to be double between the wires, the field from each individual wire must add up. Thus the current needs to be traveling in opposite directions in the wires and the currents need to be equal. Thus the answer is D.

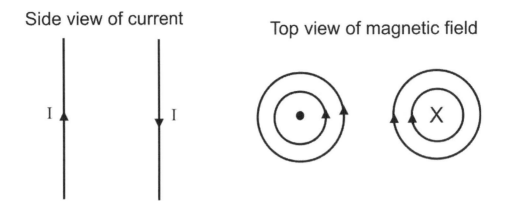

Question 10

For a full moon the order of the celestial bodies must be Sun, Earth, Moon. Thus from the moon the Earth is seen in the New phase.

Question 11

Brightness is related to power output. This is calculated using $P = VI$ so the power output / brightness is highest when the product of current and pd are highest. Current and pd are both maximum when the resistance of the resistors is smallest. This is because this directly leads to the largest current and when the resistance is smallest the bulb is a larger share of the total resistance so receives a larger share of the supply pd. The smallest resistance occurs when both switches are closed since the two branches are in parallel. The bulb is least bright when there is the smallest product of the current and pd. This occurs when the resistance of the resistors is highest. This occurs when only B is closed. So the answer is C

Question 12

This is similar to standing waves on a string - it's just standing waves in a tube. A node is formed at the closed end and an antinode at the open end. The lowest frequency note produced has a wavelength 4 times the length of the tube. So:

$$v = f\lambda \tag{18.22}$$

$$v = f_{min}4L \tag{18.23}$$

$$L = \frac{v}{4f_{min}} \tag{18.24}$$

So the answer is B.

Question 13

part a

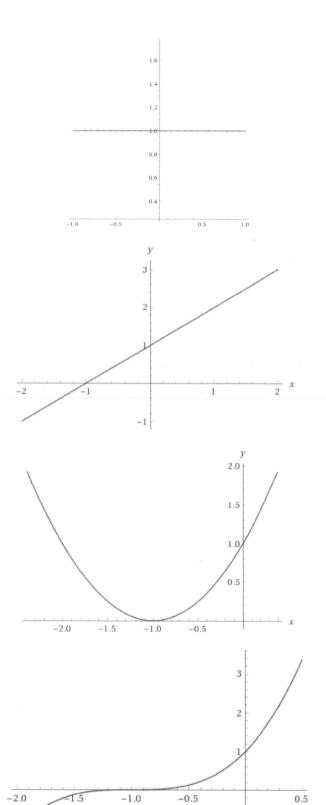

The common point is $(0, 1)$.

part b

All the graphs have a gradient which changes with x and the graphs touch or cross the x axis with gradient equal to zero.

Question 14

part a

At $t = t_{1/2}$, $N_A(t) = N_{A0}/2$ so:

$$\frac{1}{2} = e^{-\lambda t_{1/2}} \tag{18.25}$$

$$\ln \frac{1}{2} = -\lambda t_{1/2} \tag{18.26}$$

$$\ln 2 = \lambda t_{1/2} \tag{18.27}$$

$$t_{1/2} = \frac{\ln 2}{\lambda} \tag{18.28}$$

part b

$$N_B(t) = N_{A0} - N_{A0}e^{-\lambda t} + N_{B0} \tag{18.29}$$

part c

We are looking for the time taken for the number of A to fall to N_{A0}/x because then these will have decayed into B i.e.

time	N_A	N_B
0	xB	B
t	B	xB

So:

$$\frac{N_{A0}}{x} = N_{Z0}e^{-\lambda t} \tag{18.30}$$

$$\frac{1}{x} = e^{-\lambda t} \tag{18.31}$$

$$\ln x = \lambda t \tag{18.32}$$

$$t = \frac{\ln x}{\lambda} \tag{18.33}$$

This matches up to the equation found in part a if $x = 2$.

Question 15

part a

When the ray crosses a boundary from liquid to glass it refracts towards the normal, when it crosses from glass to air it refracts away from the normal. The ray in the air should not be parallel to the dashed line since $n_l \neq n_a$. When the ray crosses from air into glass it refracts towards the normal and finally when it crosses from glass liquid it refracts away from the normal. It should emerge parallel to the entry ray. The two rays in the glass should be parallel to each other.

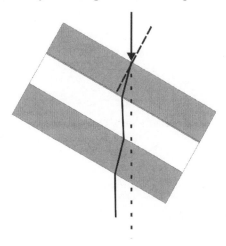

part b

Because the ray emerges parallel to the entry ray as the angle θ_i is increased the ray appears to shift further to the left. Eventually the ray leaving the apparatus disappears. This happens when a critical angle is reached in the apparatus. So to operate the apparatus the cell is rotated until the emergent light ray disappears. At this point the angle θ_i is measured.

We know that total internal refection occurs when light travels from a dense to less dense material. So in this context, there are two places TIR may occur: the glass to air boundary or the glass to liquid boundary. Which is it? We know that the critical angle for light traveling from medium 1 to medium 2 is given by:

$$n_1 \sin \theta_c = n_2 \sin 90 \tag{18.34}$$

$$n_1 \sin \theta_c = n_2 \tag{18.35}$$

$$\theta_c = \sin^{-1}\left(\frac{n_2}{n_l}\right) \tag{18.36}$$

Since the fraction n_a/n_g is smaller than n_l/n_g TIR will occur first (as θ_i is increased) at the glass -

air boundary. At the liquid - glass boundary:

$$n_g \sin \theta_g = n_l \sin \theta_i \qquad (18.37)$$

and at the glass - air boundary:

$$n_g \sin \theta_g = n_a \sin 90 \qquad (18.38)$$

So:

$$n_l \sin \theta_i = n_a \qquad (18.39)$$

part c

Require a larger θ_i so it can be measured with lower percentage uncertainty therefore need n_a/n_l to be closer to 1. This means that n_a needs to be larger - perhaps the liquid should be used rather than air between the glass.

Question 16

part a

$$E = \frac{hc}{\lambda} \qquad (18.40)$$

part b

$$\Delta E = E_p - E_q \qquad (18.41)$$
$$\frac{hc}{\lambda} = \frac{-hcR}{p^2} - \frac{-hcR}{q^2} \qquad (18.42)$$
$$\frac{1}{\lambda} = \frac{R}{q^2} - \frac{R}{p^2} \qquad (18.43)$$
$$\frac{1}{\lambda} = R\left(\frac{1}{q^2} - \frac{1}{p^2}\right) \qquad (18.44)$$

part c

For set A, substitute a set of numbers for level $p = q + 1$:

$$\frac{1}{121.57 \times 10^{-9} \times 10976731.6} = \left(\frac{1}{q^2} - \frac{1}{(q+1)^2}\right) \qquad (18.45)$$
$$0.75 = \left(\frac{1}{q^2} - \frac{1}{(q+1)^2}\right) \qquad (18.46)$$

At the point, since we know that q is going to be a low integer. We can guess $q = 1$ and check if this works. It does. Hence $q = 1$.

For set B we get:

$$0.0225 = \left(\frac{1}{q^2} - \frac{1}{(q+1)^2}\right) \tag{18.47}$$

Testing values for q rapidly gives us $q = 4$.

Finally for set C we get:

$$0.0122 = \left(\frac{1}{q^2} - \frac{1}{(q+1)^2}\right) \tag{18.48}$$

and $q = 5$.

Question 17

part a

Begin with an equation for f:

$$f = \frac{A_g}{4x^2R^2} \tag{18.49}$$

Now write an equation for A_g which is the area of the small central circle:

$$\pi R^2 \tag{18.50}$$

plus the shaded areas in the 4 corners which is the area of the square minus the area of the large circle:

$$4x^2R^2 - \pi x^2 R^2 \tag{18.51}$$

plus the area spanned by the angle theta which is the area of the sector of the large circle minus the double counted area of the sector of the small circle:

$$\pi x^2 R^2 \frac{\theta}{2\pi} - \pi R^2 \frac{\theta}{2\pi} \tag{18.52}$$

So:

$$A_g = \pi R^2 + 4x^2R^2 - \pi x^2 R^2 + \pi x^2 R^2 \frac{\theta}{2\pi} - \pi R^2 \frac{\theta}{2\pi} \tag{18.53}$$

and:

$$f = \frac{(4x^2 + \pi - \pi x^2)R^2 + \frac{\theta}{2}R^2(x^2 - 1)}{4x^2 R^2} \tag{18.54}$$

$$= \frac{4x^2 + \pi - \pi x^2 + \frac{\theta}{2}(x^2 - 1)}{4x^2} \tag{18.55}$$

$$\theta = \frac{2(4fx^2 - 4x^2 - \pi + \pi x^2)}{x^2 - 1} \tag{18.56}$$

$$= \frac{2((4f - 4 + \pi)x^2 - \pi)}{x^2 - 1} \tag{18.57}$$

$$= \frac{-2\pi - 2(4 - \pi - 4f)x^2}{x^2 - 1} \tag{18.58}$$

$$= \frac{-2\pi + 2\pi x^2 - 2(4 - 4f)x^2}{x^2 - 1} \tag{18.59}$$

$$= \frac{2\pi(x^2 - 1)}{x^2 - 1} - \frac{8(1 - f)x^2}{x^2 - 1} \tag{18.60}$$

$$= 2\pi - \frac{8(1 - f)x^2}{x^2 - 1} \tag{18.61}$$

where $B = 2\pi$ and $C(f) = 8(1 - f)$.

part b

$\theta = 2\pi - 4.5 = 1.7832$

Question 18

$$e^x + 9 = 2e^{-x} + 10 \tag{18.62}$$

$$e^x = 2e^{-x} + 1 \tag{18.63}$$

$$e^x = \frac{2}{e^x} + 1 \tag{18.64}$$

Multiply through by e^x:

$$e^{2x} = 2 + e^x \tag{18.65}$$

Make a substitution $y = e^x$ and solve the resulting quadratic in y:

$$y^2 = 2 + y \tag{18.66}$$

$$y^2 - y - 2 = 0 \tag{18.67}$$

$$(y - 2)(y + 1) = 0 \tag{18.68}$$

$$y = 2 \tag{18.69}$$

$$y = -1 \tag{18.70}$$

Since $y = e^x$ then when $y = -1$ there is no solution. When $y = 2$, $x = \ln 2$.

Question 19

part a

First consider conservation of momentum. This applies horizontally, and separately to vertical motion. The initial vertical momentum is

$$p_i = 2 \times (1 + 2 + 3 + 4) = 20 gm/s \tag{18.71}$$

If m_4 has a final vertical momentum of 4 gm/s then m_1 will have a final vertical momentum of 16 gm/s.

Since horizontal momentum was zero before the explosion then it will also be zero after the collision. The two particles moving horizontally are m_2 and m_3.

$$\frac{m_2}{m_3} = \frac{2}{3} \tag{18.72}$$

then

$$\frac{v_2}{v_3} = -\frac{3}{2} \tag{18.73}$$

Since energy is conserved then total kinetic energy before plus the 1J released must equal the total kinetic energy afterwards:

$$1 + \frac{5 \times 2^2}{1000} = \frac{0.5 \times 16^2}{1000} + \frac{1 \times (3/2v_3)^2}{1000} + \frac{1.5 \times v_3^2}{1000} + \frac{2 \times 1^2}{1000} \tag{18.74}$$

$$1000 + 20 = 128 + 2.25v_3^2 + 1.5v_3^2 + 2 \tag{18.75}$$

$$1020 = 130 + 3.75v_3^2 \tag{18.76}$$

$$v_3 = 15.4 m/s \tag{18.77}$$

$$v_2 = -\frac{3}{2}v_3 = -23.1 m/s \tag{18.78}$$

part b

m_2, m_3 and m_4 would all need to go in the same direction vertically downwards. m_1 (the particle with the lowest mass) would then travel upwards with the initial momentum of the rocket and the momentum of all the other particles moving downwards.

Question 20

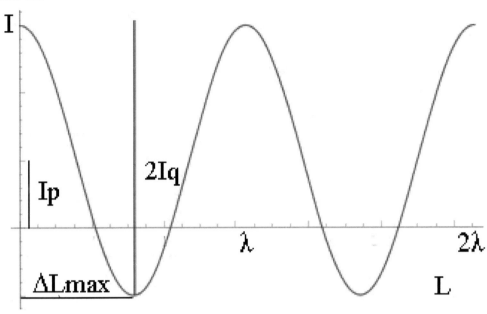

Question 21

part a

$$L_{min} = nL \tag{18.79}$$

part b

$$L_1 = \delta L \tag{18.80}$$
$$L_2 = 2\delta L \tag{18.81}$$
$$L_4 = 4\delta L \tag{18.82}$$
$$L_i = 2^{i-1}\delta L \tag{18.83}$$

part c

$$n_{min} = \log_2\left(\frac{\Delta L}{\delta L}\right) = \frac{\log_{10}\left(\frac{\Delta L}{\delta L}\right)}{\log_{10} 2} \tag{18.84}$$

Question 22

The volume of a cone is given by:

$$V = \frac{\pi}{3}r^2 h \tag{18.85}$$

Substituting the terms in the question for the total volume of the cone:

$$V = \frac{\pi}{3}\left(\frac{D}{2}\right)^2 H \tag{18.86}$$

$$= \frac{\pi}{12}D^2 H \tag{18.87}$$

The volume of the liquid is given by:

$$\frac{V}{2} = \frac{\pi}{12}d^2 h \tag{18.88}$$

$$V = \frac{\pi}{6}d^2 h \tag{18.89}$$

Where d is the diameter of the cone of liquid. Equating the two equations for V:

$$\frac{\pi}{12}D^2 H = \frac{\pi}{6}d^2 h \tag{18.90}$$

$$D^2 H = 2d^2 h \tag{18.91}$$

$$\frac{D^2 H}{2h} = d^2 \tag{18.92}$$

$$\tag{18.93}$$

By similar triangles:

$$\frac{D}{H} = \frac{d}{h} \tag{18.94}$$

$$d^2 = \frac{h^2 D^2}{H^2} \tag{18.95}$$

Equating the two equations for d^2:

$$\frac{D^2 H}{2h} = \frac{h^2 D^2}{H^2} \tag{18.96}$$

$$H^3 = 2h^3 \tag{18.97}$$

$$h = \frac{H}{\sqrt[3]{2}} \tag{18.98}$$

Question 23

The amount of of impurity removed is a geometric progression, so for y passes, the fraction of impurity x removed is:

$$x = \frac{1}{n} + \frac{1}{n^2} + \frac{1}{n^3} + \ldots \frac{1}{n^y} \tag{18.99}$$

The maximum fraction of impurity removed is the sum to infinity of the above:

$$x = \frac{\frac{1}{n}}{1 - \frac{1}{n}} \tag{18.100}$$

multiplying top and bottom by n:

$$x = \frac{1}{n-1} \qquad (18.101)$$

So when $n = 2$:

$$x = \frac{1}{2-1} = 1 \qquad (18.102)$$

That is, it is possible to remove all the impurity.

When $n = 3$:

$$x = \frac{1}{3-1} = \frac{1}{2} \qquad (18.103)$$

Question 24

part a

Equate the force of the spring kR with the centripetal force in terms of ω: $m\omega^2 R$:

$$kR = m\omega^2(R_0 + R) \qquad (18.104)$$

$$kR = m\omega^2 R_0 + m\omega^2 R \qquad (18.105)$$

$$R = \frac{m\omega^2 R_0}{(k - m\omega^2)} \qquad (18.106)$$

part b

$$F_{max} = m\omega_c^2(R_0 + R_{max}) \qquad (18.107)$$

$$\omega_c = \sqrt{\frac{F_{max}}{m(R_0 + R_{max})}} \qquad (18.108)$$

Since $F_{max} = kR_{max}$:

$$\omega_c = \sqrt{\frac{F_{max}}{m(R_0 + \frac{F_{max}}{R})}} \qquad (18.109)$$

$$= \sqrt{\frac{kF_{max}}{m(R_0 k + F_{max})}} \qquad (18.110)$$

part c

Substituting in the values given to the equation found in part b:

$$\omega_c = \sqrt{\frac{F_{max}}{1 + F_{max}}} \qquad (18.111)$$

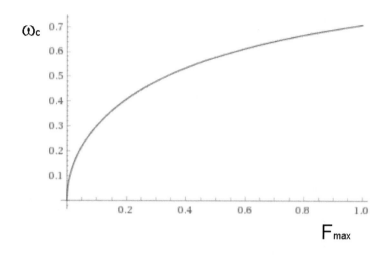

part d

This is a mass spring system which will undergo resonance when the driving rotational frequency equals the natural frequency ω_i. When this happens the mass will oscillate rather than rotate.

$$\omega_i = \sqrt{\frac{k}{m}} \tag{18.112}$$

Chapter 19

Interviews

These are a selection of previous Oxford Physics interview questions and questions of a similar style. With the advent of the internet, it is rare that the same questions are used for more than one year. Some of these questions are provided with advice and hints on how to answer them. It is your method and your thought processes that are of most interest in the interview, do not worry about estimating things perfectly (as long as they are reasonable). These questions should familiarise you with the style of questions and style of possible methods. They are not predicted questions and specific answers should not be learnt by rote. There are two sections of questions 'Fermi Problems' (estimation exercises) and 'Physics/Maths Problems'. There will often be more than one obvious method for a question - and they may give different answers.

19.1 Fermi Problems

19.1.1 Question 1

How much water flows through Amazon river?

You need to consider the width and depth of the river along with the speed of the river. Multiply all these together to get an answer. If we estimate the mouth of the river to be 2km wide and a depth of 100m and that it is flowing at a rate of 2m/s then the volume of water will be

$$Volume = 2000 \times 100 \times 2 \tag{19.1}$$
$$= 400,000 m^3/s \tag{19.2}$$

19.1.2 Question 2

How many ping pong balls fit into a double decker bus?

You need to consider the volume of the bus and the volume of a ping pong ball. A more advanced answer would also take into account that there will be some empty space between the balls. If we estimate the radius of a ping pong ball to be 2cm its volume is

$$
\begin{align}
V_{ball} &= \frac{4}{3}\pi r^3 \tag{19.3}\\
&= \frac{4}{3}\pi 0.02^3 \tag{19.4}\\
&= \frac{4}{3}\pi 0.000008 \tag{19.5}\\
&\approx 0.00003m^3 \tag{19.6}
\end{align}
$$

The volume of the bus will be around

$$
\begin{align}
V_{bus} &= length \times width \times height \tag{19.7}\\
&= 10 \times 3 \times 4 \tag{19.8}\\
&= 120m^3 \tag{19.9}
\end{align}
$$

Consider around 25% of space is wasted between the spheres the volume of the bus can be taken to be $90m^3$. To find the number of balls divide the volumes:

$$
\begin{align}
\frac{V_{bus}}{V_{ball}} &= \frac{90}{0.00003} \tag{19.10}\\
&= 3,000,000 \tag{19.11}
\end{align}
$$

19.1.3 Question 3

How many piano tuners are there in New York?

You need to consider the population of New York (approx. 10million); the number of households (approx, 4 million); the number which have a piano (approx. 1/10 so 400,000); the frequency of tuning (approx. once per year) meaning you have a requirement of 400,000 tunings per year. Each piano tuner can tune 2 per day, 5 days per week, 200 days per year (allowing for weekends and holidays) so each tuner tunes ($2 \times 5 \times 200 = 2000$ pianos per year. Thus the number of piano tuners required is $400,000/2000 = 200$. (Curiously, this is actually fairly close to the number which show up in a simple Google search).

19.1.4 Question 4

How many people can fit inside a Mini?

You need to consider the volume of the car ($2m \times 1m \times 2m = 4m^3$) and the volume of a person. If we assume a person is mostly water and therefore has the same density as water if they have a mass of 70kg they have a volume of 70litres. There are 1000 litres in a m^3 so approximately 14 people have a volume of $1m^3$. This means that $4 \times 14 = 56$ people would fit into the car. Again we need to realise there is some empty space and that people are slightly less dense than water (they float). So lets take the smallest, easy number to divide by (2) and say $56/2 = 28 people$.

19.1.5 Question 5

The Catholic Church believes that at Communion you receive the body and blood of Christ (where as the Anglican Church believe that it is just bread and wine which symbolise the body and blood of Christ). Consider whether the Catholic Church are justified in his claim.

This is quite a long, tough question but you can work through it systematically. First you need to consider the number of atoms that were once part of Jesus. Find the number of moles where n is the number of moles, m is the mass in grams and Mr is the molecular mass. Again assume the human body is made of water with $Mr = 18$ and has a mass of 70kg.

$$n = \frac{m}{Mr} \tag{19.12}$$
$$= \frac{70000}{18} \tag{19.13}$$
$$= 3889 moles \tag{19.14}$$

Each mole has 6.02×10^{23} molecules so Jesus had $3889 \times 6.02 \times 10^{23} = 2.3 \times 10^{27}$ atoms. If the Earth has a radius of 6400km, an average density of $2000 kg/m^3$ (rock is more dense than water) and an average Mr of 40 (somewhere between Iron and Carbon) then the earth has a mass, M given by

$$M = density \times volume \tag{19.15}$$
$$= 2000 \times \frac{4}{3}\pi 6400000^3 \tag{19.16}$$
$$= 2 \times 10^{24} kg \tag{19.17}$$

$$n = \frac{m}{Mr} \tag{19.18}$$
$$= \frac{2 \times 10^{27}}{40} \tag{19.19}$$
$$= 5 \times 10^{25} moles \tag{19.20}$$

This corresponds to $5 \times 10^{25} \times 6.02 \times 10^{23} = 3 \times 10^{49}$ atoms in the world. Assuming these are all mixed around uniformly over time then for every 1 Jesus atom there are

$$\frac{3 \times 10^{49}}{2.3 \times 10^{27}} = 1.3 \times 10^{22} \tag{19.21}$$

other atoms in the world. In a communion wafer which might have a mass of 1g and an Mr of 12 (roughly the same as carbon) there are

$$n \quad = \quad \frac{m}{Mr} \tag{19.22}$$

$$= \quad \frac{3}{12} moles \tag{19.23}$$

which corresponds to 1.5×10^{23} atoms. Thus in every communion water there should be an average of

$$\frac{1.5 \times 10^{23}}{1.3 \times 10^{22}} \approx 10 \tag{19.24}$$

Jesus atoms. So you could say the Catholic Church is justified in its claim!

It is now hoped that you are a little more familiar with the concept of an estimation question. Here are a number of further examples for you to try yourself, without detailed working out.

19.1.6   Question 6

What is the kinetic energy of a drifting continent?

19.1.7   Question 7

What is the heat output of a human?

19.1.8   Question 8

How big does a seed need to be to justify a bird flying up from the ground to the tree to eat it?

19.1.9   Question 9

A helium filled balloon is 50cm in diameter. What is its diameter when taken to the bottom of the Atlantic ocean?

19.1.10   Question 10

How much do the brakes of a car heat up in stopping at a set of traffic lights.

$$E = mc\Delta T \tag{19.25}$$

19.2 Physics/Maths Problems

19.2.1 Question 1

What is $\sqrt{5}$?

You know it's more than 2 ($2^2 = 4$) and less than 3 ($3^2 = 9$). Take a guestimate at 2.1 then try

$$2.1 \times 2.1 \tag{19.26}$$

$$2.1 \times 2 + 2.1 \times 0.1 \tag{19.27}$$

$$4.2 + 0.21 \tag{19.28}$$

$$4.41 \tag{19.29}$$

Try 2.2 and repeat

$$2.2 \times 2.2 \tag{19.30}$$

$$2.2 \times 2 + 2.2 \times 0.2 \tag{19.31}$$

$$4.4 + 0.44 \tag{19.32}$$

$$4.84 \tag{19.33}$$

Try 2.3 and repeat

$$2.3 \times 2.3 \tag{19.34}$$

$$2.3 \times 2 + 2.3 \times 0.3 \tag{19.35}$$

$$4.6 + 0.69 \tag{19.36}$$

$$5.29 \tag{19.37}$$

So it's 2.2 to 1dp. You can repeat until you have the required accuracy.

19.2.2 Question 2

A brick sits is a boat floating on a small pond. If the brick is thrown out of the boat into the pond what happens to the water level: does it stay the same, rise or fall?

When is the boat the brick displaces its weight in water. When in the water the brick displaces only its volume in water. Therefore the water level in the pond will decrease (assuming the brick is more dense than water).

19.2.3   Question 3

Using four number fives and any mathematical operators can you make the number 24?

This is easy!

$$5 \times 5 - \frac{5}{5} = 24 \tag{19.38}$$

A harder problem is to make 24 with just 2 fives!

$$\frac{5!}{5} = 24 \tag{19.39}$$

19.2.4   Question 4

A king has 1000 bottles of wine. One (and only one) is known to be poisoned with slow acting poison (which always kills a person after one month). The king has 10 slaves who can each drink one whole glass of wine. The king decides how to pour each glass - using wine from one or more bottles. How can he discover which bottle is poisoned?

Answer: Use binary. Label all the bottles from 1 to 1000. Pour each bottle into its corresponding glass. For example bottle number 16 ($16 = 2^4$) should be poured into only glass 4. Bottle number 528 ($528 = 2^9 + 2^4$) should be poured into glasses 4 and 9. Thus each bottle has its own unique combination of glasses and thus slaves killed. So if bottle number 72 is poisoned, slaves 3 and 6 will die since $72 = 2^3 + 2^6 = 8 + 64$. Of course this means that each bottle needs to be opened and 1000 vacuum wine savers will be needed!

19.2.5   Question 5

Astrology claims that the position of the planets at the time of birth influences a person's life. Calculate the relative gravitational attraction on a newborn baby by Jupiter and the mother. The mass of Jupiter is $1.9 \times 10^{27} kg$ and its closest approach to Earth is at $6.3 \times 10^{17} m$.

Simply use the equation for gravitational force, assuming the mass of the baby is 4kg. For Jupiter:

$$\begin{aligned} F &= \frac{GMm}{r^2} \tag{19.40} \\ &= \frac{6.67 \times 10^{-11} \times 1.9 \times 10^{27} \times 4}{(6.3 \times 10^{17})^2} \tag{19.41} \\ &= 1.3 \times 10^{-18} N \tag{19.42} \end{aligned}$$

For the mother (of mass 70kg):

$$F = \frac{GMm}{r^2} \tag{19.43}$$

$$= \frac{6.67 \times 10^{-11} \times 70 \times 4}{(0.5)^2} \tag{19.44}$$

$$= 7.47 \times 10^{-8} N \tag{19.45}$$

Thus the gravitational effect of the Mother on the baby is significantly larger than the gravitational effect of Jupiter.

19.2.6 Question 6

Milk can be added to a cup of coffee either when it is made or after 5 minutes when it is drunk. Which would result in the coffee being cooler when it is drunk?

Adding it before drinking as hotter objects loose heat quicker to their surroundings.

19.2.7 Question 7

You are at a party with a drink full to the brim of a cup with two lumps of ice sticking out of it. What happens to the drink if you leave the ice to melt? Does it overflows, stay at the brim or fall?

Assume the drink is mostly water. The ice displaces its weight in water. When it melts it turns into water (and it still displaces its weight in water). The newly melted water will have the same density as the rest of the water and so will take up the same space in the cup so the level should stay at the brim.

19.2.8 Question 8

Find the time during the period of oscillation of a ideal pendulum where its kinetic energy and potential energy are equal.

Assuming no energy losses:

$$KE + PE = Z \tag{19.46}$$

where Z is a constant. Where $PE = 0$ the pendulum is hanging vertically with a displacement of zero so Z must equal the kinetic energy at this point. This is also the point of maximum velocity.

So

$$KE_{max} = Z \tag{19.47}$$

$$KE_{max} = \frac{1}{2}mv_{max}^2 \tag{19.48}$$

$$v_{max} = A\omega \tag{19.49}$$

Since for SHM

$$s = A\sin\omega t \tag{19.50}$$

$$v = \frac{ds}{dt} = A\omega\cos\omega t \tag{19.51}$$

Therefore

$$KE_{max} = Z = \frac{1}{2}mA^2\omega^2 \tag{19.52}$$

Now, at the point where kinetic energy and potential energy are equal

$$\frac{1}{2}mA^2\omega^2 = 2KE \tag{19.53}$$

$$\frac{1}{2}mA^2\omega^2 = mA^2\omega^2\cos^2\omega t \tag{19.54}$$

$$\frac{1}{2} = cos^2\omega t \tag{19.55}$$

$$\frac{1}{\sqrt{2}} = cos\omega t \tag{19.56}$$

$$\frac{\pi}{4} = \omega t \tag{19.57}$$

$$\tag{19.58}$$

Now $\omega = 2\pi/T$ so

$$\frac{\pi}{4} = \frac{2\pi}{T}t \tag{19.59}$$

$$\frac{1}{8} = \frac{t}{T} \tag{19.60}$$

So the kinetic and potential energy are equal at a time corresponding to an eighth of the period into the swing.

19.2.9 Question 9

Take the digits 1 to 9 once only. Make a 5 digit and a 4 digit number which subtract to give 3333. A followup question is how many combinations of 5 and 4 digit numbers are there in total. The answer is 12876 and 9543. There are $3! = 6$ combinations.

19.2.10   Question 10

How does a bicycle stay upright?

19.2.11   Question 11

How does a Galileo Thermometer work. Answer: The glass bulbs have fixed density. The clear liquid has a density which is temperature dependent. Objects float when they are less dense than their surroundings.

19.2.12   Question 12

Draw a free body force diagram (i.e. all the forces acting) for the middle book in a horizontal stack of three or an inside rail carriage in a long train.

19.2.13   Question 13

Consider a helium balloon tied to a seat in a car. As the car accelerates what happens to the balloon and why: does it stay directly above the seat, move towards the front of the car or move towards the rear. Answer: it moves towards the front as it is less dense than the air around it. Watch the bubble in a spirit level for a simple demonstration.

19.2.14   Question 14

How do we detect planets around other stars? Answer: consider monitoring the gravitational wobble of the star as a large planet passes near by and the dimming of the star when a planet passes in front of it.

19.2.15   Question 15

Why is a fridge difficult to open soon after it was previously opened? Answer: apply the equation PV=nRT. When open, the fridge fills with a fixed volume of warm air. This is then cooled by the fridge reducing the temperature. This must cause a reduction in pressure in fridge.

19.2.16   Question 16

The men's high jump was won recently with a height of 2.38m. What would this height have been had the event taken place on the moon? Assume g on the moon is 1/6 that of earth. A weak candidate will probably think the answer is something like 6 times 2.38m. A strong candidate should reason that it is the centre of mass of the athlete that has to clear the bar and reason that this would be about half-way up a human body. If the athlete was 1.92m tall, this puts it approximately 1m from the ground. Thus the CoM has risen 1.38m. On the moon this could be as high as 6 times 1.38m.

19.2.17   Question 17

Without using your hands describe how you would tie your shoe laces. How many times do I need to fold a piece of paper for it be the size of an atom?

19.2.18   Question 18

How many times do I need to fold a piece of paper for it be the size of an atom?

19.2.19   Question 19

If you are given a voltmeter, battery and resistor and told to find the internal resistance of the battery, how would you do it?

19.2.20   Question 20

The power falling on an umbrella is enough to power a washing up machine, what's the rate of loss of mass of the sun?

19.2.21   Question 21

What is the power of a grasshopper at take off?

19.2.22   Question 22

Differentiate $y = x^x$

19.2.23   Question 23

Sketch $y = e^{-x} \sin x$, and talk about its turning points.

19.2.24   Question 24

Sketch $y = \frac{\sin x}{x}$, and talk about its shape and turning points.

19.2.25   Question 25

If I have ten plates to wash up, and one bowl of hot water, which way ends up with hotter water at the end; putting the plates in one at a time, washing them, then removing them; putting all ten plates in at once, washing them then removing? Neglecting losses of heat to anything other than the plates.

19.2.26   Question 26

How far away from the earth do I have to go for g to drop by 1

19.2.27   Question 27

If I split a piece of paper into 4 squares, shade one square, then pick one of the other 3 squares, split that into 4, shade one of those squares and repeat to infinity what is the shaded area?

19.2.28   Question 28

If I have a chocolate bar of A pieces across and B pieces down, how many breaks are needed to get to the individual pieces?

19.2.29   Question 29

I have a pipe with water flowing in it, how can I determine its direction of flow using any tools but not cutting into the pipe.

19.2.30   Question 30

I have a bucket draining via a hole in to a bucket beneath it, and that bucket draining into another bucket beneath it, which is sealed. Sketch graphs of the height of the water against time for the buckets.

19.2.31   Question 31

I need to chose fairly between 3 puddings in a restaurant, but only have one coin. How can I do it?

19.2.32   Question 32

Why are there seasons? (Hint: consider that during summer in the northern hemisphere, the Earth is 1 million km further away from the sun than in winter. Do the mathematics to compare.)

19.2.33   Question 33

Sketch the graph of $y = \frac{1}{x(x-1)}$

19.2.34   Question 34

Look at this analog watch. At certain times during the day, the minute hand and the hour hand will overlap precisely. Create two simultaneous equations and use them to find these times. Can you see another way of working this out without simultaneous equations?

19.2.35   Question 35

Why do you love physics?

19.2.36   Question 36

Sketch $f(x) = (x-1)e^{-x/3} + 3$

19.2.37   Question 37

Have you heard of the equation $E = mc^2$? What does it mean? How is it used everyday?

19.2.38   Question 38

Find $lim(x \to a) \frac{(\tan(x) - \tan(a))}{(x-a)}$

19.2.39   Question 39

So here we have a rollercoaster, of starting height H. After the drop, the cart goes through a loop of diameter h. What is the condition on H in terms of h for the cart to fully make it around the loop? At the top, what provides the centripetal force? So what does the person feel? What do they feel, in G-force, at three quarters through the loop? What about at the bottom after looping?

19.2.40   Question 40

A man is going to see either friend in town A or B. Who he sees depends on which bus comes first. He takes the first available bus always and he arrives at random times in the hour. Bus to town A comes at 10 past the hour and 10 minutes until the next hour Bus to town B comes at 15 past the hour and at 30 minutes past. Which friend will he see more?

19.2.41   Question 41

What is Kepler's Third Law?

19.2.42 Question 42

If the government gave you an unlimited amount of money to spend on science, what you you spend it on?

19.2.43 Question 43

a) Find a solution to

$$\frac{d^2x}{dx^2} = -\omega^2 x \tag{19.61}$$

b) Find a solution to

$$\frac{d^2x}{dx^2} = \omega^2 x \tag{19.62}$$

c) What is the difference between $\cos \omega t$ and $e^{\omega t}$?

19.2.44 Question 44

Why is this table white? Why is glass transparent? How would you measure the band gap of glass?

19.2.45 Question 45

At what speed should you swing a bucket over your head to avoid getting wet?

Printed in Great Britain
by Amazon